MONAD AND THOU

Series in Continental Thought

Monad and Thou

*Phenomenological Ontology
of Human Being*

H IROSHI K OJIMA

Ohio University Press
ATHENS

Ohio University Press, Athens, Ohio 45701

© 2000 by Hiroshi Kojima

Printed in the United States of America

Ohio University Press books are printed on acid-free paper ∞

04 03 02 01 00   5 4 3 2 1

Library of Congress Cataloging-in-Publication Data

Kojima, Hiroshi, 1925–
   Monad and Thou: phenomenological ontology of human
being/Hiroshi Kojima.
      p. cm. — (Series in Continental thought; no. 27)
   Includes bibliographical references (p.) and index.
   ISBN 0-8214-1320-1 (alk. paper)
   1. Philosophical anthropology. I. Title. II. Series in Continental
thought; 27.

BD450 .K63547 2000
128—dc21
                                                      99-054676

CONTENTS

PREFACE

THE CONTENTS OF THIS BOOK reflect my entire philosophical endeavor, which has had two focal points: the idea of the monad and the question of Thou. My first intuition of the idea of monad came to me when I was almost twenty years old, in 1945. The Pacific War was coming to a close, and even a student, such as I was at the time, could see Japan's imminent defeat. Nevertheless, none of us could imagine how the war would end. We thought only in vague terms: "perhaps all of us will die." The sky was filled with smaller American planes that had flown from the southern island, Iwo Jima. The Japanese planes had vanished, ostensibly to prepare against the threat of all-out enemy attack on the mainland. When enemy planes flew overhead we hid by throwing ourselves to the ground behind anything that would shade us from view. At times the planes flew so close to the ground that we could see the ruddy faces of the pilots aiming their machine-gun fire at anything on the ground. Although we had no weapons to fight against them, the situation increasingly resembled a duel. I would imagine the fate of the unknown pilot flying over me, perhaps the one who would kill me. I would seriously wonder whether he was happier than I, his anonymous potential victim, was. At the same time, suddenly and unexpectedly, I felt my very Being expand as if without limit toward the sky, transparent like a huge glass dome, yet dense and full of Being. I stood alone, utterly alone, in the middle of this dome and felt that I was the only one in the entire universe. The concrete enemy had disappeared, yet some invisible force that threatened my entire Being still remained. This was the pure negation of my Being. (Some years later I read Sartre's *Nausea* in translation and found something similar in Sartre's experience of *l'être-en-soi* in the root of the chestnut tree. There was a proximity to my own experience, but it was not identical, since I did not, like Sartre, feel my Being to be a kind of material presence.)

After the war, which I barely survived, this experience continually haunted my thoughts, and gradually I was unable to resist the desire to seek the meaning of the experience of my Being. This decision brought about the turning point of my life, when I began to study philosophy in 1952. The concept of the monad in Husserl's *Cartesian Meditations* struck me as having a unique and primordial importance, yet I still felt something lacking in the transcendental approach to Being. I learned much more from Heidegger's notion of Being, but I was disappointed that Heidegger did not use the idea of monad itself. As a result, I spent many years going between Husserl and Heidegger, as I sought to bridge the gap between transcendental subjectivity and the Being of the monad. This search comprises the problematic that I address: how is it possible that a solitary ego, alone in the universe, can also be a member of a community?

In addition, I became familiar with the concept of Thou through my reading of Martin Buber. From the beginning, I had a strange recognition of this concept as self-evident. With time, however, it became clear to me that there was some inconsistency between the schema of the I-Thou relation and the realm of the in-between, an inconsistency that most deeply concerns the dichotomy between the I-Thou and the I-It relations. In 1985, when I was preparing a speech to be presented at the University of Frankfurt in Germany, I finally arrived at the idea of the occurring Thou as the ultimate mediator between I and the world. At this moment my thinking gained its foundation, and it seemed that my search for the meaning of Being had virtually reached its goal.

My Being in the monad gains meaning through the occurrence of Thou, and I am thus saved from solitary thrownness into a closed universe without meaning. "Thou" is the source of meaningfulness. Wherever and whenever Thou occurs, the shadow of nihilism vanishes. The I-Thou schema that has come into common usage since Buber is produced by what I would call a somewhat halfhearted analysis of the true dialogical situation. The common use of I-Thou expresses only one direction of the activity of the ego. Rather, this activity must be doubled in real dialogue. Thus it becomes clear that the equal partner of the ego is not Thou, but rather the alter-ego, who, in becoming the passage of my Thou, discovers my ego as the passage of its own Thou.

The schema I-Thou is erroneous because in reality Thou is not on the same plane as I. On the contrary, Thou is the transcendent (second-person) dimension, which is able to completely mediate the first-person dimension (the Being of monad) and the third-person dimension (either other monads or objects of kinesthesis). Without Thou, I and the "He, She, It" as a totality would either be silently segregated from each other or fall into conflict with each other. Yet the idea of monad is indispensable because Thou can occur only through and by way of the total Being of I, "He, She, It." Modern science has insisted on one particular kind of kinesthetic relation alone (the I-It) and has completely forgotten not only the mediating transcendent second-person dimension (Thou) but also the first dimension (I) and the third dimension (He, She, It) in their total monadicity, and as a result the I-He, She, It intermonadic relation. Asian culture, by contrast, may be able to make a relevant contribution to this question, as this book will discuss.

This book consists of fourteen articles written on different occasions over the past twenty years. I have tried to smooth out the transitions between them to the best of my ability, but this attempt may not always have been successful. In such a case, I must ask for the reader's generosity. Regrettably, my thought has never had a remarkable response in my own country. By contrast, it has been given much more serious attention in the United States, and I feel happy that this book is being published through the kind and helpful efforts of some friends in America, the same country that, as an anonymous and enormous force, first motivated me to begin to philosophize fifty years ago.

ACKNOWLEDGMENTS

THIS BOOK WOULD NEVER have appeared without the continuous and strenuous efforts of Professor Steven Crowell (Rice University). Since we first met in Seattle in 1991 his penetrating as well as warm sight has kept incessant attention on my thought. His effort extended not merely to the usual intellectual matters but included as well the tiresome cobbling together of a first readable text from an incompletely formatted diskette sent by me from Japan. The stupendous benevolence shown by this younger colleague and friend from a foreign country inspires me and fills me with deep gratitude to him and with reverence for the Spirit that has moved him.

Dr. Elaine Miller (DePaul University) contributed her valuable time and ability to make my manuscript speak better English and to make sure that my footnotes were in proper order. I appreciate the quality of her work and her patient, cooperative attitude with the author. Without her help, no text suitable for an English-speaking readership would have been possible.

I am also grateful to Professor Tullio Maranhao (University of St. Thomas), who, at a conference in Houston in 1996, first suggested the possibility of publishing my book in English. Since then his encouragement has continued unabated.

Dr. Elizabeth Behnke (Felton) kindly read through my still very incomplete manuscript and gave many valuable suggestions.

I would also like to register my cordial gratitude to many unknown people in the United States who worked in various capacities to support the publication of this book.

Earlier versions of some of the chapters have previously appeared in print. I am grateful to Kluwer Academic Publishers for permission to publish revised versions of the following articles: "The Potential Plurality of the Transcendental Ego of Husserl and Its Relevance to the Theory of Space," from *Analecta Husserliana* 8 (1978): 55-61; "The Modern Age as a Transitional Period," from *Analecta Husserliana* 20 (1986): 369-82; "The Phenomenology of the Thou," from *Analecta Husserliana* 22 (1987): 337-42; "The Transcendental

Reflection of Life without a Transcendental Ego," from Blosser, Shimomisee, Embree, and Kojima, eds., *Japanese and Western Phenomenology* (1993), 55-68; and "The Vertical Intentionality of Time-Consciousness and Sense-Giving," from Hopkins, ed., *Husserl in Contemporary Context* (1997), 79-93.

My thanks go to Alber Verlag for permission to publish English-language versions of "Zur philosophischen Erschließung der religiösen Dimension—Überlegungen im Anschluß an Descartes, Husserl, und den Zen-Buddhismus," in *Philosophisches Jahrbuch* 85 (1978): 56-70; and "Monade und Dichtung," in *Philosophisches Jahrbuch* 91 (1984): 325-40.

INTRODUCTION

THIS BOOK INVESTIGATES the human being in its individual totality and universal communicativity from the standpoint of phenomenological ontology. I pursue the theme mainly in confrontation with the texts of Edmund Husserl, Martin Heidegger, and Martin Buber. I find the point at which all their thoughts tend to converge is the Being of the human body, which has, however, never been adequately investigated—not by these thinkers nor by any previous Occidental philosophers so far as I know. I find that the human ego in its most primary state is the somatic ego, which, as embodied, inhabits the life-world. But I find also that the human ego is not able to unify its own inner schism because it is already being pulled by two transcendent forces—objectifying and subjectifying (projecting) forces—which are much stronger than itself and always motivate it in opposite directions.

In section 1 (chapters 1 through 4), I take up the transcendental ego of Husserl in order to establish my thesis that, contrary to Husserl's view, this ego always functions in cooperation with other egos and is consequently a priori intersubjective. In chapter 1 the invalidity of Husserl's solipsistic concept of the transcendental ego is demonstrated through a confrontation with his theory of how the back of a physical thing is appresented. The functional plurality of egos that comes into view here itself originates from the impersonal transcendental subjectivity that is a priori transcendent to every ego; such subjectivity is, specifically, the ability to objectify everything. Only through the objectification of the unobjectified body, then, can the impersonal transcendental subjectivity coincide with every ego. Hence what is usually called the "transcendental ego" ought more precisely to be called the "transcendentalized ego," which is only a reflective aspect of the concrete, somatic ego. In chapter 2, Husserl's idea of transcendental reflection as the fundamental mode of his transcendental ego is discussed in order to show that the agent of transcendental reflection is not the transcendental ego, as he thought, but rather the somatic ego. This destruction of the illusion of an idealistic ego is above all necessary in order to open the way for the discovery of the true ego. Chapter 3 thematizes the vertical intentionality of time-consciousness from the standpoint of the somatic ego. With the discovery of a new type of intentionality in it—one that is not objectifiable (nonreflective)—a relation between vertical intentionality and the act of sense-giving, which Husserl's reliance on reflection could never uncover, is brought to light. Chapter 4 brings together the main points of section 1 and, by ascertaining the impersonal transcendental subjectivity (not transcendental ego) and the pre-thetic Being of the world as two indubitables, prepares for section 2, where the Being of the somatic ego as monad is discussed.

In section 2 (chapters 5 through 7), I explore the concept of monad, which originates in Leibniz but is taken up anew by Husserl as a model for the concrete ego. I find, however, that Husserl's concept of monad is a hybrid that lacks consistent definition. I therefore offer a new and deepened idea of monad, which expresses the genuine totality and individuality of the self and underlies every human somatic ego. I try to illuminate this idea from three different perspectives: (1) religiousness, (2) poetry, and (3) intersubjectivity. In chapter 5 I argue for a basic similarity between the space-time continuum in Zen Buddhism and the monad as a complex of the pre-thetic self and the pre-thetic world. Chapter 6 discusses Japanese haiku as the specific product of the monadic complex of poet with Nature-monad. By way of a critique of Iso Kern's argument concerning Husserl's fifth Cartesian Meditation, chapter 7 shows the limit of the appresentation theory as an account of what mediates between one monad and another.

In section 3 (chapters 8 through 10), the structure of the body is treated as the dimension where two different kinds of subjectivity meet, yet without complete mediation. Chapter 8 takes up the historical development of theories of the body in Occidental philosophy from Feuerbach through Marx, Bergson, Scheler, Heidegger, Sartre, and Merleau-Ponty. In this critical observation, the double subjectivity proper to the human somatic ego becomes progressively visible in its full scope. We find the transcendental subjectivity and the monadic projection together, corresponding to two layers of the body: *Körper* (the physical body) and *Leib* (the bodily flesh). These two layers are indeed united by the somatic ego, but only incompletely, because they are simultaneously controlled by the opposite (objectifying and subjectifying) principles mentioned above. Chapter 9 traces the relation between natural science and modern technology as a function of the interaction of double subjectivity proper to the somatic ego. Two centuries after the birth of natural science, the image projecting monadic subjectivity absorbed the all-objectifying transcendental subjectivity and produced modern technology. Modern technology is therefore an incomplete mediation of double subjectivity, which could not overcome its own schism but on the contrary is fed by that very schism. These dual subjectivities are also the remote origins of the modern science and the economic mass production that, by now, seem to be self-generating as products of hidden dualistic moments of the modern age. Barely mediated by scientific technology, these subjectivities are beyond the control of any human ego. No one knows where this modern world is going. Chapter 10 explores the level of practice, where the pre-thetic Being of the world proves to be upsurging living power with imagination, while the thetic Being of things emerges as the restricting force unto death of the former. The power of life struggles with the force of things and endeavors to assimilate the latter in the form of food, utensils, and machines. However, it never succeeds completely. At the same time, the power of life is intrinsically determined by self-contradiction: *teleology without telos*. Only by becoming aware of this contradiction is the way opened to the true mediator of dual subjectivity: Thou.

In section 4 (chapters 11 and 12), I try to locate the true mediator of the dualism that has its ground in the inner schism of the human body. Chapter 11 addresses the unhappy dichotomy of I-Thou and I-It relations in Martin Buber's work and tries to explicate the difference between these relations by using the paired concepts Consciousness and Being. It turns out that the I-Thou relation is between "Beings seen from inside" one another, while I-It is a relation between a complex "Being seen from inside = Being seen from outside" and a simple "Being seen from outside." However, a genuine encounter necessarily demands the complete synthesis (and not a mere complex) of "Being seen from inside" and "Being seen from outside," and that is no longer explicable in terms of the paired concepts of Consciousness and Being. The solution to this ultimate problem is entrusted to chapter 12. There I discover, by a reapprehension and deepening of Buber's thought, the second-person dimension,

"Thou." Though Thou abides and occurs autonomously and independently from "I" (ego) — that is, it does not have the form of I-Thou — it is what mediates the first-person dimension (monadicity) and the third-person dimension (transcendentality) inside of, and in between, human bodies. In other words, "Thou" is the ultimate mediator of the fundamental subjectification (Being seen from inside) and objectification (Being seen from outside), which are both immanent-transcendent to the ego. The phenomenal functions of Thou are (1) language, (2) love, and (3) spiritual creation, all of which occur through, and in between, I (ego) and He, She, It (alter ego). Only by encountering Thou and by becoming the path of the occurring Thou is a human (or even nonhuman) ego able to experience a genuine encounter with the alter ego outside, and the unity of its Being inside. Reason as the absolute of modern thought is only the partial, restricted occurrence of the occurring Thou. Thou is the source of meaningfulness in general and of authenticity in human being.

Section 5 (chapters 13 and 14) addresses the problems mentioned above with particular reference to the cultural tradition of Japan.

SECTION I

CHAPTER ONE

Looking at the Back of a Thing

The Potential Plurality of
Husserl's Transcendental Ego

THE TEXT OF THE *Cartesian Meditations* suggests that Husserl was motivated to construct a theory of "Others" mainly in order to repudiate the charge of solipsism that had been brought against him.[1] Husserl calls this criticism "what may seem to be a grave objection."[2] Indeed, one might suspect that herein lies the Achilles' heel of Husserl's phenomenology. According to Husserl, the world and nature as a whole are constituted as noematic meaning through the intentional act (noesis) of the transcendental consciousness. World and nature as a whole form the immanent transcendence of the transcendental consciousness of the ego. Since this transcendental ego is taken to be *my* ego, one might say that the entire world here is nothing but my world. In other words, the whole world is given as nothing but a view or perspective of mine. The wholeness of the world remains only as the limitless horizonality of this perspective as it develops panoramically before my eyes.

Can such a world really contain an ego other than mine? Does my intentionality, in other words, constitute other consciousness than my own? Given that all the objects of the world are, according to Husserl, constituted solely through my intentionality, it seems that nothing will remain that is not constituted by me. In order for Husserl's theory of world-constitution to avoid the charge of solipsism, the consciousness of other egos must necessarily be constituted by my consciousness. Husserl confronts this problem in the fifth Cartesian Meditation.

However, we cannot help wondering whether this was actually a pseudoproblem, even though Husserl himself seems not to have thought so. This doubt arises from the very ground of our interpretation of the relation of Husserl's transcendentality to the natural attitude of the human being. Even given that the phenomenological reduction excludes any naive positing of the objective world as a whole, the unlimited horizonality of the transcendental consciousness remains. This horizonality will prove to be a priori incompatible with any strictly single perspective and thus with solipsism, because it will itself imply the potential plurality of the transcendental perspectival consciousness; this claim will be the focus of our argument.

ACCORDING TO MICHAEL THEUNISSEN, Husserl's effort to develop a theory of "Others" is motivated by the attempt to constitutively establish the "objective" world.[3] In my opinion, however, the theoretical establishment of the "objective" world cannot be considered the *aim* of the theory of "Others." Rather, both objectives coincide: the "objective" world, for Husserl, also means "a single world for everyone," a world that envelops me and others equally originarily. The theory of the "objective" world and the theory of the Other cannot be separated; both are aspects of the transcendental foundation of the natural attitude.[4]

In the natural attitude, I am always with others in an "objective," single world that is for everyone. I am one of many egos scattered throughout world-space. I am not an absolute, solitary ego, but an average ego, one that is already mediated and penetrated by others. Once we adopt this point of view, another side of Husserl's egological theory of world constitution becomes evident. If the ego in the natural attitude is always already penetrated by the existence of other egos, then even the phenomenological reduction would be incapable of transforming it into a solitary ego, just as it is unable to change the "objective" world into a singular, horizonless perspective. Rather, the egological ego will more likely anticipate the potential plurality of the transcendental ego, just as the perspective of the phenomenologically reduced world anticipates other perspectives as its horizonal background.

It is true that Husserl himself was not sufficiently aware that the transcendental ego might be a priori plural. He chose instead a detour through the phenomenological reduction to a primordial sphere, together with the introjection of each ego into other bodies (empathy), as a means of reaching other transcendental egos. Husserl believed, indeed, that by excluding all alien elements from the domain of each constituting ego, he could establish the primordial sphere of the self, namely, the monad. In fact, however, the a priori plurality of the transcendental ego survives this reduction. It is not only after the introjection of each ego into other bodies that other egos are found. Anonymous other egos already function within the primordial sphere of my ego. If this is true, then the overcoming of solipsism or the constitution of other consciousnesses through my consciousness was never a problem. Other consciousnesses will not be constituted by my consciousness; rather, they are equiprimordial with mine. The intentionalities of other egos are not noemata of my intentionality; rather, they are co-noeses with mine.

To support my argument I will take up Husserl's concept of "appresentation." Husserl writes, "An appresentation occurs even in external experience, since the strictly seen front of a physical thing always and necessarily appresents a rear aspect."[5] Appresentation, thus, is a kind of copresentation of analogical apperception. In my primordial sphere things always appear together with their rear aspects, which I, from my perspective, cannot see. An analogical apperception of the unseen side, a kind of copresentation, accompanies every perception of a thing. Every perception contains something beyond merely sensory reception. Husserl attributed this to the noetic composition of the transcendental consciousness of my ego.

But is it really my intentionality that appresents the backs of things? I can grasp the world only from my perspective. I never see things from more than one place at any given moment. How do I appresent their rear aspects? Do I imagine them through memory? If that were the case, nothing but the recollected image of the reverse side would confront me, simply represented and superimposed above the current presentation of the obverse side, but not as the rear aspect at this very moment. In this case, the rear side could not be given as my image of recollection.

In the same way the attempt to reduce the appresentation of the rear side to the retention of an impression that has just passed away cannot hold true, since the appresented rear side shows no inclination to stray from the obverse side but remains immobile together with it. Thus the appresentation of the rear side can equally not be the result of my retention of an impression.

Husserl also calls the appresentation an empty intention, one that is not yet filled with sensory *hyle.* Thus he considers it possible, by revolving things, to transform an appresentation into a presentation, that is, to fulfill an empty intention. Here I must object, however, that defining an appresentation as an empty intention to be fulfilled by turning or reversing the position of things proves quite problematic. In order even to turn a thing over, I must know in advance that it has another side! Thus the back of a thing cannot be defined by my empty intention, to be fulfilled in turning the thing around. Rather, my intention directed toward the reverse side is empty, or imperfect, because it is not originally my intention.

In that moment I can constitute the back of a thing from neither a recollected image, nor a retention, nor an empty intention. From Husserl's standpoint, namely, from the point of view of a single transcendental consciousness, the appresentation proves to be an enigma. However, from the standpoint of multiple interpenetrating transcendental consciousnesses, the enigma disappears. The consciousnesses of others are already performing their functions before being constituted by my consciousness through my self-introjection. In other words, the intention of another anonymous ego aiming at the thing from another side at this very moment defines the back of the thing as itself. The back is nothing other than the front confronted by another ego. The appresented existence of the back of a thing can never be founded without the intentionality of an anonymous other consciousness behind the thing.

But how is my intentionality directed from here related to the intentionality of others from other sides? My intentionality is a priori mediated and penetrated by the intentionalities of others. In other words, I always necessarily anticipate the cooperation of other egos as I am intending the front of a thing. These egos are indeed anonymous, but their functions are nonetheless actual. Therefore the unity of the presentation and the appresentation of a thing, often emphasized by Husserl, means that each thing is constituted not by me alone, but by me together with others simultaneously. I recognize the other anonymous intentionalities acting within my own intentionality, not as part of it, but as equally original co-operators. This is what we mean by the phrase: the potential plurality of the transcendental ego. This is, of course, a kind of intersubjectivity, but I would prefer to call it interintentionality. It is an immediate, impersonal intersubjectivity without the mediation of bodies. Here other transcendental consciousnesses are not constituted by my transcendental consciousness. Rather, both participate in the same horizon around the constituted thing. While we acknowledge the unity of the presentation and the appresentation of a thing, I find myself as a transcendental ego set in this single universal horizon beyond my single perspective, knowing that all other transcendental egos also participate in this horizon. Thus one might say that this spatial horizon is what transcendentally founds the so-called objective world-space for everyone. It will thus aptly be called the transcendental schema of interintentionality.

HUSSERL'S INTERSUBJECTIVITY, BY CONTRAST, is made possible by my introjection of myself into other bodies. According to this theory, intersubjectivity in this sense founds an "objective" world common to everyone. In fact, however, Husserl's intersubjectivity already presupposes an "objective" world for everyone. Let us examine his argument. He writes, "As reflexively related to itself, my animate bodily organism (in my primordial sphere) has the central 'Here' as its mode of givenness; every other body, and accordingly the 'other's' body, has the mode 'There'. . . . By free modification of my kinesthesias, particularly those of locomotion, I can change my position in such a manner that I convert any There into a Here, that is to say, I could occupy any spatial locus with my organism."[6]

The implications of this statement are problematic. If Husserl really stood on the central Here of his monad, he would never describe his situation in such a way, for in that case no There could be transformed into the central Here. My central Here is absolute and thus unchangeable.[7] By contrast, every There might approach and be absorbed into the central Here or might detach itself and distance itself from the Here. My body as a central Here will never move about; rather, things in front of me will approach me or distance themselves. One must question the "locomotion" of Husserl's central Here. The central Here moving about is no longer the center, since it is already situated relative to a certain unmovable plane (in space) that consists of equally unmovable Theres. On this plane every There is already a potential Here, and even the "central" Here is a potential There. What is this plane or space other than an "objective" world for everyone, which is beyond the difference between the central Here and every There, which is constituted of homogeneous Here = Theres? Husserl makes a critical mistake in describing the moving Here, because this description concerns the fundamental construction of intersubjectivity. He writes, "Since the other body there enters into a pairing association with my body here and, being given perceptually, becomes the core of an appresentation, the core of my experience of a co-existing ego, that ego . . . must be appresented *as an ego now coexisting in the mode There,* 'such as I should be if I were there.'"[8] Thus we might say that the essence of Husserl's theory of intersubjectivity lies not in a pairing-association nor in appresentative empathy, but rather in the possibility of removing the center from Here to There. He believed that only the removal of Here provided the ego with the possibility of changing There into Here. The pairing only forms the factual motive for this removal. Thus he writes, "Not only the systems of appearance that pertain to my current perceiving 'from here', but also other quite determinate systems, corresponding *to the change of position that puts me 'there',* belong constitutively to each physical thing" (emphasis added).[9]

However, as we have seen, the absolute central Here as such will never be removed. If it could be shifted to a There, it would no longer be absolute but rather relative (Here = There), and the space in which such a Here moves will have an unfixed center whose coordinates could thus be arbitrarily displaced. Even the imaginary removal of the "as if I were there" already anticipates this kind of space, which is a kind of "objective," homogeneous space quite independent of the position of the center. That is to say, this space potentially (or impersonally) has its center of coordinates equally upon every There (Here = There). Thus it is clear that Husserl's theory of intersubjectivity presupposes an "objective" homogeneous world-space where a plurality of perspectives potentially (or impersonally) predominates.[10] This space, in which I know that everything can be and is seen both from the Here out and from a multiplicity of Theres out (simultaneously) prior to any movement of the body, is nothing other than a space where the presentation of There is always accompanied by the appresentation of Here. In fact, the Hereness in every

There is still egologically potential, but it is nonetheless actual as impersonal intentionality. In other words, Husserl's theory of intersubjectivity presupposes the existence of other intentionalities or consciousnesses before it thematizes the bodies of others. Thus we might say that Husserl proceeds by simply factually projecting an indefinite anonymous intentionality of others onto a determinate body.[11] It would be more apt to call this the embodiment of a preexisting intentionality rather than the introjection of ego into a preexisting body. In this respect, our impersonal interintentionality is far in advance of Husserl's intersubjectivity.

We have said that the interintentionality of the transcendental consciousness is possible only insofar as it is guided by the transcendental schema of the spatial horizon. This schema is not contained in my consciousness. Rather, my consciousness participates in this spatial schema in which other consciousnesses can also participate. Modern philosophy began with the discovery of this schema in the form of infinite space, but it failed to grasp the schema's essence because consciousness was rigidly bound to *my* ego, and space was driven into mere objectivity. The phenomenological reduction of the objective world, the core of Husserl's method, would have liberated space from mere objectivity if it had been adequately performed. Space as the schema of interintentionality is neither mere subjectivity nor mere objectivity. It is the place where subjectivity and objectivity meet. The very fact that everything appears to me from my perspective with its distinct horizonal composition immediately indicates the existence of intentionalities other than mine. Moreover, the relation between the schema of space and interintentionality suggests an analogy to the relation between Reason *(Vernunft)* as a transcendental schema of thought and cointentionality as transcendental apperception, which is, however, no longer an ego.

CHAPTER TWO

Transcendental Reflection without a Transcendental Ego

THE DEVELOPMENT OF TWO KINDS of subjectivity, the pure ego and noesis, found in the theory of intentionality of Husserl's *Ideas Pertaining to a Pure Phenomenology* leads to a paradox between the transcendental ego and the psychological ego in human subjectivity in *The Crisis of the European Sciences and Transcendental Philosophy*. Husserl tried to resolve this paradox by way of the self-objectification of the transcendental ego into the psychological ego. I will here be seeking a more comprehensive solution.

HUSSERL'S TRANSCENDENTAL EGO is in the mode of self-reflection from beginning to end, at least ostensibly. In the period of the *Ideas*, however, this fact is not yet so obvious. As Husserl wrote in the *Crisis*, "It is naive to remain within the subject-object correlation conceived in an anthropological and mundane manner, and to misinterpret the phenomenological presentations of my first writings as those of this correlation."[1] The pure ego (as the transcendental ego was called at that time) has been too easily misunderstood to be a subject who directly has to do with real or ideal objects in the world. The assertion that the transcendental ego constitutes the world intentionally may have augmented this misunderstanding.

Indeed, the pure ego of the *Ideas* is the pole from which the ray of intentionality begins its path toward the transcendental object *x*, which is the other pole — a still unknown something beyond the immanent realm of consciousness. But this ray of consciousness that forms a bridge between the pure ego and the object *x* is mediated by a stream of consciousness filled with immanent varieties of animated *hyle*. The object *x* as one pole of intentionality is given as something invariant only through this varying stream of animated *hyle*. Now what animates this *hyle* is the sense-giving aspect of intentionality (noesis), which synthesizes the *hyle* as phenomena of the objective sense (noema) relating to *x*. In Husserl's words, the intentional experience consists of two essential sides: noesis and noema. Thus the intentionality of the transcendental pure ego that aims at object *x* is always mediated by the sense-giving act of noesis (including its *hyletic* material) and its correlate, noematic sense. Husserl states, "It is clear, then, that this relation [of the full noesis to the full noema] cannot be the same as that which is meant in discussing the relation of the consciousness to its intentional object. . . . We become aware that in discussing the relation of the consciousness to its object we are referred to the innermost moment of the noema. It is not the . . . core [of the noema] itself, but something which makes up, so to speak, the necessary central point of the core."[2]

Husserl differentiates here between the noema as sense and the intentional object *x* of the pure ego, but in other places he also clearly refers to the difference between noesis and the pure ego. Noesis is an immanent element of our stream of consciousness, while the pure ego is always transcendent to our consciousness. Therefore, we must differentiate between the sense-giving act of noesis and the intentional gaze of the pure ego.

To Husserl, however, the gaze of the pure ego accompanies all my experiences, much like the "I think" *(ich denke)* of Kant: "Apart from the ways in which it relates or behaves, it is completely empty of essential components, it has no explicit content at all, it is indescribable in and for itself: pure I and nothing more."[3]

A gaze emerges from this empty ego toward the intentional object and its experience by the ego. This experience, however, is divided into two layers: that which relates to the subject of experiences (noesis) and that which relates to the object of experiences (*hyle* and noema). Therefore the pure ego experiences the noesis in itself as its own mediating agent. This is a kind of self-reflection: "The reflection (is the) self-orientation of the I to its experiences and at the same time the performance of acts of the cogito in which the I is oriented towards its experiences."[4]

Husserl calls the problem of the constitution of the object of consciousness through noesis "the functional problem."[5] The word "function" here has something of a teleological meaning, namely that of aiming at the unity of a concrete object as *telos.* The difference Merleau-Ponty draws between act-functionality and functional intentionality in *The Phenomenology of Perception* seems to have its ground here. Although Husserl does not refer to the functional intentionality of noesis in the *Ideas,* we might, following the discussion above, be able to free noesis from complete dependence on the act-intentionality of the pure ego and treat it as a relatively independent form of intentionality mediating between the act-intentionality of the pure ego and the object *x.* In contrast to the emptiness of the pure ego, noesis has an abundant variety corresponding to the variety of the noema. The pure ego illuminates and reflects upon the variety of this noesis and of the noema as its agents rather than concentrating on the transcendent object (an empty *x*) directly. This *x* will vanish later when the functional intentionality of the noesis is combined with the psychological ego, and the pregivenness of the object is referred to the potentiality of the world-horizon itself instead of to the *x* as an unknown thing-in-itself.

I HAVE INDICATED THAT IN *Ideas* the act-intentionality of the pure ego gazes upon the functional intentionality of noesis while being mediated by it, and thus possesses a kind of reflexivity upon it. This reflexivity remains obscure insofar as Husserl concentrates on the proof of the apodictic evidence of the immanent object that emerges from the flowing unity of noesis and *hyle:* profiles of noema.

Here even the relative independence of noesis against the pure ego is attenuated, since when the existence of the world becomes questionable and everything flows together, the only thing that remains constant is the empty gaze of the pure ego, just as in the case of Cartesian doubt. Husserl's somewhat enigmatic and polemical words later in the *Crisis* refer to this circumstance: "I note in passing that the much shorter way to the transcendental epoché in my *Ideas* . . . has a great shortcoming: while it leads to the transcendental ego in one leap, as it were, it brings this ego into view as apparently empty of content . . . so one is at a loss, at first, to know what has been gained by it."[6]

What then saves the pure, or transcendental, ego from this emptiness of content? The establishment of noetic functions as acts of the psychological ego through its own corporeal body and the incarnate union, so to speak, of the pure ego with this empirical ego. Already in *Ideas II* Husserl writes, "From the pure or transcendental I we differentiate . . . the real mental subject, or the mind, the identical psychological being, which, connected with each human- and animal-body, makes up the substantial-real double-being man or animal."[7]

At the same time, Husserl differentiates between two types of reflection: "We distinguish pure reflection, the reflection upon the pure I essentially belonging to every cogito, from the reflective thematical experience founded on the full-grown empirical apperception; the intentional object of this latter reflection is this empirical I, the I of empirical intentionality."[8] The first reflection accompanies every cogito by virtue of the act-intentionality of the pure ego. The second reflection is a new one—one that thematizes not only every noesis but also the unifying pole of empirical apperception, particularly concerning a corporeal body: the empirical ego. Husserl's empirical ego, or psychological subject, becomes possible only as the unifying pole of the various noeses that virtually constitute a special noema called "body." This noematic object is very special in nature, because it is intended not only as an object but also as organ controlled by the empirical ego.

Here the question inevitably arises: How is the relation between these two egos, namely the pure and the empirical ego, to be understood? Husserl answers: "Every developed subject is not merely a stream of consciousness with a pure I, but it has also accomplished a centralization in the form 'I'. This I is an apperceptive unity constituted from its own attitudes and habits and abilities, whose core is the pure I."[9] This so-called composite I, formed of two egos, is called the "personal I" or the spiritual I. Spirit, for Husserl, is the simple unity of the transcendental and the psychological, which constitutes the personality of human beings and tends to penetrate into corporeal and material things, granting them a cultural Being: "The Spiritual sense melts together with sensory phenomena in a certain way, by animating them, instead of merely being tied to them in a parallel juxtaposition."[10]

This interpenetration, or fusion, of both egos, however, does not exclude the possibility of their distancing themselves from each other in the reflecting-reflected relationship of self-responsibility and self-cognition: "The mind belongs to the person as a founding underlying ground."[11] The same may be seen from the perspective of the person: "The person is the subject who is self-responsible, the subject who is free and enslaved, unfree."[12]

Thus at first the emptiness of the pure ego would seem to be overcome in that it has become the core of human personality, with its abundance of psychological variety. However, this unity of egos in *Ideas II* is not yet phenomenologically founded. How can these egos, totally different in their character, one transcendent and one immanent, one pure and one empirical, one empty and one various, coincide? How can they overcome the distance that exists between them in the mode of original reflexivity and unify themselves with each other? Husserl offers no answer anywhere in *Ideas II*.

IN THE LECTURES IN *First Philosophy* (1923–24) and the *Encyclopedia Britannica* article (1927), both of which followed the composition of the *Ideas,* Husserl tried to solve this problem of the doubling of the ego. He concentrated on strengthening the psychological ego against the pure ego and at the same time emphasizing the mode of reflection. He pursued this direction to the point that even the method of the phenomenological reduction itself underwent a remarkable transformation. The former (Cartesian) approach to the reduction as the elimination of the general thesis of the natural attitude had resulted, in a sense, in the empty domination of the pure ego over pure consciousness and in the apodictic evidence of the flowing immanent object that had nothing to do with the reality of the world. The new approach, or the psychologist's approach, as Husserl called it, began from the experience of the psychological ego with reference to the natural world; for example, "I see a house." Absorbed in the perception of the object (the house), the ego is not aware of itself. Only through the reflection upon itself does it become aware of itself. Through this reflection it becomes a patent, rather than a latent, ego to itself.

Nevertheless, the reflecting ego is not yet different from the reflected one; they are the same ego split into two. The difference between them is not ontological, but only modal. Up to this point this reflection is nothing other than a psychological one, one that every psychologist performs in the study of human mental experiences. What differentiates phenomenologists from psychologists is the inhibition that the reflecting ego imposes upon itself to avoid confounding itself with the reflected ego through an unwarranted "thesis of existence" *(Seinssetzung)*. The ego that perceives a house in front of it usually believes in the existence of this object. The psychologist who is reflecting upon himself or herself also assumes this thesis. A phenomenologist who is reflecting upon himself or herself, by contrast, may not assume this thesis of existence together with the other, reflected ego. He or she should be an uninterested observer of the phenomena, making no judgment about the existence or nonexistence of the perceived object.

Through such a phenomenological reduction, which is expanded beyond the particular intentional relations of the present to embrace the whole of experience universally, phenomenologists obtain the transcendental subjectivity that has as its object the universe of psychological experiences. This universe originally contains the positionality *(Dasein)* of noematic objects and implies, therefore, a kind of world filled with life-experiences. From here to the life-world is only a short step. In this way Husserl establishes a remarkable parallelism between phenomenology and psychology. Pure psychology free from physical objectivism is the foundation of phenomenology. Phenomenology itself—to the probable astonishment of the phenomenologist of the *Ideas*—is even called a priori psychology: "Therefore pure psychology is in itself identical with transcendental philosophy as the science of transcendental subjectivity."[13] With regard to the problematic relationship between the double egos, Husserl's thought in *First Philosophy* seems to be most consistent, since he does not use the word "transcendental ego" at all, in order to avoid giving the impression that another ego distinct from the psychological one exists.[14]

THIS CONSISTENCY WAS SOON DISRUPTED with the publication of the *Encyclopedia Britannica* article just three years later. In an interesting

letter to Husserl during their cooperation on the article Martin
Heidegger writes, "And only in the last few days have I begun to
assess how far your emphasis on pure psychology provides the clarifying ground, that is, the ground first and foremost for unfurling the
problem of transcendental subjectivity and its relation to the purely
psychological in its full determination."[15] Now in the last version of
the article itself we read:

> Arisen out of the methodological transcendental epoché, this
> new kind of "inner" experience opens up the limitless tran-
> scendental field of Being *(Sein)*. This field of Being is the par-
> allel to the limitless psychological field. . . . And again, the
> transcendental ego [or I] and the transcendental community
> of egos, conceived in the full concretion of transcendental life
> are the transcendental parallel to the I and we in the customary
> and psychological sense, concretely conceived as mind and
> community of minds, with the psychological life of conscious-
> ness that pertains to them. My transcendental ego is thus evi-
> dently "different" from the natural ego, but by no means as
> second, as one *separated* from it in the natural sense of the
> word, just as on the contrary it is by no means bound up with it
> or intertwined with it in the usual sense of these words. It is just
> the field of transcendental self-experience (conceived in full
> concreteness) which in every case can, *through mere alteration of
> attitude,* be changed into psychological self-experience. In this
> transition, an identity of the I is necessarily brought about; in
> transcendental reflection on this transition the psychological
> objectification becomes visible as self-objectification of the
> transcendental I, and so it is as if in every moment of the natu-
> ral attitude the I finds itself with an apperception imposed
> upon it.[16]

The expression "transcendental ego" resurfaces here along with a
discussion of its relation to the psychological ego. According to Husserl these egos are different, but not in the sense of two different
things. They share an identity through the transitional change of attitude that occurs between them. Moreover, the psychological object
of reflection, that is, the psychological ego, is regarded as the self-
objectification of the transcendental ego, a self-objectification that
charges itself implicitly with natural or psychological apperception.

We must conclude from these assertions that Husserl now decisively privileges the transcendental side. The relationship between the two egos is now reversed, so that the reflexive relation based upon the psychological ego is now supplanted by the self-objectification of the transcendental ego.

However, through this procedure the former difficulty returns. On the one hand, if transcendental subjectivity is only a reflexive mode of the psychological ego, it would be impossible to call it another ego and for it to reobjectify itself as the psychological ego. On the other hand, if the transcendental ego exists, and objectifies itself as the psychological ego, then this relation is the self-relation of the transcendental ego and not that of the psychological ego. In other words, the transcendental reflection of the psychological ego and the self-objectification of the transcendental ego cannot be the same thing, because the agents themselves and the direction of their movements are completely different (see figure 2.1).

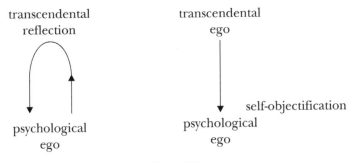

Figure 2.1

IN HUSSERL'S LAST BOOK, the *Crisis*, this problem was not resolved. Section 53, entitled "The Paradox of Human Subjectivity: Being a Subject for the World and at the Same Time Being an Object in the World," addresses the paradoxical difficulty I have traced in this chapter. Husserl asks, "But can we feel at ease or be satisfied with the mere fact that humans are subjects for the world and at the same time objects in the world?"[17] My answer: If this circumstance expresses the reflexivity of a single ego in the world toward itself and the surrounding world, then there is no difficulty, because it is no paradox at all. But if this statement is interpreted as expressing a split in the ego in any way or to any degree, then it immediately becomes an unresolvable paradox.

The subsequent section, entitled "The Resolution of the Paradox," still contains the idea of the self-objectification of the transcendental subject found in Husserl's earlier writings: "I am the I who stands beyond all natural existence . . . and who is the I-pole of transcendental life at any given time."[18] Husserl asserts, however, that the I must be reduced to an original solitary I with a body in order to resolve the paradox. This I reminds us, not without reason, of the "monad" of the *Cartesian Meditations*.[19] In the *Crisis* Husserl refers to the I as "the originary I, the ego of my epoché, which can never lose its individuality and personal indeclinability. That it makes itself transcendentally declinable for itself . . . only seemingly contradicts this fact."[20]

Only by starting from this originary but concrete solitary ego, he says, can we understand that every human being carries in itself a transcendental ego, not as a real part or layer of its mind, but rather as the ground of self-consciousness. Husserl asks whether this self-objectification of the transcendental ego into the world applies to the insane as well, and he answers in the affirmative. He intimates that the same is true of animals and children too. In the same vein, he suggests that problems concerning genesis, history, personality, birth, death, and unconsciousness could also be treated in this context. Husserl describes an interesting example with reference to the problematic of the self-objectification of the transcendental ego. A person within the natural attitude is in the condition of transcendental naïveté. The transcendental ego remains anonymous for him or her. But once this naïveté has been exposed and the transcendental reduction performed, that person cannot remain in his or her former condition. He or she may indeed return to ordinary daily life and engage in a job, but a new apperception flows into his or her mind, filled with new words, and becomes the background of his or her constitutional life, although his or her transcendental insight and intent is no longer engaged.

This example clearly demonstrates Husserl's belief that the transcendental ego and human being are one and the same being, only that the former is the source of the latter's ongoing genesis. The self-objectification of the transcendental ego is not only its self-reflection but also its self-realization into the world through various processes and degrees. In this sense its transcendentality is genetic and histori-cal, as it is itself.

WHAT, THEN, OF HUSSERL'S RESOLUTION of the paradox of human subjectivity? Some objections remain. The historical and genetic identification of the transcendental ego and the psychological ego does not sufficiently explain the reason why these *two* egos must exist. Moreover, Husserl always privileges the transcendental ego. The psychological ego, or the mind, only passively receives what the transcendental ego offers it. But the existence of the transcendental ego without the foundation of the psychological ego cannot be estab-lished with evidence. When the psychological ego falls asleep, or even faints, the persistence of the transcendental ego can never be proved by any phenomenological intuition. Therefore, to presup-pose even a relative independence of the transcendental ego from the psychological ego can be nothing other than idealistic conjecture or metaphysical dogma, without any phenomenological warrant whatsoever.

Husserl's phenomenological description at this point could be rendered more consistent by taking note of the transcendental reflexivity of the psychological ego. This ego lives with its own corpo-real body amid a life-world. As a "psychologist," it reflects upon itself without the benefit of the phenomenological reduction. As a "phe-nomenologist," however, it reflects upon itself while availing itself of the reduction and suspending all "positing of existence" *(Seinsset-zung)* with respect to the entire life-world. This is the transcendental reflection of the psychologist, so to speak, a reflection that makes transcendental phenomenology possible.

The reflection is performed solely and completely by the psycho-logical ego, not by the transcendental ego. Its object, however, is the self-same psychological ego itself. The reflection is, therefore, a spe-cial mode of the (nonreflective) psychological ego, not the result of a split in it in any way. Through this reflection the ego transforms it-self to acquire the transcendental aspect in itself. This acquisition does not vanish when the psychological ego returns to its nonreflec-tive stance. It is much the same as when one is out hiking and, by reflecting upon a geographical map, acquires a new practical knowledge of one's orientation in the surrounding terrain. As Merleau-Ponty said, the transcendental reduction performed by the psychological ego cannot be complete and must be performed repeatedly, because this reduction originates in a mode of reflection of the nonreflected ego, a mode that must be gradually assimilated into a primary nonreflective mode by the same ego.

We can now reinterpret the genetic self-realization of the transcendental ego in Husserl's account in the opposite direction such that it becomes the special reflective-nonreflective mode of the psychological ego or of life itself.[21] Life does not need a transcendental master directing and dominating it from above. It has within itself the light that enables it to reflect upon itself and to enrich its own content. Is this not what Husserl wanted to convey with the expression "the transcendental life"? The task of phenomenology should not be to establish the predominance of the so-called transcendental ego, but rather to secure the light inherited from life itself and to develop the wisdom gained by it to illuminate the opacity of the life-world.

From the standpoint of the psychological ego the transcendental dimension of reflection ontologically resembles nothingness, but once this "nothingness" penetrates the psychological ego everything in it changes.[22] This is the meaning of the transcendental reflection (or reduction) of human life. This reduction, or nonreflective reflection, must be performed in two different directions: toward the entirety of the natural objects of life and toward the world of life itself. Husserl was acquainted only with the former and was prevented from discerning the latter by the illusion of the self-objectifying transcendental *ego*. The reduction of the world, as a result, was virtually bequeathed to the Existential Philosophers, especially to Heidegger. Both dimensions of the transcendental reduction must now be unified from the new perspective of self-reflecting *transcendental life*.[23]

CHAPTER THREE

The Vertical Intentionality of Time-Consciousness and Sense-Giving

IN CHAPTER 2 I ARGUED THAT the agent of transcendental reflection is not the so-called transcendental ego but rather life itself, that transcendental reflection is a derivative mode of the originally nonreflective consciousness of life, and that the phenomenological reduction, as the cardinal method phenomenology employs to approach the matter itself, should therefore take account of both the reflective and the nonreflective (nonpositional) stance toward life itself. In other words, Husserl's psychological ego, or "somatic ego" (I prefer this locution in order to emphasize the ego's relation to the body), is not the worldly self-objectification of the transcendental ego, as Husserl would have it, but rather a type of Being-in-the-world whose self-awareness is at once reflectively and nonreflectively conscious.

Reflection as a mode of self-consciousness has been overvalued ever since Husserl took it as the only legitimate way to approach the matter itself. In his book *Lebendige Gegenwart*, however, Klaus Held has already found that the anonymous ego of life that stimulates the temporalization of the living present cannot be treated by transcendental reflection in principle, since the latter grasps everything in flowing time, and thus always comes too late to seize anything emerging at the source of the original present.[1] One might nonetheless question this analysis in the following manner: if we cannot grasp the anonymous ego at all, on what basis can we presume to discuss it in such a way? Just as the life-world is not given solely through transcendental reflection as self-observation but also through incarnate monadization, or the "in-flow" of the worldly apperception of the transcendental ego into the body, so too the somatic ego will not be given solely through self-reflection but also through the reflective-nonreflective mode of the self-consciousness of life. This latter mode is crucial to our quest for the somatic ego.

Sartre introduced the concept of *être-pour-soi* or *conscience non-positionelle de soi* in connection with this problematic, but he failed to connect it structurally to any reflective mode of self-consciousness. The nonreflective and reflective modes of self-consciousness are dialectically or circularly connected to each other, and no one can grasp either one of them without referring to the other. Indeed, self-reflection has as its necessary premise the nonreflective cognition of self, while the latter cognition progressively assimilates reflective recognition in the flow of time and thus builds itself up.

Access to this pregiven somatic ego is, of course, a result of the phenomenological reduction in the wider sense and thus apodictically evident to the phenomenological consciousness, although not adequately, in the same way as the pregiven world is given unthematically to the transcendental reflective consciousness. The somatic ego is originally the proper correlate, or the proper inhabitant, of the life-world. Its proper prereflective status, however, has long since been buried under the veil of what might be called "Husserlian Reflectionism."

In order to clarify some fundamental aspects of the transcendental somatic ego, we will here take up the problem of time. Time belongs to the consciousness of the somatic ego as the indispensable form of its intuition and recognition. Beyond the variety of many popular interpretations of time, everyone would likely agree upon the following point: namely, that there are two ways of understanding the "present" in time, one as now-moments that flow one after the other toward the past, and the other as that which remains still at the origin of the flow and never flows itself. The latter of these two presents may be called the fountainhead of the flow. Husserl himself combined these presents, calling them "standing-flowing present." By contrast, I will emphasize the qualitative difference between these two presents, even though they are dialectically or circularly connected. It is clear that the standing present plays the role of origin or zero-point to the flowing present. If there were no standing present as origin, the flow itself might dry up. In this sense, the former precedes the latter and makes it possible. Therefore the standing and the flowing present are essentially different from each other. This relation reminds us at once, and with reason, of the relation between the nonreflective and the reflective mode of consciousness of life. Here too the former precedes and makes the latter possible. It is no accident that there is a correspondence between the structure of time and the modes of life consciousness, for the standing present is nothing other than the temporal form of presencing proper to the nonreflective mode of consciousness, and the flowing now is the form of presencing proper to the reflective mode of that consciousness.

Generally the standing present is conceived of as a dividing point between the future and the past through which time flows continually in one direction, namely from the future toward the past. However, this image does not correspond to the true standing present. This image is only a shadow of the standing present, which, objectified and relativized by objectifying reflection, is made to correspond to such an image. Standing at the quasi-future-perfect viewpoint, this reflection incorporates the anticipated future—as if it had already passed—into the past dimension, and joins it seamlessly to the actual time flow moving from present to past. Insofar as the time flow from future to present is fictitious and not originary, the popular image of the standing present as a dividing point between past and future is also fictitious and not originary. It deprives the standing present of an absolute nature and makes it indefinitely shiftable along the stretched linear time flow as the "historic present." This relation between the true standing present and the fictitious one reminds us of the relation between the "Here" *(Hier)* of the ego and the "There" *(Dort)* of the alter ego in the Husserlian monad, insofar as the latter is the shadow of the former. Like the absolute Hereness of the ego, the true standing present cannot be grasped thematically from any reflective standpoint because it is the dimension of the absolute encounter between consciousness and transcendent objects as well as the absolute encounter between consciousness and its own Being-in-the-world, namely the kinesthetic living body *(Leib-Körper)*.

Hence the standing present is not to be treated as one of many nows comprised in the linear flow of time. The standing present is not on the same level as the flowing now, just as the nonreflective mode is not on the same level as the reflective mode. Therefore, for example, to talk about the proper length of the standing present without referring to the flowing nows would be meaningless. As the form of phenomena appearing to the nonreflective mode of life-consciousness, the standing present has a deep structure, the analysis of which will be the main theme of this chapter.

Husserl called the intentionality that constitutes the structure of the standing present "vertical intentionality" in contrast to "horizonal intentionality," which constitutes the stream of flowing nows.[2] Both intentionalities include the retention (memory in the first order) of primal impressions that make up the originary content of the consciousness of the standing present as it perceives transcendent objects in the world. Every retention contains intentionally within itself the retention of a former retention, and the former retention contains the retention of a further former retention, and so on. This nesting structure of retention develops either in a vertical direction or in a horizontal direction, according to Husserl; that is, it either sinks into the standing present or extends into the succession of flowing nows. In other words, in the stream of time we can see every preceding now mirrored into the following now, successively, now by now, somewhat in the way that Leibniz's monads relate to each other. In this way the standing present, as always the last successor, contains all the nesting memory of the retained pasts. At first glance, Husserl's theory of retention seems to succeed in explaining how we grasp the duration of an immanent or transcendent object—for example, the melody of a piece of music or the substantial continuity of natural things—in the flow of time.

However, when we examine the matter more closely, it becomes clear that this theory of retention cannot explain the duration of objects, for whether we look at a now-point that has just flowed away and find in it the sinking succession of retained past moments, or else from a bird's-eye view look over the flowing succession of now-points in a series such that each contains the retained memory of each past succession, what connects the different nows to each other is the effect of vertical intentionality that accumulates past moments into momentary simultaneity (Leibniz's monad). However, mirroring presentations of each other cannot connect monads temporally to each other at all, for here the horizonal intentionality is dominated solely by the isolated and self-enclosed presence of vertical intentionality. There is nothing in empty flowing to really connect each flowing now to the next. Here we might recall Bergson's argument that duration never comes from perception itself but only from the dimension of life.[3] Indeed, this statement seems to contradict Husserl's concept of a "time-object," which is something perduring in the flow of time. However, the duration of the time-object is a constituted one, that is, not the duration of the flow of time itself, but that of noematic meaning reflecting into time, for example, as a "tone" or "book." Husserl himself asserts this by saying that "the original time flow has no duration."[4]

It is interesting, thus, to hear from John Brough and others that Husserl changed his theory of retention from about 1911 on and regarded it as belonging to a deeper stratum of absolute time-consciousness rather than the stratum of the time-object.[5] In any case, duration is not caused by retention; rather, retention must be constituted by duration as an essential attribute of life.

The conscious flow of passing nows and the standing present as its origin have a common immobile bottom ground called life (or the *Leib*-layer of the somatic ego). This life never flows (contrary to many current interpretations of it) but stays still as a kind of *nunc stans* extending in indefinite continuity from the immediate present in the direction of the past. For example, my "I," as a time-object, is always changing in the flow of time. My I of five years ago and my I now are quite different as time objects. For the sake of the continuity of life itself, however, both I's are always perceived to be exactly the same (except, perhaps, in a psychiatric case). This is to say that my identity as "I" has its ground in the standing present of life or of the somatic ego in its nonreflective stance. My somatic ego is always presented to itself as the same ego. The *Leib*-layer of the somatic ego underlying the I of five years ago persists in the standing present in the broadest sense, even though my I is passing away and thus varying as a time-object. Therefore I can ascertain that my I of five years ago and my I now belong to the same standing present, as the somatic ego in its nonreflective stance. This is what I do each time that I recognize my identity. The duration of time objects, for example, of a melody or of sensory data, is achieved through a reflex of the identity of my somatic ego. When the flowing nows with their contents are grasped in a quasi-direct relation to the continuity of my life-ego, that is, of their immobile ground, they appear under the phase of duration. (That the duration given through noematic sense is also a modification of this type of duration will be indicated later.) Each flowing now is not connected to the next through the retained memory of other nows mirrored into itself, but only through its continuous ground, namely, through life and the somatic ego. Only such duration causes the retention of the flowing now, because it flows away from the original present while nevertheless remaining still in the same present in a wider sense (with relation to life). Held describes retention understood as such a phenomenon of "flowing yet standing" in the following way:

> Every kind of presentational synthesis is founded upon my "still-holding-in-grip" something that is slipping away in the present field. However, in principle, letting-slip-away precedes this holding-in-grip, for holding is possible only if something is slipping away. This distinction must not be understood in such a way that retention seems to be caused by the co-operation of two different forces. Rather it is an indissoluble unity of holding-in-grip and letting-slip-away—which does not exclude a change in the width of the present field through the variability of the synthesizing hold or interest. In all the change of interest remains the primal phenomenon: Holding-in-grip in letting-slip-away.[6]

Despite Held's comment, in our analysis of retention we must recognize that two different forces, divergent force and convergent force as it were, do seem to be working here, and related to this, we must distinguish two different kinds of standing present: (1) the standing present as the direct origin or fountainhead of the flow of time, and (2) the standing present as the immobile absolute ground of the flow of time. These two types of standing present are not at the same level, but rather are mediated and founded by each other. They share the nature of remaining still and not flowing, but the two remain still in very different manners. In brief, the difference is between a momentary simultaneity and an absolute stretched-simultaneity. One might even say in anticipation that everything in the phenomenon "time" occurs, in the end, between these two kinds of simultaneity.

The distinction between these two types of simultaneity becomes more important when we find that they correspond exactly to the double structure of the somatic ego, that is, to the extensive kinesthetic body *(Körper)* and the bodily-flesh *(Leib)*. On the one hand, the nonreflective consciousness of the kinesthetic body lives in the first type of standing present (momentary simultaneity), while, as soon as it turns into the reflective mode, it finds the just-now objectified extensive body beginning to flow away into the past as a time-object. On the other hand, the similarly nonreflective (although in another way) consciousness of the bodily-flesh lives in the second type of standing present (absolute stretched-simultaneity), as mentioned above concerning the identity of the ego. This latter consciousness can in principle never change into the reflective mode. From the above analysis, the phenomenon of retention will be explained as a combination of the second type of standing present (stretched-simultaneity) and the reflective mode of the first type of standing present (a flow of nows). Retention will be considered a special kind of reflective-nonreflective mode of life-consciousness where the retained impression flows within and through the convergent thickness of the standing-present of life.

We will now return to the vertical intentionality of the first kind of standing present, momentary simultaneity, in order to further clarify the relation between the somatic ego and the standing present. Husserl's notion of vertical intentionality captures the truth of time consciousness, even if it fails to account for the genesis of retention in flowing time. Vertical intentionality shows that time never ceases to flow, while time consciousness itself does not flow. Time consciousness contains within itself the presentation of the flow while remaining in a constant present. However, we must recognize that this passive type of intentionality forms only a part of the intentional acts that belong to the momentary present. The passive absorption of primal impressions into the present only provides the material to constitute a distinctive kind of memory, namely, undated memory. We not only retain a musical melody that we have just now heard, but we also remember it as something that has no date. We say that we have memorized or learned it by heart, or, as in Japanese, that it has been planted in our body. This kind of memory, which was philosophically discovered by Bergson, has its root in the kinesthetic dimension. Even when we memorize a verse or a sentence, this is not an intellectual phenomenon, but rather principally a kinesthetic one, for here the meaning of the verse or sentence has little importance since it is hardly more than pure phonetic activity.

Recall that the nonreflective consciousness of the extensive kinesthetic body lives in the momentary standing present. This body is
not an object but rather the subject of nonreflective consciousness,
which is nonpositionally conscious of itself as a kinesthetic schema of
physical movement. This schema forms the nonobjectifiable content
of undated memory. A memorized verse or sentence is a kinesthetic
schema of the oral organs, which, if animated, can be repeated indefinitely. A kind of iterability such as that emphasized by Jacques
Derrida with relation to the ideal presentation of the standing
present can now appear as the fundamental nature or *nunc stans* of
the nonreflective corporeal subject.[7] Thus the nonreflectively self-
conscious kinesthetic body-subject not only accumulates every flowing past into itself, but also typifies and schematizes this material into
iterative undated memory. These memories are sedimented into the
memorizing subject itself, and thus are neither time objects nor objectifiable. Rather, they are planted deep into the anonymous body
where they lie still until they are called up again to act in some pro-
tentive dimension.

Husserl discusses the I as substratum of habitualities in the *Cartesian Meditations:*

> The ego grasps itself not only as flowing life, but also as the *I*
> who experiences this and that, lives through this and that cog-
> ito, as *one and the same.* . . . For example, if in a judgment of a
> certain matter I make up my mind for the first time in favor of
> a Being and a Being-thus, this fleeting act passes away, but from
> now on I am the I abidingly determined in such and such a way,
> I am so convinced. This means, however, not merely that I re-
> member the act or will be able to recollect it further down the
> line. . . . As long as this conviction holds for me, I can *come back*
> to it repeatedly and over and over again find it as mine, as ha-
> bitually my own, that is, find myself as the I who is convinced —
> determined as the persisting I through this abiding habit; it is
> the same for every determination, every value-judgment, every
> volition. I make up my mind — the experience of the act flows
> away but the determination persists —[8]

Although Husserl uses the words "determination" or "conviction" here, this description will also apply to undated memory, for
"habit" is a kind of undated memory that is repeatedly actualized in

daily life. Husserl takes this I of habituality to be a second pole confronting the pole of the transcendent object. However, he never recognizes that this ego is a nonreflectively self-conscious corporeal
body in the momentary present. Therefore, in order to make the
real figure of this subject clearer, I will address its functional intentionality toward the object in the world.

According to Husserl, perception is "givenness in the flesh" (leib-
hafte Gegebenheit).[9] This metaphorical expression is pregnant with
meaning, for it is evident that the bodily flesh as the ground of the
immanent flow of time has its correlate in the transcendent realm as
the pregiven horizonal world called "the earth."[10] The bodily flesh
and the earth are two aspects of one and the same ultimate ground,
which Merleau-Ponty called the "flesh" (chair).[11] We can find the
same substratum underlying the immanent consciousness as well as
beyond it in the transcendence of objects in the world (like Kant's
"thing-in-itself"). This substratum is the product of neither metaphysics nor mysticism, but forms the primal-doxa of the theory of the life-
world. Our perception in the momentary present is a givenness in
the flesh, that is, the severing of sensual manifestation from the horizonal flesh into the mold of extensive solidity. This severing might be
called the "dehiscence" of the flesh (Merleau-Ponty).[12]

The flesh is given to perception in the schema of solidity (res extensa). Perceived things are given together with their unseen sides.
Where does this solidity of perceived objects come from? The Husserl of the Ideas seems to ascribe it to the form of manifestion of the
noema, and to treat it as an ideal problematic within regional ontology. He writes:

> The regional idea (Idee) of a thing, its identical x with a deter-
> mining sense-content, posited as a Being—prescribes rules to the
> manifold of appearances . . . It becomes clear . . . that every ap-
> pearance of a thing conceals within it a stratum that we call a
> thing-schema (Dingschema): it is the spatial figure merely filled
> with "sensory" qualities—without any determination of "sub-
> stantiality" and "causality." . . . Even the idea pertaining to a
> mere res extensa is a title for a plethora of phenomenological
> problems.[13]

However, it is preferable to ascribe the schema of solidity to
the activities of functional intentionality and to the nonreflective

consciousness of the kinesthetic body. This body is itself extensive
and solid. It has in itself, parallel to the dynamic undated memory
of kinesthesis, another more standing memory of solidity as the
bodily schema. The latter functions as the infrastructure of the
former. That is to say, we grasp ourselves nonpositionally as something voluminous or solid enveloped by a delicately curved surface. Every physical movement is apperceived by us as a change in
this figured solidity. As we are the subject and the pole of our
functional intentionality toward the transcendent object, this solid body-schema functions as the paradigm for constituting the object as solidity, as *res extensa*. We sever the manifold of sensory
appearances emanating from the horizon of flesh according to
this paradigm and arrange it solidly, including the unseen sides of
the figure. We sometimes arrange it incorrectly, however, for example, when we take a billboard of a human figure standing on
the street for a real person. We mistakenly introduce solidity,
which never belongs to the flat billboard, into its sensory manifold, and apperceive it as solid and voluminous.

In such a way the physical body-subject of functional intentionality constitutes the object as object in space. Here the nonpositional
consciousness of the body makes the positional consciousness of the
object possible. However, one might ask about the act of sense-
giving. Is there any constitution of the object without sense-giving?
Of course the physical (kinesthetic) body-subject is founded and mediated by the bodily-flesh as another moment of the somatic ego.
Both moments function cooperatively in the frame of the same somatic ego. Therefore the sense-giving act of the bodily-flesh is inseparable from the solidifying act of the physical body. The whole analysis
of the structure of object-constitution depends upon the adequate
synthesis of two kinds of standing present (momentary- and
stretched-simultaneity), including their living subjectivity.

IN THE FOLLOWING SECTION I will touch upon the problem of sense-
giving, insofar as it is inseparably involved with the phenomenon of
the vertical intentionality of time. The problem of sense, or meaning, is one of the most crucial and delicate issues within current phenomenology. Here is not the place to treat it comprehensively, but

according to the nature of the matter itself it is impossible to leave it untouched.

After reading Husserl's detailed description of intentional acts, especially in the fifth and sixth *Logical Investigations,* one cannot help noticing the lack of enumeration of the kinds of intentionality.[14] Husserl distinguishes between the objectifying *(objektivierende)* act, which is the foundation of all kinds of intentionality and is given by presentation *(Vorstellung)* or judgment *(Urteil),* on the one hand, and the nonobjectifying *(nichtobjektivierende)* act, which comprises questioning *(Frage),* commanding *(Befehl),* wishing *(Wunsch),* willing *(Wille),* and so on, on the other. He writes:

> By comparing the name and the statement *(Aussage)* with the expressions of the group in question [e.g., How is π a transcendent number? The driver must hitch up the carriage! May heaven help us! etc.] we find a fundamental difference as follows: the acts of presentation or judgment, which are "expressed" in a name or a statement are indeed sense-giving (or sense-fulfilling), but still not always sense-laden, and they are not objective *(gegenständlich)* in naming and predicating, but object-constitutive *(Gegenstände konstituierend).* On the other hand, and exactly contrarily, we find in all the expressions in question that the "expressed" acts become objective *(gegenständlich)* though they are ostensively sense-giving *(bedeutungsgebend).*[15]

Husserl discusses sense or meaning here as *Bedeutung,* and not yet as the noematic *Sinn.* Therefore we cannot yet be certain from this quotation whether intentional acts accompanied by particular inner experiences (questioning, commanding, wishing, etc.) could function as noematic sense-givers at all (although, in fact, in the *Ideas* Husserl seems to affirm this point).[16] However, even in the dimension of linguistic expression it is problematic to understand these acts as mere objects constituted by the objectifying acts of intentionality, as Husserl did.

Rather, we find here an entirely new genus of intentional act, one that might be called a *nonobjectifiable* act of intentionality. The nonobjectifiable act coincides not only with the Husserlian nonobjectifying acts (questioning, commanding, wishing, willing, etc.), but also (in another way) with his objectifying acts themselves (presenting or stating) as a congruent structural moment. These nonobjectifiable acts intend some inner strata of Being: kinesthesis, including the cognitive schema of the body *(Körper)*, the somatic ego, and the self- or world-Being *(Leib* in a broader sense). These Beings are transcendent to or on the borderline of the objectifying consciousness but are never objectifiable by their very nature. For example, when I wish for something to happen, my wish comes from my self-Being, which is continuous with the world-Being, and combined with the objectifying intentionality it is censored by my somatic ego. I know this clearly enough to state it as it is, though this process is never objectified. The process occurs through the phenomenologically reduced self-awareness of my nonobjectifiable act of intentionality, but never through any objectifying reflection. In this case the phenomenological reduction signifies (1) the bracketing of the Being of every object in the world, and (2) the suspension of belief in the Being of the self and of the world as horizon. Only this reduction makes the existence and function of the nonobjectifiable act of intentionality visible, because the origin of belief in Being as such lies in this very kind of intentionality. The phenomenological reduction is therefore nothing other than the self-approach and self-catharsis of this intentionality. As Husserl was not yet aware of the ontological difference between the Being of an object and that of the world, his reduction remained incomplete and unsatisfactory, especially with reference to the Being of the world.

Here some remarks about the somatic ego are in order. This ego, developed from the psychological ego of Husserl, lives in the "life-world" with its own "body." To call it, in the Occidental tradition, a "psycho-physical Being" is very naive in a phenomenological sense, since this name expresses little more than the fact that this ego belongs to two different dimensions at the same time. The somatic ego could be more appropriately described as dwelling at the borderline of two dimensions: objectified and nonobjectifiable. Various things in the world are objectified (or objectifiable), but the world itself is essentially nonobjectifiable. The human body is on the one hand objectified (or objectifiable) as the *Körper,* but on the other hand it is nonobjectifiable as pure flesh *(Leib).* Therefore the somatic ego, living in the world among various things including its own body, belongs to these two different dimensions (the objectified and the nonobjectifiable) simultaneously. In other words, this ego is the origin of the two intentionalities, namely the objectifying and the non-objectifiable. While with the former intentionality the ego intends various (transcendent) objects and reflects upon itself as object *(Körper)* in the world, it also intends with the latter intentionality either the world as horizon or its *Leib* as its self-Being (which is congruently continous with the Being of the world), or, especially in the act of imagination, both at the same time.

In this way the somatic ego is neither immanent to objectifying consciousness nor transcendent to it, but lives just on the borderline of both areas in its conscious body. Of course the objectifying consciousness means something different here from the stream of pure consciousness in the *Ideas*, because my objectifying consciousness (it is not only mine, but one of ours) is a priori interintentional and cooperative among plural intentionalities whose proper form is not only temporal but also spatial, in the sense that space is the schema of cooperation of this interintentional consciousness.[17] Regrettably I was unable to touch on this point in the explication of the cognitive *Körper* schema (solidity) in the first part of this chapter. As a matter of fact, this *Körper* schema is primordially constituted by such an interintentional consciousness at the zero-point of a nonreflected space that corresponds temporally to the standing presence of vertical intentionality. Thus my body *(Körper)* is coupled a priori with other things of the world including the bodies of others. Therefore the objectifying consciousness not only flows reflectively according to a temporal schema but also abides nonreflectively and cooperatively in space (i.e., in the momentary standing-present) around various objective Beings in constituting them within a common cognitive *Körper* schema (solidity). My objectifying consciousness is not enclosed in temporal inwardness but is penetrated by the intentionalities of others and in turn penetrates freely into space. Thus we can say that the somatic ego lives on the borderline between time (the flowing now) and space (standing present), or on the borderline of the immanence and transcendence of objectifying consciousness, and that it is a priori simultaneously—and in a complex way—intersubjective and a genuine individual.

The dimension of kinesthesis, which is founded by the cognitive *Körper* schema, consists in the conversion of dated memory into undated memory, or of objectifying intentionality into nonobjectifiable intentionality. Dated memories of the movement of the body in the stream of objectifying consciousness become concentrated as undated sediment and schematized by the nonobjectifiable act of consciousness to become the corporeal schema. When a baseball player swings a bat repeatedly before a mirror as an exercise, he is trying to bring about this conversion. He wants to be able to swing the bat in the same correct form in the game without looking into the mirror (without objectifying himself), namely, through nonobjectifiable intentionality. This sedimented form (schema) is further connected to objectifying intentionality in the movement toward a pitched ball in the batter's box.

We also find this type of cooperation between the objectifying and the nonobjectifiable act in the case of the application of the cognitive schema of the body *(Körper)*. Here, again, the nonobjectifiable intentionality toward this schema (solidity) is functionally coupled with objectifying intentionality toward the spatio-temporal area, enabling the cognition of extended beings in general. This fundamental schema of solidity is very important because it represents the deep structural relationship between consciousness and the body. It points out that even the fundamental objectifying consciousness cannot function without the foundation of the body *(Körper)*. If this consciousness were pure nothingness, as Sartre would have it, it would never be able to grasp the corporeal solidity of things. The objectifying act of consciousness is entirely based upon the solidity of the body *(Körper)* as a nonobjectifiable schema.

It will already be clear to everyone who has followed our argument up to this point that the vertical intentionality of time consciousness is another name for the nonobjectifiable intentionality of consciousness viewed from the perspective of temporality. Nonobjectifiable intentionality functions in the momentary standing present when it intends the kinesthetic and cognitive *Körper* schema, while it functions in the stretched standing present when it intends the Being of the self or of the world or of both of them simultaneously, as in the case of imagining.

The nonreflective stance, which was connected to vertical intentionality in the first part of this chapter, will become somewhat clearer when this stance is interpreted as eminently that of the nonobjectifiable act in itself. The reflective stance, by contrast, will be interpreted as eminently that of the objectifying act in itself.

We will now turn to the main theme of this part of the chapter: the problem of sense-giving. Through the coupling of the nonobjectifiable act with the objectifying act, the somatic ego with its self-Being *(Leib)* intends the sensory manifold by way of the cognitive and kinesthetic *Körper* schema. This manifold is then objectified and severed from the horizonal world-Being, but it still contains de-totalized Being as a whole within itself. This Being of the object, which is de-totalized from world-Being as a whole, still sustains the inner relation to the original Being from which it was cut off. Such an ontological relation of an object to the world as a whole includes as its quality the projected tool-aim-systematic described by Heidegger in *Being and Time*, but it has an essentially broader and richer content because it is the ontological and semantic positioning of that object within the entire world. This Being of the object with its inner relation to the entire world should be called "noema," or the noematic sense in our new perspective.

Indeed, here the noema not only forms the center of the synthesis of sensory multiplicity *(Auffassungssinn)* as in the case of Husserl,[18] but also is what gives the objectified its ontological relation toward the somatic ego with its kinesthesis, and toward the entire world. This is exactly what a child asks whenever he or she encounters something objectified but not yet known. In the case of its identification with something he or she already knows, what appeals to the child most as a mark of identification is not the object's shape or any of its sensory qualities, but its noema as the ontological-semantical relationship. Yet the noema is not just individual Being, but has already been typified through one's own experiences; one surely encounters many things with the same noema.

Although Husserl's objectifying act comprises meaning *(Signitive)* intention *(Bedeutungsintention)* on the one hand and intuitive intention (noema as its material moment) on the other, in mutual congruence, hitherto we have treated only the latter, because the phenomenological relationship between linguistic meaning *(Bedeutung)* and noematic sense is not yet sufficiently clear to be treated here. Husserl himself confessed his wavering with respect to this problem.[19] J. N. Mohanty is pessimistic about the possibility of theoretically unifying these essentially different meanings.[20] Donn Welton, too, recognizes at least a dialectic, if somewhat external, relationship between these two aspects after struggling with this problem.[21]

This issue is very important because it concerns the very nature of the so-called ideal identity of linguistic meaning itself. Does logical-linguistic meaning *(Bedeutung)* have a Platonic ideality that is independent of any nonobjectifiable Being of an object? Or is the so-called strict identity of meaning rather a result of the *Ereignis* (occurrence) of the Being of the world, which is not mine, but perhaps "Thine," through the Being of the object? In any case, the newly discovered intentional relationship between kinesthesis and noema in the constitution of the object seems to suggest the key to solving the enigmatic relationship between the sign and linguistic meaning.

CHAPTER FOUR

Perception and Imagination

The Point of Contact between Phenomenology
and Ontology

IN THIS CHAPTER I will explicate the dimension of pregiven Being that lies beneath vertical intentionality and the sense-giving act, the two foci of chapter 3.

In order to avoid unnecessary equivocation concerning the names "phenomenology" and "ontology," I will specify from the outset that the theme of this chapter will be the relationship between Husserl's own phenomenology and the phenomenological ontology historically derived from it primarily by Heidegger and Sartre. Moreover, I will defer a discussion of the historical and factual relationship between these schools of thought for now and focus instead upon the methodological and purely theoretical relationship between them. In other words, I will consider why and how the philosophy of the human being that adopts material and individual "Existentialia" rather than eidetic categories was derived from the Husserlian phenomenology that consistently referred to itself as an eidetic science or strict science of essence. How and why was phenomenological "ontology" born from the phenomenology that suspends the general thesis of Being through the phenomenological reduction or epoché? How does the life-world that the later thought of Husserl reached differ from the dimension of existence or *Dasein* in Heidegger and Sartre? Finally, what is the true relationship between perception, the principal topic of Husserlian phenomenology, and imagination as it is addressed by the phenomenological ontologists? These will be the main themes of this chapter.

As is well known, the treatment of these themes becomes

more difficult when we consider the remarkable transformation in Husserl's thought during his lifetime. However, even here we will come to see a movement that might be characterized as a ceaseless approach to an ultimate goal motivated by a kind of inner necessity rather than a simple history of changing thoughts, although doing so requires an interpretation that goes beyond Husserl's own words. Similarly I will interpret the Existentialist philosophers in such a way as to deepen or broaden their views on "Being-in-the-world." I believe that only in doing so is it possible to discover the real point of contact between phenomenology and phenomenological ontology. By exposing this point of contact we may be able to do away with the equivocation that has haunted the term "phenomenology" in general.

THE DEVELOPMENT OF HUSSERL'S PHENOMENOLOGY

Husserl's Cartesianism

In his last book, *The Crisis of European Sciences and Transcendental Phenomenology* (1938), Husserl referred to the "transcendental reduction" developed in the *Ideas Pertaining to a Pure Phenomenology and to a Phenomenological Philosophy,* which had been published about twenty-five years before, as the "Cartesian way," and he stated that this method was so riddled with difficulties that it should be exchanged for an entirely new one. Landgrebe, Husserl's former assistant, writes in his paper "Husserl's Farewell to Cartesianism" (1963) that Husserl's "phenomenology of pure consciousness" conceived as a "strict science" began to change remarkably from the time of his lecture "First Philosophy" given in the winter semester of 1923-24.[1] What, then, is the Cartesianism of Husserl, or the Cartesian method of reduction? Why and into what was it supposed to have changed?

It is obvious that Husserl's perspective in the *Ideas* is strongly influenced by Descartes. For example, Husserl's epoché, or bracketing, of the general thesis of the natural attitude, or of the *Dasein* of the world, is always considered in comparison with Cartesian doubt. The general thesis—by means of which the "real" surrounding world is consistently known not only conceptually but also as existing "reality"—does not consist, of course, of an articulated predicative judgment about existence. It is surely something continuously existent for the duration of any attitude during natural waking daily life. Husserl writes:

> We can deal with a potential and unexpressed thesis in exactly the same way as with an expressed thesis of judgment. Such a procedure, which is possible at any time, is, for example, *Descartes's attempt at universal doubt,* undertaken for the sake of a completely different goal, in order to bring out a sphere of absolutely indubitable Being. We start from this point, but we emphasize at once that the attempt at universal doubt will only be useful for us as a methodological expedient, in order to select certain points that will be brought to light through it, summed up in its essence. . . . *We do not abandon the thesis that we have performed, we do not change our conviction* . . . yet, we put it so to speak "out of action," we "switch it off," we "bracket" it. . . . In the attempt to doubt . . . an "exclusion" is performed in and with a modification of the anti-thesis, namely, with the *"supposition" of non-Being* which thus makes up the common ground of the attempt to doubt. In the case of Descartes this supposition is so predominant that one can say that his universal attempt to doubt is properly an attempt at universal negation. This we will leave aside. . . . *We select only the phenomenon of "bracketing" or "exclusion,"* which is obviously not bound to the phenomenon of the attempt to doubt, though particularly easily drawn from it, and which on the contrary can also appear in other combinations and no less on its own. In relation to every thesis we can practice this particular *epoché* in full freedom.[2]

Husserl furthermore explained that "instead of the Cartesian trial of universal doubt, we could now let the universal *epoché* in our sharply defined new sense step in."[3] Thus we can see that the Husserlian epoché has at least some elements in common with Cartesian doubt, although it excludes the antithetic tendency of the latter. Nevertheless, if, as Husserl later states in *Experience and Judgment* (1939), doubt is an undecided condition floating between two beliefs, the phenomenological epoché that suspends judgment on the thesis or antithesis concerning the existing world will be regarded as a kind of controlled doubt in a broader sense.

In the case of Descartes, too, it is not always essential that doubt involve the idea of the nonexistence of the world. This occurs only after the introduction of the "evil genius" from the outside, while the essence of doubt originally lies in a situation such as wavering between the real world and the world of dreams or imagination, just as one might, for example, between a square tower and a round tower. As will become clearer gradually, the most important thing in the attempt to doubt is to keep one's attention consistently on the (doubted) world and not to turn one's eyes away precisely from the world, lest the doubt would result in the so-called turn to the subject.[4] In this turn Descartes does argue, "I exist indubitably insofar as I am thinking," while Husserl insists that whether the world exists or not, pure consciousness remains as a "phenomeno-logical residue" that will become a field of phenomenology, a "science of consciousness" in a new sense.[5]

However, Husserl's Cartesianism in the *Ideas* is more radical than Descartes's. While Descartes's cogito literally loses its relation-ship to the world of things through the turn to the subject and needs the mediation of God to recover it, Husserl's pure consciousness, a kind of absolute Being, "preserves all worldly transcendences . . . in itself, 'constitutes' them in itself."[6] For Husserl, "Consciousness (Ex-perience) and real Being *(reales Sein)* are anything but coordinate kinds of Being,"[7] and "immanent Being is indubitably absolute Being in the sense that it in principle *nulla 're' indiget ad existendum"* (needs no thing to exist),[8] while the transcendent world of things *(res)* is completely dependent on consciousness.[9] In other words, "the world itself has its entire Being as a certain 'sense' that presupposes abso-lute consciousness as the field of sense-giving."[10] Through such a se-mantification of Being nothing is omitted from the world. It is just as in the case where "nothing is taken away from the fully valid geomet-rical Being of the square when one . . . denies that it is round."[11] Hus-serl states further that "the entire spatio-temporal world is . . . a Being that consciousness posits and is to be intuitable and determin-able as identical only through harmoniously motivated multiplicities of experience—but *beyond this* is nothing."[12]

In Husserl's attitude, in which he on the one hand insists that "between consciousness and Being a veritable abyss of meaning opens,"[13] and on the other hand makes the real world completely de-pendent upon consciousness, we can understand his Transcendental Idealism as a radicalized Cartesianism. What, then, forced him in a later period to transform this Cartesianism? As I have already mentioned, in his last book, the *Crisis,* Husserl writes that "the much shorter way to the transcendental *epoché* in my *Ideas Pertaining to a Pure Phenomenology and to a Phenomenological Philosophy* which I called 'Cartesian' . . . has the great disadvantage that while it leads, in one leap, as it were, to the transcendental ego, because of the necessary lack of preliminary explication, it brings the ego to light in a seeming emptiness of content in which one is perplexed as to what is to be gained by it and how a new and philosophically decisive science, a fundamentally new kind of science, is to be gained from it."[14]

What is this seeming "emptiness" of the transcendental ego? Shortly before the passage from the *Crisis* cited above, Husserl states, "What is given with and in this deliberation *(epoché)* is the discovery of the universal, the in itself enclosed and absolutely self-sufficient correlation between the world itself and world-consciousness."[15] It is remarkable that here the consciousness produced by the *epoché* is no longer called a pure consciousness but rather a world-consciousness, and that the correlation between consciousness and the world is emphasized rather than the self-sufficiency of consciousness itself. If we go back to *First Philosophy,* Husserl says, referring, for the first time, to the new, second way of reduction, "To survey my life is therefore at the same time and in correlative expression: to survey the world,"[16] and "So the reflection upon my whole life brings forth not a mere life without the objects experienced in life, without its real and ideal worlds, but precisely together with them as correlates."[17] Referring to this passage of *First Philosophy,* Ludwig Landgrebe also says, "It was claimed that after the reduction to the 'apodictic' evidence of I am in accordance with the critique of mundane experience, not only an empty point-like consciousness remains, but rather a consciousness of 'I am and I am experiencing this world.'"[18] This means that the experience of the horizonal world itself is already included within the stream of perceptive experience itself. Through this analysis, Landgrebe tells us, Husserl cut to the heart of that dimension of world-consciousness that Kant points to in the preface to the first *Critique* by saying, "How this should be possible we are as little capable of explaining further as we are of accounting for our being able to think the abiding in time, the coexistence of which, with the changing, generates the concept of alteration."[19]

The various citations above coincide in the suggestion that for the Husserl of the *Crisis* not only does the relative weight of the world vis-à-vis consciousness remarkably increase, but in addition the world is discovered as the necessary correlate of consciousness even after the phenomenological *epoché*. Here his Cartesianism, which insisted upon the absolute lack of necessity of any "thing" for the Being of consciousness, is repudiated as a kind of "seeming emptiness."

Now Husserl's farewell to Cartesianism does not result from any external cause, but rather from an inner failure immanent to his Cartesianism itself; in other words, the phenomenological *epoché* thought of as doubt in a broader sense already comprises elements that deny the absolute self-sufficiency of consciousness, as Husserl himself insists. According to Husserl, "Consciousness . . . forms an in-itself closed . . . correlation with other consciousness, the correlation of the stream of consciousness."[20] He continues, "Perception itself is what it is in the continuous flow of consciousness and is itself a continuous flow: on and on the now of perception changes into the connecting consciousness of the just-passed, and simultaneously a new now lights up, and so on."[21] The phenomenological time as the form of such a stream of consciousness is synthesized by a pure ego: "When the reflective grasp is oriented to my experience, then I have grasped an absolute self whose existence is in principle not negatable; that is, the insight that it is not is in principle impossible; it would be nonsense to think that an inner experience *given in such a way* is *not* in fact."[22] This will be called the Husserlian discovery of the indubitable existence of the self, a self that unifies the stream of inner experiences as flowing life.

Almost from the beginning to the end of his life, Husserl contrasted the spatiality of transcendent things to the temporality of consciousness in a so-to-speak metaphysical way, and took it to be self-evident that self-consciousness flows. In fact, however, herein lies a most difficult problem, a problem that also concerns the Kantian "refutation of idealism." Namely, what flows in time must always have as its precondition what does not flow at all; the former is recognizable as a flow only in contrast with the latter, which persists in time, without which "flow" itself does not have any meaning (e.g., a river flows only against the immobile bank or a riverbed).

But as the Husserlian pure ego, which gives temporal form to the stream of consciousness while reflecting upon it, is itself never encountered within the stream of consciousness, Husserl states, so it can never be this indispensable persistence in time. Nothing persisting in time can be found anymore at all. Thus, insofar as the very precondition of the flow of the stream of consciousness remains ambiguous, it is clear that the absolute self-sufficiency of consciousness required by Husserl's Cartesianism will be undermined from its ground.

This collapse is connected, however, to another more serious difficulty. The inner experience of the stream of consciousness comprises not only immanent-real experiences, but also intentional experiences. Namely, the real elements immanent to the stream of consciousness are divided into the material stratum of sensory *hyle* and the formal stratum of noesis as intentional *morphe;* the latter inspires life into multiplicities of the former, unifies them through sense-giving, and constitutes the noema, the nonreal, ideal element of consciousness as the intentional correlate of noesis. This noematic sense constituted by noesis has an identical center around which its defining contents and characters are concentrated. On the other hand, the "gaze" of the pure ego, the subject of entire intentional acts, penetrates into the act of noesis and then into the identical center of noema, ultimately reaching the putative object *x:* "Each noema possesses 'contents,' namely its 'meaning,' and relates itself through them to its object."[23] Our problem concerns precisely this intentional object *x.* Husserl says that this object *x* "is the junction of predicates or their 'carrier,' but never their unity. . . . Predicates are unthinkable without it and yet to be distinguished from it."[24] Furthermore, "The intentional object is always known in the continuous or synthetic process of consciousness, but is given again and again as 'other.'"[25]

Therefore this *x* is to be regarded as the ultimate aim of the pure ego in its intentional constitution through the noesis-noema structure or the "transcendental guidance" of the constitution of a particular object as sense-giving.[26] Indeed, the predicates or characters of the noema are not thinkable without the *x* as their subject. At the same time, however, Husserl states that if the noematic description has been adequately performed, "the identical intentional 'object' distinguishes itself evidently from the changing and changeable 'predicates.' It distinguishes itself as the central noematic moment, as *the pure x in abstraction from all predicates.*"[27] Furthermore, "The sense (the objective sense), such as we have defined it, is *not a concrete essence* in the entire continuance of the noema, but is a kind of abstract *form* inhabiting it."[28]

In other words, the *x* is gained in full evidence only when it is abstracted from all predicates, possible as well as real, that are attached to *x* as its own attributes. This situation implied a kind of hermeneutic circle: on the one hand, for the pure ego that has experienced the *epoché*, the *x* must be found before its constitution, as a guide for the gaze oriented toward the noema through the stream of hyletic multiplicities. But on the other hand, this *x* is nothing other than the identical central point that must be purely abstracted from the noematic predicates and characters to be constituted from now on. Therefore we must inevitably confront the fundamental difficulty that the *x* is necessary before its constitution but is not given until after that same constitution. How does this situation imply anything but a setback for the activity of the pure ego? Here we can also see the confusion of the semantic and the spatial unity of objects in Husserl's thought. To overcome this difficulty, as we shall see later, we shall have to think that the object *x* is evidently and adequately given in every changing multiple *hyle* together with a noematic sense pregiven in the world, and that consciousness is already that of the pregiven world before it is a consciousness of some "thing" or a putative object *x*.

Overcoming Cartesianism

We have seen in the previous section the reason the Cartesianism of Husserl's middle period was destined to collapse in relation to its two inherent structural faults. As mentioned above, the absolutism of consciousness began with the phenomenological *epoché* and the turn to the subject. Now, however, with the failure of this absolutism, a new way of performing the *epoché* had to be found. I will paraphrase Husserl's new procedure, since his own explanation in *First Philosophy* does not always seem to the point.

The new procedure will no longer be a "turn to the subject" but rather will involve keeping a persistent gaze at the world without turning the eyes away, while refraining from any judgment about the existence or nonexistence of the world and instead remaining floating between the two positions. This description coincides for the most part with what Husserl suggests in the latter part of *First Philosophy*. For Descartes, already, the thesis "I cannot doubt but I am doubting" was valid, as he states in his final work, *Recherche de la verité.* Is the truth of philosophical doubt nothing other than the thesis that the indubitable can be demonstrated only within the structure of doubt? For Descartes, as we have seen, this indubitability is attributed only to the ego. However, when we gaze at the presencing world while doubting or suspending a judgment of its existence or nonexistence, what is shown to be indubitable is not only the doubting ego or self. Rather, a new world arises that is inseparable from the doubting self and presses itself upon it as also indubitable. This world is, of course, no longer the natural world, since we refrain from any straightforward thesis about things or about the world itself. Much less is it the dimension of the noematic sense constituted intentionally by the ego. This world is not constituted and posited by any activity, but rather is given passively to the self from the outset. The attitude of the ego or self toward this pregiven world might be called the "pre-thetic," passive, prime belief.

In general it is true that a belief is always followed by the possibility of doubt. However this prime belief, which is to be found only through doubt, is in principle indubitable and apodictic because it is the precondition of doubt itself as the floating mediator of belief in existence and nonexistence, or of general thesis (intention) and general anti-thesis (empty intention). Through the process of doubting every thesis of Being concerning the world, and beyond the antagonism of thesis and anti-thesis, we find the indubitable apodicticity of the pre-thetic world as well as that of the pre-thetic doubting self. To bracket the thesis of the natural world does not mean to immediately return to the immanence of the stream of consciousness. In order for consciousness to flow as a stream an intuition of some "persistence" in time is indispensable, as mentioned above; this persistence is nothing other than this world received passively as pre-thetic Being. The transcendent thetic world of things and the immanently real stream of consciousness arise only afterward and in parallel out of this primordial pre-thetic world, separated from each other as the objective and the subjective side through the reflection of transcendental subjectivity.

Indeed, every thesis is doubtful. However this doubt itself occurs only on the precondition of a certain indubitable primary belief. The latter is comprised of the primary belief in the doubting self and in the pre-thetic world, both in complete correlation with each other. The mistake of Cartesianism lies in the fact that it recognized only the former belief, which it mistook for a belief in an ideal ego, and that it overlooked the latter belief in the world completely. What is

most remarkable here is that this world does not belong to Husserl's
so-called dimension of *doxa,* namely, the object of thetic or positional
belief. Using a Heideggerian expression, this world is not the integration of thetic beings, but rather Being as a kind of nothingness. We
might also say that it is a new historical Being, the potential Being
that produced Existential philosophy or phenomenological ontology
in the first half of the twentieth century. We can already and unexpectedly, however, find a well-couched expression of this world in
Husserl's *Experience and Judgment,* one of his latest works: "Before every employment of the activity of recognition, objects are already
there for us and are pre-given in simple certainty,"[29] and "These [pu-
tative] objects become the continuous core of acts of recognition."[30]
These objects-to-be, which are pre-given, stimulate us and rise up to
us from their positions amid the surrounding world:

> The environment is co-present as a *realm of pre-givenness,* of *pas-
> sive* pre-givenness, that is, always readily given there without
> any involvement, without a grasping gaze turning toward it,
> without any awakening of interest. All activity of recognition,
> all grasping attention to a single object has as its precondition
> this region of passive pre-givenness.[31]

Husserl continues, "We can also say that a particular world precedes
any cognitive involvement as its universal ground,"[32] and

> This *universal ground of world belief* is that which preconditions
> every praxis, as much the praxis of life as the theoretical praxis
> of recognition. The Being of the world as a whole is self-
> evidence which is never doubted. . . . *Consciousness of the world
> is consciousness in the mode of certainty of belief,* which is not gained
> through an act of positing Being occurring properly in corre-
> lation with the life, an act of grasping as existent, or even an act
> of predicative existential judgment. All of these are already
> preconditioned by world-consciousness with the certainty of
> belief."[33]

We may ask, however, does Husserl adequately grasp this world in
truth? Indeed, he attained a quite correct recognition of pregivenness, indubitable certainty, and the passivity of the world. However,
he fails, it seems, to gain an authentic insight into the profound relevance of the "pre-thetic" character of the world insofar as we can tell

from *Experience and Judgment.* As a result he did not discover the pre-thetic self (Existence) thematically as the necessary indubitable correlate of this world. His regress to the ideal region of "transcendental subjectivity" begins anew.

That he did not recognize the authentic meaning of the "pre-positionality" of the world is clearly shown by the fact that he identified this world immediately with the life-world, the field of intersubjective daily praxis. However, as he himself acknowledged elsewhere, this world is the *precondition* or the universal basis of all praxis; therefore it is the precondition or the basis of the life-world and is not the life-world itself.

If we confuse the reduction to the pre-thetic world with the reduction to the life-world, the pre-thetic self will inevitably become entangled in a chaos of various theses through the reduction, among them the kinesthetic thesis. According to this account Husserl must again refrain from any commitment to the general thesis of the world and must insist on the reduction to solitary transcendental subjectivity as the second stage of the *epoché,* as can be seen in *First Philosophy* and in the *Crisis.* As a result, the life-world, including the psychological ego, becomes an integration of intentional objects that must be constituted by transcendental subjectivity alone, though on the basis of anonymous pregivenness. One cannot deny the (somewhat lukewarm) resonance of Cartesianism even in Husserl's latest period of thought.

We must overcome Husserl's Cartesianism. Nevertheless, I will not repudiate Cartesian or transcendental subjectivity at all, even though I will insist that its origin is beyond the egological dimension. It is very plausible that the phenomenological reduction as the fundamental doubt hovering between the general thesis (existence) and general anti-thesis (nonexistence) of the world reveals not only the pre-thetic world with its self but also primal positional subjectivity— that fundamental *impersonal* intentionality that includes the differentiation between the thesis and the anti-thesis, or the anonymous freedom of positing affirmatively or negatively—to be indubitable. This subjectivity and its positing also form the precondition of doubt as do the pre-thetic world and the self: without these indubitables doubt itself becomes impossible.

This primal positional subjectivity, once immanently acquired by a pre-thetic self, corresponds to the "objectifying intentionality" of

Husserl, which is the foundation of every personal intentionality. As such, it was called by him the pure or transcendental ego in its personal aspect. However the life-world is not constituted by this Cartesian subjectivity alone.

The pre-thetic self (Existence) is not purely passive, but rather passively active. In the next section this pre-thetic self will be revealed to be the proper subject of imagination. It participates, together with transcendental subjectivity, in the constitution of the life-world. Thus positionality in a broader sense and its neutrality modification, which are merely placed side by side in Husserl's system of thought, will now appear in close cooperation with each other in moving toward the constitution of the life-world.

If Husserl had been consistently faithful to the suspension of the general thesis of the natural world and the pre-thetic character of the suspended world, he would have avoided the confusion of the pre-thetic world and the life-world, and would have dispensed with his partiality to transcendental subjectivity through the thematic discovery of the pre-thetic self, namely of Existence. The pre-thetic self prepares and assists the thetic act of transcendental subjectivity, while functioning in necessary correlation with the pre-thetic world. The paradox of human subjectivity that Husserl emphasized in his latest period, the paradox articulated as "I am a subject towards the world and at the same time an object in the world"[34] is simply a pseudoparadox when viewed from the perspective of the pre-thetic self as Being-in-the-world.

The Pre-thetic World and the Self

As we have seen, Husserl virtually arrived at the pre-thetic world, but because he did not completely overcome his Cartesianism he could not grasp its essence adequately and could not find the pre-thetic self living at the center of this world. Since I am regarding this pre-thetic dimension as the core of Existence, both the point of contact and of the separation of Husserlian phenomenology and Existential ontology seem to lie in this pre-thetic dimension, which consists of the pre-thetic world and the pre-thetic self.

According to Husserl, "If we take up the field of passive pre-givenness as it is, before the egoic activity exerts any sense-giving work upon it, it is not yet a field of objectivity *(Gegenständlichkeit)* in the original sense."[35] However, "This field is not a mere chaos, a turmoil of givenness, but rather a field of certain structure, of nuances and of articulated particulars."[36] Husserl considers the law of association to be the dominating principle of this passive sensuous field: "The unity of a sense-field is first of all a unity through associative fusion (homogeneous association); its order and its articulation as well as every grouping and equality in it are worked out by association."[37] From this passively pregiven sense-field the ego is stimulated in various ways, and if the ego responds, an active "devotion to" and an "interest in" begin to be produced. The interest of the ego tries to grasp the stimulation in its various manifestations. It is quite striking that Husserl calls this manifestation an "image" (Bild). He says, of course, that it has nothing to do with a reproduction but rather is the manner in which one looks at something or how one is looked at by someone: "In this sense every object of external perception is given in an 'image' and it constitutes itself in synthetic transition from image to image, whereby images come to synthetic co-incidence as images (appearances) of the same."[38] A certain subjective kinesthesis on the side of the ego corresponds to each image, and along the process of its action one image after another appears. Nevertheless, what the "identical" or the "same" is around which these images coincide with each other still remains an enigma.

At this point we are aware that this stage of transition from the pre-thetic, pregiven world to the general thesis of the life-world, on the side of the world, must correspond exactly to that of the transition from the pre-thetic self to the transcendental corporeal (somatic) ego, on the side of the subject. The pre-thetic self as the primordial form of Existence is necessarily thrown into the common general-thetic world by the radical reflection of transcendental subjectivity, and it is given the kinesthetic vestment of voluminosity (body-schema) and becomes a corporeal ego. This voluminosity or spatial corporeity of the ego accompanied by the nonreflective transcendental consciousness is able to constitute a similar voluminosity analogically around any image given from the world at a stroke through the transcendental principle of coupling. This is to say that to constitute an object in the life-world we need no complete synthetic convergence of images. A certain given image will associatively call up an optimum image and then, tout à coup, an inner horizon will be established around it through transcendental coupling (what Husserl describes in section 38 of the Cartesian Meditations as primal foundation or *Urstiftung* through passive synthesis seems to coincide with this, at least as a result).

Therefore, the pre-thetic world and the pre-thetic self do not suddenly disappear even in the establishment of the general thesis of the life-world by transcendental subjectivity. Rather, the pre-thetic world remains as the dimension of the optimum image of the object and its meaning, and the pre-thetic self remains as the dimension of imagination and projection.

Now I must briefly touch upon a difficult question, namely, the relationship between the phenomenological *epoché* and neutrality modification, since I now refer to the pre-thetic dimension discovered by the *epoché* as the dimension of image and imagination, as Husserl himself did to a certain degree.

The neutrality modification described in the *Ideas* is the universal modification of the modality of the thetic (or positional) character of the noematic object (e.g., being, being possible, being probable, being questionable, etc.), which brackets these modalities and neutralizes them. As a result, the neutralized theses lose their original validity and take the form of an "as it were" (being as it were, being possible as it were, etc.).

According to Husserl, the act of imagination or fantasy is the neutrality modification of positional representation or of remembrance in the broadest sense. By contrast, the neutrality modification of ordinary perception occurs when, for example, we look at the picture on a television and appreciate it as the image of certain reproduced beings. This reproducing image is neither the glass plate of the television tube nor the group of sparkling colored points upon it, but rather a neutralized perceptive object floating—"being, as it were"—before our eyes. In this way we find at least three types of image in Husserl:

1. fantasy as a neutrality modification of remembrance
2. the reproduction of an object through a perceptual object (physical analogon)
3. perceptive occurrence in genesis as a stimulus to object-constitution (perceptive image: *Wahrnehmungsbild*)

In addition, if we expand the concept of "analogon," we might call the third type of image a kind of analogon, specifically a mental analogon, of the object *x*, its profiling reproduction.

Of the image in general we can say, with Husserl, that: "It stands before us, neither as being nor as non-being, nor in any other thetic modality."[39] We must take notice of Husserl's description of the modality of the image, because the phrase "neither as being, nor as non-being" coincides with our description of the pre-thetic world, which is discovered as the indubitable residue between the general thesis and the general anti-thesis. Moreover, the image is also indubitable because we cannot doubt what is neither being nor non-being. Thus the pre-thetic dimension is at last identified with the dimension of the image. It is quite remarkable that the two dimensions, the pregiven world-horizon and the imagination, which have been regarded as completely different, can now be identified with each other.

However, as Husserl insisted, it is unnecessary, and indeed incorrect, to immediately identify the phenomenological *epoché* and the neutrality modification, since the *epoché* as fundamental doubt concerns not only negatively the disclosure of the pre-thetic dimension of the image, but also positively the disclosure of indubitable transcendental subjectivity. It is nonetheless incorrect, however, to think that the *epoché* and the neutrality modification are acts that are completely independent of each other, because the *epoché* concerns the constitution of the life-world not only from the perspective of transcendental subjectivity but also from the perspective of the pre-thetic neutral dimension, namely from the dimension of image in its broadest sense. In this sense *epoché* includes the neutrality modification as its indispensable basic element, as a Japanese phenomenologist, Satomi Takahashi, already insisted in 1930.

In fact, what stimulates us to devotion and interest in the constitution of the life-world out of the pre-thetic world is not an "object" immediately. Rather, it is an optimum obverse image of a certain object *x* buried in the background of the pre-thetic world, a relief, as it were, on a wall. It is called the "perceptive image" by Husserl, and I call it the profile analogon of *x*. To use a metaphor, it is a "physiognomy" that indexes the object to be. Guided by this pre-thetic index, transcendental subjectivity, which is already incarnated, projects an appropriate voluminosity upon the object in one stroke through the principle of coupling, and thus posits it. This is a non-Cartesian constitution of the object that does not make use of any paradoxically pregiven intentional object *x*.

Husserl neglected the pre-thetic self of imagination and hence missed the categorical function of the body-schema, which is based upon the spatial voluminosity vested in the pre-thetic self in the form of the transcendental facticity of Existence. Therefore Husserl seems to be caught up, to the very end, in the prejudice of the ideal principle of constitution, namely, by the ultimate positing of reality by reason alone. In reality, however, the pre-thetic self of imagination keeps up an intentional relationship with the perceptive object in whose core an image, as its obverse profile, remains. Husserl aptly called this intentional relationship "still holding in one's grip."

The image is posited by the pre-thetic world and in the pre-thetic world as its founding horizon; it is the phenomenon of Being-in-the-world, not immediately of the *eidos* nor of reason. Therefore the meaning of the object with its proper image must be reexamined from the point of view of the self-imaging world, now revealed passive-actively to the incarnated (somatic) ego, to transcendentally factic Existence. We will return to this problem of meaning later.

I wish to note, incidentally, that this pre-thetic world has a structural similarity to the universe of "pure experience" described by Kitaro Nishida. In Nishida's first book, *The Inquiry into the Good,* this pure experience is described as an experience in which the subject and the object are not separated from each other but are somehow fused. This condition is grounded by the coincidence of the synthetic forces within the subject and object with the fundamental synthetic force of the universe from which the subjective and objective forces diverged.[40] In the same way, our pre-thetic self and the image diverge from the pre-thetic world; they are both founded by the synthetic force of the pre-thetic world as the primordial monad, and are inseparably related to each other as subject and object. Insofar as Nishida insists that his universe comprises the total unity of intellect, emotion, and will, it is undoubtedly broader than our pre-thetic world, which is eminently limited to the region of the imagination. Nevertheless, we are certain that Nishida's universe contains the pre-thetic world within itself as an indispensable dialectical moment.

REEXAMINING THE PHENOMENOLOGICAL ONTOLOGY CALLED EXISTENTIAL PHILOSOPHY

On the basis of the above explication, we will now proceed to examine phenomenological ontology, or so-called Existential philosophy. We will do so in order to clarify the real point of contiguity of Existential philosophy with Husserlian phenomenology. We have already found one point of convergence in the pre-thetic world of the image, toward which Husserlian phenomenology consistently made an approach. This world of the image might be considered the most probable contact point of phenomenology and Existential philosophy. Indeed, the fundamental concept of "Being-in-the-world" common to Heidegger and Sartre cannot be understood without taking the pre-thetic world into consideration, since this mode of Being-in (*In-Sein*) goes beyond a simple general thesis.

However, as we shall see, Husserl thematizes the pre-thetic world alone as what is passively pregiven to intentionality and as the fundamental basis of the life-world, while neglecting the "pre-thetic self." In Heidegger and Sartre, in contrast, the pre-thetic self is seriously thematized as Existence, while the pre-thetic world itself is treated only in a quite restricted or distorted manner.

Heidegger

Just as we had difficulty in considering the development of Husserl's thought, we are troubled by the remarkable, indeed catastrophic, transformation in Heidegger's thought and its unfinishedness. I will refrain from discussing the problem of the "turn" *(Kehre)* in Heidegger's thought and confine our discussion to the consideration of Heidegger's work from the time of *Being and Time* (1927) to the publication of *Kant and the Problem of Metaphysics* (1929).

Let us begin by considering Heidegger's "ontological difference," namely, the difference between Being and beings, which he emphasized over and over again. What Heidegger calls "beings" are clearly something thetic, which encompasses the realm of the possibly thetic. However, Heidegger insists that an ontic (intentional) commitment to this thetic being is possible only under the precondition of a preliminary preontological understanding of Being. Heidegger expresses this phenomenology's aim as to "let [this Being of beings] be seen from itself as it shows itself from itself."[41]

At first glance the attitude Heidegger describes of receiving the emergence of Being passively without actively constituting it through any intentionality reminds us of the passive acceptance of the pre-thetic world described by the later Husserl. On the one hand, indeed, Husserl's all-positing transcendental subjectivity is concealed in the background for Heidegger's view, but on the other hand

Heidegger postulates an activity more active than any intentionality in Existence or the transcendence of self, which is the ability to understand and interpret the meaning of Being. The Being called Dasein, that is, a human, is the one concerned most decisively with the question of Being. This Being called Dasein is concerned with Being in its own Being, as its own possibility:[42] "The essence of Dasein lies in its Existence."[43] In other words, Existence is Dasein's ecstatic manner of Being, in which it is always "in advance of itself." In addition, Dasein has the essential structure of "Being-in-the-world." This world is not simply a sum total or integrated whole of beings (the general thesis), but rather a "how *(wie)*" of the Being of the entirety of beings as well as the aim of the transcendence of Dasein, which defines this "how" of Being.

Heidegger writes, "Dasein transcends means: it is, in the essence of its Being, world-forming *(weltbildend),* and indeed 'forming' in the following multiple senses, that it makes the world occur and together with the world gives itself an ultimate view (image), which is not properly grasped, but functions just as a model *(Vorbild)* for all the unconcealed beings including Dasein itself."[44]

This model is comparable to Plato's Idea of the Good. Heidegger continues, "Temporality is, as the ec-static horizontal unity of temporalizing, the precondition of the possibility of transcendence and therefore also of the possibility of intentionality founded by transcendence."[45] The intentionality at the origin of every thetic act is thus regarded as possible only through the temporal transcendence of Dasein. In this sense, Dasein as that transcendence that precedes every intentionality and founds intentionality can quite aptly be called the pre-thetic self.

What Dasein transcends are beings that are not arbitrarily thrown together or gathered up; rather, "however [they are] individually defined and articulated, [they] are passed over as a whole in advance."[46] It is only through this transcendence that "the world happens as world," and beings are given meanings.[47] Heidegger's Dasein, which transcends the general thesis in its entirety in advance, will also in this sense be appropriately called the pre-thetic self.

We must remain aware, however, of the fact that the prescription of corporeity is almost completely missing from Heidegger's Dasein. Heidegger seems to deliberately evade this question, judging from the following passage from *Being and Time:* "corporeity, which conceals in itself its own problematic, [is] not to be treated here."[48] In any case, the characteristics of "dis-tance" and "orientation" taken by Heidegger to be the spatiality of Dasein cannot even be thought of without the corporeity and kinesthesis of Dasein. As I see it, this incomprehensible elision of corporeity has much to do with the retreat and demotion of all-positing intentional subjectivity to a position behind the transcendence of Dasein, since the co-originality of this so-called Cartesian subjectivity with Dasein will be indispensable for the constitution of its corporeity.

If we take the above points into consideration together with Heidegger's designation of those beings that are not Dasein as "Being-ready-to-hand" *(Zuhandensein)* and "Being-present-at-hand" *(Vorhandensein)*, it will soon be clear that Heidegger's Dasein is the pre-thetic self with a very incomplete characterization of corporeity. If we return, for the moment, to the pre-thetic world as the correlate of a pre-thetic self like Dasein, what does Heidegger mean when he calls the world the aim of transcendence?

Heidegger says that the openness *(Da)* of Dasein has the structure of "the state in which one may be found" *(Befindlichkeit):* "In *Befindlichkeit* Dasein is always brought before itself, it has always found itself, not as perceptive self-discovery, but as finding itself in a mood *(gestimmtes Sichbefinden)."*[49] In another place Heidegger writes, "Such a disposition by mood . . . lets us be penetrated by it and be found in the midst of beings as a whole."[50] This way of being of Dasein is called its "thrownness" *(Geworfenheit):* "In the state of being-found essentially lies a kind of disclosive directedness to the world, out of which whatever matters can be encountered."[51]

At first glance the world disclosed in being-found-ness or in a mood seems directly to refer to the pre-thetic world. However, this is not the case, for mood is, so to speak, the shadow (the apprehension), which the pre-thetic world itself casts upon the common objective world that is virtually concealing the pre-thetic world itself.

Thus the world found through mood is not yet or not always the pre-thetic world. To reach the pre-thetic world, Husserl needed the phenomenological *epoché* or radicalized doubt. To reach the same world, Heidegger now needs a determinate mood: anxiety. Heidegger believed that anxiety is not anxious about any being within the world, but rather about the world itself. In other words, anxiety would seem to be anxious for the absence of the pre-thetic world, which is the indispensable correlate of the self. My interpretation is supported by Heidegger's characterization of anxiety as that which individuates and discloses Dasein as the *solus ipse*.[52] Individuation is the necessary condition of the exclusive correlation between the pre-thetic self and its world, which will not allow any direct intervention of others as the monadic structure.[53]

The difference in Husserl's and Heidegger's methods used to approach the pre-thetic world necessarily introduces a difference in the ways they characterize this world. Husserl found that the image that comes from this world stimulates us to the constitution of the object. Heidegger, by contrast, will see in the image that emerges from the world the aim *(worumwillen)* or goal of transcendence (project) of the pre-thetic self, when it is freed from any corporeity (positionality). Indeed, every image is the phenomenon of the Being of the pre-thetic world, but what is new in Heideggerian transcendence is that the whole Being of the pre-thetic world is grasped as concentrated in or converged upon an image. On account of the peculiar concentration or convergence of Being, the image becomes not only the phenomenon but also the meaning of the Being *(Seins-sinn)* of the pre-thetic world. This ontological semantification seems to be even more important considering that the origin of every nominal meaning (essence) of objects could be found here.

This meaning of and as the world is also the meaning or the possibility of the Being of the self, Dasein, and contains in itself a new type of futurity as the advancement to one's own possibility. Beings within the world are given meanings from the future, as their optimum images with voluminosity represent the ultimate aims of the putative projections by the transcendence of Dasein. For example, the meaning of a pen is the Being of the pre-thetic world into which and by which we project the image of a pen. I cannot agree with Heidegger when he defines the meaning of a being that is not Dasein through its relevance *(Bewandtnis)* in the chain of utility *(woraufhin)*, which is subordinate to and joins with the ultimate aim of Dasein's primary project *(worumwillen)*.[54] If this were the case, the meaning of the being would be restricted by its particular situation and position in the chain and could never reach its Being as such. I would like to draw its meaning out directly from the primal aim *(worumwillen)*, in and as the image of which the being is thematically focused upon the background of the chain of other utensils. In other words, I will not define the meaning of a pen from the paper or the ink or the desk, but rather from the aim of our projection concerning the pen itself, namely, to write.

Husserl's noematic objective sense (X), which is immobile during the multiple changes of perception, might be the Being of the pre-thetic world converged into the optimum profile of this object as the aim of our projection. Such a meaning is never constituted by Cartesian subjectivity alone because it originally belongs to another pre-thetic dimension. But the transformation of this meaning of the object, which is still mine *(je-meinig)*, into the essence or *eidos* seems to require the mediation of a transcendental subjectivity intending all temporality and all locality, or in other words the primal copresencing of egos. Then the future pro-jected meaning must be re-collected anew from the infinite past as a kind of *anamnesis*.

Thus we have found that Heidegger's Dasein is deeply rooted in the dimension of pre-thetic Being, and while he explicated several new aspects of this pre-thetic Being, he nevertheless treated it only within a very limited scope, as the transcendence or the projection of the self.

Sartre

For the sake of convenience, I will restrict the scope of our discussion to Sartre's work up until the time of the publication of *Being and Nothingness* (1943).

Sartre splits the domain of pre-thetic Being into nothingness and material Being-in-itself. On the one hand, then, the pre-thetic world becomes the nothingness of imaginative consciousness, the antithesis of material Being as a whole, and on the other hand the pre-thetic self becomes the transcendent material body, the residue of that same material Being as a whole, which is also the Being to be of the self. As a result, the human being is always automatically posited in a kind of "lacking" or "deficient" condition vis-à-vis Being.[55] On the other hand, the Husserlian transcendental subjectivity of all-positing intentionality is ontologically connected to presencing of material objects, and loses its freedom of negating the positionality, as this function is now transferred to the imagination alone.

From the outset Sartre takes the phenomenological *epoché* to be the liberation of the consciousness from any ego immanent to itself: "The ego is not the possessor of consciousness, but the object of consciousness."[56] Such consciousness, free from any parasitic ego, becomes the domain of pure spontaneity and the power of the nullification or limitation of material Being as a whole. As the ground of absolute freedom it cannot receive any stimulus. Rather, it needs a partner to whom it could demonstrate its freedom and spontaneity. Thus a metaphysical Being called Being-in-itself, which has full density and inertia as the recipient of consciousness's nullification, is produced. This Being-in-itself lets consciousness explode within itself as nothingness and embraces like a vermiculate hole.[57]

The human as consciousness is this nothingness, which thetically intending the objectified thing, non-thetically drags a body as its Being with itself. Sartre writes that "Consciousness is a Being for which in its Being, its Being is in question insofar as this Being implies a Being that is not its own."[58] Sartre calls such a human "Being-for-itself."

A human is an ontological lack, and insofar as it is a Being-for-itself, lacks an identity with itself. As consciousness is the nullification of Being-in-itself as a whole, and the thetic object that it intends as its own Being is the residue of Being-in-itself nullified, consciousness is in a mode of lack and thus must be haunted by possibility, which is precisely what is lacking from Being as a whole.

But the problem still remains whether or not the self-decomposing nullification of Being-in-itself as a whole could in itself comprise and produce thetic objects in a genuine sense. For example, in the past dimension its own thetic Being (the objective body) appears for Being-for-itself. This might be its own figure exposed to hunger or severely judged by another person. Insofar as this is posited not by its own imagination but by its own transcendental subjectivity, for the time being it lies in reflected three-dimensional objective space, not immediately in nullified Being-in-itself (the field of the imagination). Therefore, if we do not immediately take every act of positing to be the de-totalizing nullification of Being-in-itself without good reason, such thetic figures do not always signify the condition of lack. Only once they are taken back to the pre-thetic self as its thrownness or facticity could they become motivation for the transcendence to the future, stimulating the self from the inside. Hunger does not always produce "possibility" in the form of "fulfilled hunger," as Sartre says,[59] nor does the severely judged self always want to recover the freedom that others deprived him or her of. Rather, these situations are only possible and potential motivations to the transcendence of the pre-thetic self. Therefore they can sometimes disappear and not become motivation. Such a possibility is already cut off by Sartre, however, insofar as he does not allow any motivation by the internal stimulus of the self.

Similarly, since, as Sartre writes, "Every [nonreflective] positional consciousness of an object is at the same time a non-positional consciousness of self,"[60] and since this object is always haunted by the absent Being of the self as "value" through the so-called circuit of selfhood, the presented object seems to be posited not as a bare thing but rather as an available utensil. Consequently my non-thetic body, which confronts this utensil, must possess a sedimentation of the kinesthetic scheme that would operate this utensil. This means that this non-thetic body is not only pre-thetic but also has already been penetrated by transcendental subjectivity through a variety of physical training, and thus is so to speak ontologically alienated. Such a body is no longer the material Being-in-itself as plenitude without any gaps, but rather might be called the "biological organism," as Sartre referred to the human being in his later thought.

Moreover, material Being is the Being of passive inert power proper to resistance, which generally accompanies only positional perception, although it is sometimes distributed by empathy through corporeal coupling beyond the limit of direct perception. This means that material Being is only proper to particular thetic beings already scattered separately from each other in space. Thus Sartre's "monolithic" material Being as a whole with no gaps seems in this sense to lead to a paradoxical situation. In my opinion, such a complete fusing totalization is possible only for the pre-thetic Being proper to the imagination.

Therefore, it will not be necessary for us to think that Sartre's Being-for-itself as a kind of pre-thetic self (Existence) is always forced ontologically toward transcendence as a deficient mode of Being-in-itself as a whole with no gaps, namely as a "Being that is not what it is."[61] Rather, the pre-thetic self stays in inner correlation with the pre-thetic world unless it is stimulated from inside by anxiety and forms together a primal unitary domain preceding any differentiation into material Being as a whole (thesis) and imaginative consciousness (anti-thesis). In order to confirm this, first the Sartrian view of imagination as the nullification (negation) of material Being-in-itself must be overcome.

According to Sartre in *The Imaginary* (1940), "Image also comprises an act of belief or a thetic act. This act can take four forms and only four: it can posit the object as nonexistent, or as absent, or as existing in another place, and it can also be 'neutralized,' that is, it can be not positing its object as existent. Two of these acts are negations, while the fourth corresponds to a suspension or neutralization of the thesis. The third, which is positive, presupposes an implicit negation of the natural and present existence of the object."[62]

Thus, while the perceptive consciousness posits the object as in itself existing, the imaginative consciousness posits the object as something negative. However, according to a footnote Sartre places here, the fourth act still remains a kind of positional act.[63] Why is the neutralization of the object, the act of "not positing the object as existent" still a kind of positional act? Is this a kind of positing of an image-object (e.g., a photograph) as "nothingness" before my eyes? This is not exactly the case, for as we have already seen, the neutrality modification of the thesis involves transferring an object into a new domain called "pre-thetic Being," which is beyond thetic and anti-thetic Being. Sartre, too, says that "the image is an act which intends an absent or nonexistent object in its corporeity through a physical or mental content, which is not given properly, but with the qualification of being an 'analogical representation' of the intended object."[64] Therefore, if the intention of looking at the analogon of an object is still a thetic act, as Sartre insists, it is because, for example, when I look at a television screen, I posit the playing person also as an object *x*, which is nonexistent or absent or in another place, through the image floating before me as pre-thetic Being.

Thus we find that all four types of imaginative act include the thetic acts of transcendental subjectivity in the objective space-time horizon: (1) an absent object means one that is posited in another present in the same place; (2) an object that is in another place means that it is literally posited now in another place; (3) a nonexistent object, for example, a Siren, means something that is either posited in various points of real space-time scattered part by part, as Descartes assumed in the *Meditations,* or posited in a fictitious (virtual) space-time horizon that is quasi-objectively definable; (4) a physical analogon means an auxiliary perception, which when neutralized becomes an image and helps us to intend any of the above-mentioned three types of object. These objects are indeed not present before our eyes, here and now, but rather are posited firmly in certain points of the outer space-time horizon by our transcendental subjectivity.[65] I should add here, however, the more important fifth type of image to Sartre's four types, namely, (5) the image that radiates forth, here and now, from the pre-thetic world and stimulates us to the constitution of the object, which Husserl called the "perception-image," and which I will call the "physiognomy" of the object. The perception is nothing other than the constitution of the object by way of and on the occasion of this self-giving image here and now. Therefore the difference between perception and imagination consists only in the manner in which the intentional object of the image is constituted thetically in the external horizon of our transcendental subjectivity. In other words, perception is distinguished only in the specific loco-temporal coincidence of the standing presence of the image in genesis with the self-presencing of the positional act of transcendental subjectivity (selbt-gebende Gegebenheit), which is lacking in imagination in the proper sense.

However we must not forget that the image always retains within itself an inner relation to the pre-thetic world from which it is born. This becomes evident when we think of the meaning of the object constituted. The noematic meaning of an object is not the representation of that which material Being as a paradoxical whole lacks, as Sartre argues, but is rather the convergent representation of the Being of the pre-thetic world out of which and into which the optimum image of the object (physiognomy) as the ultimate aim of putative projection is born. This meaning will be idealized as the *eidos* in the process of realizing the primal copresence of my somatic cognitive ego and other egos by way of the free variation of the optimum image through the pan-temporality and pan-locality of impersonal transcendental subjectivity.

In this way, by introducing the total cooperation of transcendental subjectivity, Sartre's view of imagination is to be completely revised. As I have already mentioned, every object, whether it be presencing or not, has as its proper physiognomy the optimum image, the phenomenon of the pre-thetic world, so that the difference between perception and imagination turns out to be nothing more than the difference of position that the object of each act has in the external horizon, or in other words, the difference in the manner of cooperation between the imagining pre-thetic self and positional transcendental subjectivity. It will no longer be necessary to think that perception is the thesis of Being and imagination is the thesis of nothingness or non-Being. As a result, perception and imagination are not exclusive of each other, as Sartre thought, but rather are twins born from the same origin and coexisting on the same horizon of experience. Otherwise neither the *epoché* as radicalized doubt nor the recognition of objective meaning nor the kinesthetic movement of the body, including the speech act, are possible.

Thus we can free Sartre's material Being and his ontology from their narrowness and can connect them to Husserlian transcendental subjectivity and to our pre-thetic world.

CONCLUSION

Not only have we found in the pre-thetic dimension of the image the most salient point of contact between Husserlian phenomenology and Heideggerian and Sartrian phenomenological ontology, but we have also found, through the reinterpretation of the phenomenological *epoché* as radicalized doubt hovering between the general thesis and the general anti-thesis, a new theoretical framework into which both disciplines can be fitted, *mutatis mutandis,* as congruent constituents of a completely new philosophical understanding of the human being. This framework stretches between primal transcendental subjectivity as the origin of perception and the primordial pre-thetic Being of the world as the origin of imagination as between two indubitables through the radicalized *epoché.*

To use a metaphor, these two indubitables can be compared with the Heaven and Earth of the first chapter of Genesis in the Old Testament. Primal transcendental subjectivity as the basis of the objectifying intentionality of perception could be called the origin of the modern Western sciences, like the enframing *(Gestell)* of Heidegger. The primordial pre-thetic world of image is the realm of upsurging images that ante-predicatively predicate the world itself as a sole, hidden subject, for example in Japanese haiku poetry,[66] or in old Chinese landscape paintings. This pre-thetic world as a hidden subject is what Nishida meant when he said, "To see the shape of the shapeless; to hear the voice of the voiceless."[67] This world is often called "nothingness" beyond the affirmation and negation of Being, and might be called the origin of the Oriental arts.

Therefore in this new framework we find ourselves as human Being suspended, as it were, between Heaven and Earth, or between East and West, as a very intermediate Being. At the same time, we are struck to find that no ultimate ability immanent to ourselves really mediates these poles. We are not primal transcendental subjectivity as an ego that is able to posit everything including its own essence, nor are we primordial world-Being as a nature-monad that produces everything as its own image. We are rather a Being-in-between with double subjectivities, defined by both extremities, whose somatic in-betweenness should be the theme of investigation for future philosophy, perhaps even for the several coming centuries.

SECTION II

CHAPTER FIVE

Immanence and Transcendence to the Monad and Religiousness

IN THIS CHAPTER the idea of monad, namely, the complex of the pre-thetic world and the pre-thetic self, will be directly thematized for the first time, but for the present mainly with relation to religiousness.

BEYOND A DOUBT WE ARE TODAY living in a world where religion has much less of an influence than before. There are remarkably fewer people who still want to seek the ultimate truth of the world in religion. Instead, most people seem to seek not only relative truth, but even the highest truth of the world almost unconsciously in the achievements of science, especially of the positive (natural and social) sciences. What happens, then, in these sciences? People and things are methodologically thrown into an infinite, empty spatio-temporal lattice or network, or homgenized by an enormous, anonymous subjectivity, and wait for a metamorphosis into abstract quantity through various measurements. In such a case the human ego is forced from the beginning to be separated from the body (and the brain) and must become an empty gaze into the void of time and space. The human ego no longer has a proper place in the world. Instead, the body, including its brain, becomes totally reified and is treated as a homogeneous element of that empty world. Then it gradually becomes clear to us that behind both the separation of the ego from its body and the total deprivation of Being from the entire world lies one and the same fact: the common Being of the ego and the world has been completely lost. We know that such loss happens not only in the realm of the sciences, but also more and more in our daily life (e.g., in education). This is the price that human beings have had to pay for the recognition of the positive sciences not only as the relative, but also as the highest truth.

It is true that religiousness means, in a specific sense, the immanent transcendence of the ego and of the world, but once these both have lost their common Being, religiousness is necessarily robbed of its ground, for the transcendence of religious intentions occurs only upon the firm ground of this common Being. In this sense, I will call this common Being the potential dimension of religiousness. Behind the complete regress of religion today there lies, in my opinion, the threat of incessantly losing this ontological dimension, which will be called "monad" later on in this book.

As is well known, this threat had its first explicit formulation in the seventeenth century in the philosophy of Descartes through the definition of the ego and the world, respectively, as *res cogitans* and *res extensa,* between which no inner relation exists. Since then it has been generally recognized that the developing natural sciences received their philosophical foundation upon this complete separation of the ego-subject and the world-object, while traditional religiousness was fatally robbed of its principal dimension. It will therefore not be meaningless to consider the quintessence of Cartesian philosophy again. It might by chance even guide us to another conclusion of his doubt than the above-mentioned common view. I will attempt to demonstrate just such another conclusion in what follows.

To begin with we will discover the primordial Being of the ego through the analysis of Cartesian doubt and further attempt to thematize the Being of the world this ego inhabits. However, we find this Being of the world not in Descartes, but far later, in his successor Husserl, who brings Leibniz's concept of monad into the twentieth century. Next we will examine the inner correlation between time and space in Husserl, because his "living present" seems to be neither solely temporal nor solely spatial, but rather spatio-temporal, or, in other words, voluntary-horizonal. In Husserl, at last, the Will-ego of Descartes seems to come to the fore and might perhaps begin to constitute a continuum with the world, even though still in a provisional way. This living monadic unity of the ego-Being and world-

Being would be, in my opinion, very close to our potential dimension of religiousness. Furthermore, Zen Buddhism forms a kind of immanent transcendence of the ego-world continuum or the spatio-temporal continuum. I will attempt to make this clear by reflecting on some quotations from some Oriental literature.

WHAT KIND OF EGO did Descartes discover? He proceeded through the famous method of doubt. He wanted to doubt everything doubtful in order to reach at last whatever was indubitable. In *Meditations on First Philosophy* he pointed out the three regions of possible doubt: first, external sensibility, which sometimes deceives us with respect to the scale and form of things; second, sensibility, which is particularly concerned with our own bodies; third, abstract thinking, for example, that of mathematics, which lets us recognize $2 + 3 = 5$ as true. The sensory intuition of a distant square tower, he said, often deceives us, so that it seems to be round. The sensory intuition of a huge statue on top of a tower deceives us so that it seems to us to be small. In fact, it is clear that the form or the scale of a thing is defined not only through perceptual data but also through the apperceptive synthesis of the perceptual data. Only through this apperception can a person take the tower for round or square without seeing the back of it, or take the statue for large or small without any measurement. Therefore doubt hits precisely the correctness of this formal (spatial) apperception; it is concerned with possible modification or revision, that is, with the possibility of the Being-otherwise or of the not-Being of the spatial definition of a thing. We might say that such a function of consciousness belongs generally to the imagination.

The shadow of the imagination in Descartes's doubt becomes much clearer if we turn to the second area. Descartes says, "How often does it happen that I imagine while sleeping all these usual things, that I am here, that I sit before the fireplace wearing clothes, while, in truth, I am lying in bed undressed! . . . When I think on this with more attentiveness, I see clearly and distinctly that wakefulness and dreams can never be distinguished with certain proofs."[1] The correctness of self-perception as well as the existence of my own body are doubted here. They could be the mere images of a dream during sleep. As seen above, in the first case external reality is brought to partial connection with the imagination through the performance of doubt. Through the same performance of doubt, now bodily reality is put under the total guidance of the imagination.

In the third case, however, Descartes has to barely appeal to the Evil Genius who always endeavors to deceive humans, in order thereby to secure the possibility of error in the mathematical sciences. He goes on to write, "I will believe heaven, air, earth, color, shape, tone, and all external things to be nothing other than the deceiving play of dreams which this Spirit sets as a trap for my imprudence. I will regard myself as if I had no hands, no eyes, no flesh, no blood, and generally no sense, as if I had only falsely believed that I possessed all of these."[2] Here the enormously fantastic character of Cartesian doubt can be seen to its fullest degree.

Thus we might say that Cartesian methodical doubt consists of the bringing of the given (whether it be sensory perception or mathematical ideas) to the possibility of Being-otherwise or not-Being through the imagination. Who, then, is the subject of performance that mediates reality and possibility in this way? Through methodical doubt Descartes at last found the Being of the subject, namely, of the very doubting ego itself, to be the only indubitable fact. He calls this ego *res cogitans,* a thinking thing. He writes, "A thinking thing! What is it? Now, a thing that doubts, has insights, affirms, negates, wills, does not will, and that also has imagination and perception."[3] Therefore we can say that the ego of Descartes is defined as reason, will, imagination, and sensuousness. Since, however, according to Descartes, the last two abilities, imagination and perception, do not belong to the essence of the ego, the ego is essentially constituted by reason, which he gives more weight, and by will.

Nevertheless, in my opinion the essence of the doubting ego has little to do with reason, as has already been seen above. This is because (1) the ego is individual and seemingly can never be identified with reason, for reason should be, for its part, essentially universal or beyond the individual, and is never to be individuated. (The concept of the "ego beyond the individual," incidentally, is contradictory, for this could never be plural, whereas the ego must originally take both the singular and the plural personal pronouns). Indeed, I admit that in order to doubt, something must be given beforehand that is to be doubted. Every doubt is preconditioned by something that is given as true. Therefore, if we call reason that which claims something is true, then reason must be the precondition of every doubt. If the doubting ego is indubitable, then its necessary precondition, truth-claiming reason, must also be indubitable. Whether this reason can be called the "ego" is another question, however. Insofar as reason is never individuated, it will be impossible to call it "ego"; (2) Reason may make either a definitively affirmative (thetic) or negative (anti-thetic) judgment upon any reality or any mathematical calculation, or altogether refrain from any judgment thereof, but essentially it can never doubt them at all. Even according to Descartes himself, doubt belongs to the will, not to reason.[4] Therefore the Being of the doubting ego, which is discovered by methodical doubt, will be nothing other than the will, which performs the destruction of all uncertain givenness through its self-consciousness, namely, through the imagination.

Therefore, when Descartes identified the Being of the ego discovered through doubt as reason, he committed a fatal transgression. Insofar as the ego is discovered only by doubt, it can be nothing other than the free will, whose free self-consciousness is the imagination.

This is also proved by the schism between the reason and the will that runs through the Cartesian thinking-substance. Descartes perceived the origin of all errors of judgment to lie in the contradiction between reason and will. Human reason is finite, but human will is infinite, he writes. In cooperating with the reason in order to judge, the will functions as the selector of ideas properly offered by reason—but sometimes spontaneously beyond the area of reason's illumination. All errors of human judgment originate here, according to Descartes. Though Descartes writes that the human spirit is indivisible, in fact, reason is separated from the will by something like an abyss.

Descartes also often uses the phrase "the light of nature" *(lumen naturale)* instead of "reason." This phrase appears most frequently in the Third Meditation, where he argues for a demonstration of the existence of God. He writes, "There is no other ability that I trust in the same way as this light, and that could teach that this [what this light proves] is not true."[5] As the *lumen naturale* is generally regarded to be nothing other than reason itself, we can immediately inquire into the relationship between this light and the ego.

Already in the Second Meditation, Descartes declares, "I am, exactly said, only a thinking thing, namely . . . reason." Correspondingly, reason, or the light of nature, apparently is the ego itself. However the phraseology "The light of nature proves to me that it is true" or "I can trust the light" shows that the light and the ego do not necessarily make up a closed unity. Rather, the light seems to illuminate the ego so to speak from above, and this ego seems to grasp the truth only insofar as it participates in this light. In this sense, Descartes's ego cannot immediately be a reasoning substance here, but rather something that ek-sists toward (looks to) the light of reason.

Therefore, when we find in Descartes, on the one hand, the free infinite Will that makes errors when it functions beyond the illuminating area of reason, and, on the other hand, the ego that must be illuminated from above by the light of reason in order to reach the truth, we have grounds to identify this will and the ego, while reason as "the natural light" becomes valid as transcendence toward the whole egological area.

As a consequence, the identification of reason and the ego in Descartes becomes quite problematic. If we consider this problem in detail, we see that Descartes's ego as will and the ego as reason cannot make up any well-rounded unity, and that the analysis of the procedure of doubt almost necessarily shows the first ego (ego as will) to be the only possible one.

This ego as infinite will is originally transcendent toward all areas of the intentional consciousness. It makes the imagination function as its intimate tool, but it itself is not the imagination. It is able to invalidate all sensory perception, and it can also reject the light of reason; on the contrary, it can also receive sensuality and the light of reason into itself. Even when the ego receives sensory perception or reason, it does not immediately become a universal beyond-individual ego in general, as the idealists assume, but rather on the one hand an ego-less, impersonal, logical thinking emerges, and on the other hand the ever egoic, practical, voluntary ability to judge comes forth. Descartes falsely called the first impersonal ability "ego," while in the process of doubt he encountered the latter egoic ability. (Incidentally, what mediates these two abilities actually is not the ego in general or the transcendental ego, but rather something primarily personal, which Buber called the in-between of I and Thou).[6]

Thus in Descartes the true ego, the ego of the infinite will, is almost completely concealed, because it is rather violently absorbed into reason. The impersonal ego-less light of reason is regarded as "ego"; as a result the loss of the Being of the ego inevitably came to the fore.

THIS EGO AS WILL, which was concealed by Descartes in the way we have discussed above, is now redisclosed by Husserl as life. Moreover, Husserl seemingly grasps this life in inseparable correlation with the existing world, with the life-world or the monad. Husserl writes, "It belongs to the self-evidence that preconditions all scientific thought and all philosophical questioning that the world is, always is before-hand, and that every correction of an opinion . . . is always precondi-tioned by the existing *(seiende)* world. . . . Objective science, too, asks questions only on the ground of this constantly existing world, which is pregiven from pre-scientific life."[7] Furthermore, "To live is to con-stantly live in world-certainty. To live awakened is to be awake to the world, to be consistently and actually conscious of the world and of oneself as living in the world, to actually experience and to perform the certainty of the Being of the world."[8] What, then, is life itself in Husserl? It is quite remarkable in this context that in the *Cartesian Meditations* (1931) the stream of consciousness is called the "stream of life." Moreover, many new expressions appear such as "original life," "reflecting life," "intentional life," even "transcendental life." Life itself, however, is never thematized but is always treated as some-thing self-evident.

Already in *First Philosophy* (1923–24), however, we find the fol-lowing words: "Reflection is originally such a one in the will. The sub-ject indeed makes a decision of the will directed toward his whole future life of recognition when it defines itself as the philosophical subject."[9] Again, Husserl writes, "When we speak of recognition in a pregnant sense, for example, of scientific recognition, it is clear that every such act is not a mere judgment, but here a line of endeavor or will runs through judgment that is not clear-sighted, which termi-nates at last in a corresponding clear-sighted judgment, or recogniz-ing judgment in a pregnant sense, and gives the voluntary character of the acquired truth to its contents. Therefore judgment and will in-terpenetrate each other everywhere."[10]

In 1933 Husserl wrote, "May we or must we not presuppose a universal drive-intentionality that unifies every ultimate present as a standing temporalization and drives forth from present to present, so that the contents of every object are those of drive-fulfillment, and thus intended before the goal."[11]

Here it becomes clear that Husserl's "life" is a kind of will, and is primarily grasped as something that founds intentionality; that is, it is grasped in connection with objective recognition or perception. However, life as such, namely, life as the ego itself, is never to be mediated by objective recognition or perception; it is an immediate, nonreflective, living life. How is it to cognize and how does it exist? This life as ego can, in my opinion, be grasped only in its own space and time. That is to say, this ego can be grasped only in its original correlation with the world. This space and time are, of course, not identical with objective, empty space and objective, streaming time. The ego itself as life has its own space and its own time. In other words, the ego exists as a kind of space and time. It spreads out space from itself around itself and establishes time from itself before and after itself. The authentic ego as the self is the unity of a self-extending space and a self-pouring and -accumulating time.

We will confront the space-time structure of the authentic ego with Husserl's corresponding structure of the monad and the living present. In the *Cartesian Meditations* Husserl writes, "Clearly—and this is of particular importance—the self-essential *(eigenwesentlich)* element of the I as ego stretches itself out not only to the actuality and the potentiality of the stream of experiences, but also to the constitutive systems as well as to the constituted entities. . . . This is also valid for all my self-proper *(selbsteigene)* habitualities, which constitute themselves as abiding convictions as a result of self-proper establishing acts. . . . Besides, here also belong transcendent objects, for example, objects of external sensuousness . . . if I as the ego take into consideration purely that which is really originally constituted as the appearing spatial-object by my self-proper sensuousness, [by] my self-proper apperception *as something concretely inseparable from them.*"[12] This self-essential region, that is, the region that emerges after the methodical exclusion of every other ego, to which belong not only the immanent temporality of the stream of my experiences, but also the kinesthetic habituality of the ego and the spatial objects constituted by the ego, is called the "monad" by Husserl. Husserl writes that "My living body *(körperlicher Leib)* has its givenness as the central here in the monad as being related back to itself." This "central here" is also called the "zero point."[13]

The spatial objects in my monad are correlated, not only through sensory perception but also through the kinesthetic apperception of the incarnated ego, not unidirectionally but reciprocally, to my body as its only center. What is important is the character of this correlation in the monad, which Husserl calls "inseparable." Is it then transcendental-constitutive, or doxic-mundane? In other words, has this correlation something to do with phenomenological thing-phantoms, or with naturally posited things? The answer is not always one or the other. In this sense, the concluding words of Ulrich Claesges's *Edmund Husserl's Theory of Space-Constitution* are interesting: "The fact that the kinesthetic consciousness is univocally definable neither as a mundane consciousness nor as a transcendental consciousness as the in-itself complete ground of the Being of all beings and of the recognition of them forces us to a renewed consideration of the 'transcendentality' of Husserl's phenomenology."[14] These words point to the essential ambiguity of the force of correlation within the Husserlian monad. Moreover, here in the monad the functioning lively Being (force) of the will seems to not yet play a patent role.

Now let us turn to the Husserlian theory of time. Husserl called the temporality of the functioning life of the ego the living present. This present as present belongs to the now, but to the standing-flowing now. It is not a punctual now, but rather always has a breadth or thickness that involves the horizons of the immediately having-been and of the immediately coming-up. Husserl called these horizons retention and protention. When the functioning ego intends a particular spatial object while moving itself, the standing core of the living present corresponds to the ever-visible obverse side of the thing, while both horizons of retention and protention correspond to the just concealed or coming-into-view back or lateral sides of the thing. Protention always anticipates what is coming into view and retention preserves what has passed away. This breadth or thickness of the present is originally constituted by the practical interest of the functioning ego. Husserl says, "The present extends as far as we speak of a reality that is still actual for us. This has, however, a varying meaning and a varying breadth, and relates mainly to praxis."[15] Here we can see the voluntary character of the Husserlian standing-flowing present very clearly.

But these analyses refer only to the temporality of object-consciousness or of the inner horizon of a thing, not to the temporality of monad-consciousness or of the outer horizon of a thing. From Husserl's manuscripts, it is clear that he tried again and again to thematize the nonflowing, pretemporal present of the functioning ego. This anonymous present could possibly correspond to the consciousness of the monad. It is especially interesting that he suggests several times in the manuscripts that in a more radical phenomenological reduction even protention and retention would be bracketed, and then only the pure now would remain as authentic original presencing. It seems, however, that this more radical reduction, too, did not methodologically succeed in clarifying the monadic presencing as a pure presencing.

Therefore, we regrettably find in Husserl only the seed of the solution of the problem of the inner relationship between space and time. In his theory of space-constitution there is no argument concerning the temporal (self-accumulating) components of the inner relating forces of the monad, while in his theory of time there is no argument that addresses the teleological manner of self-presencing of the monad. Therefore we are necessarily forced to investigate the space-time structure of the ego on our own, beyond Husserl's theory.

WE HAVE ALREADY REMARKED that the genuine ego as will or life has its own space and time. It extends space and pours out time. What character does this space have? Let us proceed once more by way of the Husserlian theory of things. Husserl says that if we perform the phenomenological reduction, a spatial thing appears to us not only as the presentation of its obverse side, but also simultaneously as the appresentation of its reverse side, that is, as its copresencing anticipation. This latter sometimes plunges us into disappointment (e.g., we find another shape or color there than we anticipated), but appresentation as the necessary horizon of the thing-experience has presumable evidence. We cannot see a thing without the anticipation of its hidden sides. This anticipation is indeed, as an impression, to be articulated as protention and the retention in the stream of consciousness under the condition of the phenomenological inner-time analysis. However, we must recognize that insofar as this anticipated hidden side of a thing is regarded as the back "side" or any extended side, that is, as a hidden obverse side, three-dimensional, objective space is already presupposed. For how could we, as Husserl insists, identify a perspectivally perceived ball as a sphere and a die as a hexahedron without projecting them beforehand in some way onto objective, homogeneous, three-dimensional space? The inner horizon as the back of a thing, namely, the hidden front of a thing, is possible only under the condition of the existence of the outer horizon as the objective, homogeneous space that is open to plural perspectives simultaneously.[16]

Now according to Husserl's theory in the *Cartesian Meditations*, too, this objective three-dimensional space is constituted only through the mediation of intersubjectivity, that is, through the community of monads. Therefore the ego to which the appresentation of the reverse side of a thing is given together with the obverse side must already be an intersubjective ego, which is mediated by the alter ego, but not the originally individual ego as such. I can see a tree in the garden and, performing the phenomenological reduction, can have an appresentation of the back of its trunk, or intuit the impression of its reverse side in retention and protention. Already there, however, there is an anonymous alter ego, for the back of the trunk as appresentation is just the front side that is hidden over there. To regard it as something that has just passed away or that is just coming into view is to regard it as something preserved for now as a hidden obverse side somewhere. However, this hidden obverse side can be assumed only through the presupposition of the anonymous gaze of an alter ego, which sees it now from another side or from any other place than my own. Therefore, the gaze of the ego, which exists in its proper space and time as *absolutely solitary,* will never grasp the back side as the hidden front. This is to say that the genuinely individual ego will never appresent the back of anything. Protention and retention, too, will not occur to it, for, as becomes clear later, this ego has nothing but the fixed and standing present that never flows. It has only the breadth or the thickness of the fixed present and sees only the duration of the obverse side of a thing therein. There is no appresentation of the reverse side for it, because it does not occur to it. In other words, it sees things with its own eyes alone, without the mediation of the gaze of any alter ego.

Husserl called presentation the authentic occurrence and appresentation inauthentic occurrence. However, for the ego as individual will the reverse side is the authentic inoccurrence. It never appears as the back "side," because it is nothing more than the hidden front that appears through the mediation of the alter ego. Originally and essentially the "back" as such does not appear. In order to appear, it must be transformed somehow into the front side, even in a concealed manner. In the case of the solitary ego, however, there is no way to change the back into the front. If one turns the thing, a new "front" indeed appears, but at the same time a new back emerges, which preserves the silence and nonoccurrence of before. To see in this new back the color or the shape of the old front that has just passed away already presupposes the gaze of the alter ego that sees it now from the opposite side. What appears is always the front side, either presented or appresented, and not the back itself. The latter preserves its silence and inoccurrence. The back of the thing eternally retains the silent inoccurrence in space and time of the genuine ego. But in preserving the inoccurrence, it remains there. We might say that it cries out without a voice, or appears without a figure (Nishida).

Here the Being of the back of a thing is never grasped from the outside, because it does not become the (hidden) front side, that is, the appresentation. It is to be grasped always only from the inside of a thing. This Being, which is to be grasped only from the inside, is essentially different from that which is grasped from outside. The latter is the Being that is to be grasped by transcendental subjectivity in its potential plurality. It is the Being of the front side and therefore is the Being of a thing-phantom that appears in objective, three-dimensional space. This transparent thing-phantom has nothing but plural front sides, including the hidden sides, and no back in the original sense. We can see it simultaneously from all directions in the sense of "drafted side views." The Being of the back, by contrast, is to be grasped only from the inside of a thing. We can intuit it only through going deeper into its core, not by turning it around. Therefore, the back is the depth of a thing. Everything present to the genuine individual ego as will has such a Being, namely, its depth. The reverse is equally true; whenever things have such a depth, they are beings in front of the ego as will.

Now the ego as will or life also has the same Being as the depth of a thing, which is to be grasped only from the inside. The Being of the ego is never to be grasped from outside, namely in objective space. The Being of the ego, which is to be grasped only from the inside, is nothing other than the will or life. However, we could also call it the (bodily) flesh *(Leib)*, insofar as it is grasped as the nonobjectifiable starting point of praxis. The nonobjectifiable flesh as the practical starting point is my Being, which stands before and in the middle of the Being of things in the monad. My Being as flesh and the Being of things correlate with each other inseparably (I believe that the "inseparable" correlation of the ego and the constituted object in the Husserlian monad has its original source here). When I intuit one, the other is intuited at the same time. Therefore, we can say that both constitute a kind of ontological pairing. All the pairing has a common pole in my (bodily) flesh. The Being of all things relates to my body as if to a sole pivot, but they also correlate with each other. For example, the Being of a book relates to that of the table on which it lies. The Being of the table, too, relates to the wall against which it stands. And the Being or the depth of each of these things penetrates the other at the line of intersection (e.g., at the line of intersection of the front aspect of the table and the wall behind it) and makes up a continuum before me, of which the relieflike raised facades are the fronts of these things. The continuum of Being stretches behind and beyond my body, too, where my look does not reach, only distanced by a tactile-kinesthetic inter-space (e.g., I feel the ceiling-surface with the top of my head). At the same time a visual-kinesthetic inter-space opens up before me, which distances the facade of the continuum, that is, the fronts of things, from me. In this way the ego as my (bodily) flesh stands surrounded by a wall of the continuum of Being, whose depth stretches far beyond it, and all around it.

As mentioned above, the genuine ego stretches out its own space. The space of Being spreads out around me and reaches to an infinite depth. I reside at home in the middle of the infinite Being-space of this continuum, but in solitude. I am at home because my Being correlates itself inseparably and intimately with the Being of space. I am in solitude because no one else resides in this space but I.

I will call this space the "monad" in the genuine sense. It is authentically the most primordial region in the Husserlian sense. Only here is my absolute individuality preserved. What, then, is the relation of the spatiality of my ego to its temporality? I have said that the monad resides only in the standing-present. Here time does not flow. In the same way that the monad can always stretch out more and more and can potentially occupy the whole of objective space, the thickness of the present, which is the time-modality of the monad, can extend more and more and accumulate the entire past and future, insofar as the objective time-dimension can be figured as an infinitely stretching line. In this sense time pours out here, while it is accumulated in the thickness of the present.

As is the size of the monad, the thickness of the present is in itself completely without limit. As we have already mentioned, both are to be defined and restricted only through practical, voluntary interest. If I recollect any especially interesting memory, it is not kept retentionally within the flowing present, but rather is fantastically represented in the standing present; the latter has a thickness that exactly corresponds to the kinesthetic duration between now and the pertinent point in time that has passed. With respect to the future the same structure holds. It is also remarkable that this temporal thickness corresponds univocally to the size of the presencing monad. For example, if I represent to myself some beautiful natural scene that I will visit next week, my monad expands from here to that place, and possesses the size that corresponds to the kinesthetic duration from here to there. Therefore, the definitive size of the monad and the definitive thickness of the present correspond to each other through the mediation of the kinesthesis of my life. However, it is also the case that without any practical teleology and without kinesthesis, the infinite size of the monad and the infinite thickness of the standing-present correspond to each other through the mediation of my Being as will. Here space and time are not separated from each other. Rather, they are two sides of one and the same matter. We have reached at last the original unity of the ego and the world, or that of space and time. We will call this unity *the continuum of life,* or the monad in the genuine sense.

AS WE MENTIONED at the beginning, religiousness is established only upon the firm ground of the Being of the ego. Therefore, we called this ground the potential dimension of religiousness in general. Now this dimension manifests itself to us in its concrete figure as the continuum of life. Religiousness, then, could be generally described as the immanent-transcendence from this continuum. Regardless of the multiplicity of kinds or ways of transcendence, without a fundamental relation to the pure individual character of this dimension religiousness in general will be impossible.

Will anyone object in the following way? "Is this dimension of the continuum not a pure abstraction? For in reality we always live with other people, intersubjectively, in an objective world. Does this solipsistic continuum not have at most a speculative, that is, fictitious meaning?" No, we will answer, the continuum of life is the concretion of the most original and purest ego itself. Whenever we speak the word "I" and refer to only one Being existing in the world, we refer to this continuum, consciously or unconsciously.

In the midst of the objective world, where the loss of Being proceeds unceasingly, this continuum remains indeed concealed; we have lost sight of ourselves. Nevertheless, we are involuntarily seeking our lost selves. This situation appears in the teleology of the modern world, especially as its technology. Technology always has its specific *telos* and this *telos* is somehow or other related to the ultimate goal, which is our-selves, as Heidegger said. However, technology does not know what this goal is. Unconsciously and eagerly, through technological development, it seeks its concealed goal, the *telos X,* which it has, however, no means to thematize. This is one of the ironic ways in which we most passionately seek our concealed selves today.

I cannot here argue how religiousness has pursued transcendence in various historical figures. I will thematize only some phases of Zen Buddhism. Furthermore, as my theme is not the religious truth of Zen itself, but rather its relation to our religious dimension, I can only suggest how some fundamental characters of Zen are analogous to those of the continuum of life.

One of the fundamental characteristics of the truth of Zen is anti-teleology. In the sixth century Chinese Emperor Wu (Bu, in Japanese) saw Dharma, the founder of Zen Buddhism, and asked, "I have built many temples, appointed and fed many monks. I have made a great effort for the sake of Buddhism. What is it worth?" Dharma answered, "Nothing."[17] Zen does not appreciate any expediency. Hence there necessarily emerges a distinction between the aim and the means. Among the means we must distinguish between good and bad, appropriate and inappropriate. Such distinction is the essence of healthy human understanding. This differentiation occurs, however, only when we have removed ourselves from the goal. By contrast, when we already reside in the goal, we must no longer choose anything. We are beyond all duality. Therefore, the anti-teleology of Zen means that the ego already resides here in its home. This is to say that Zen is not only transcendent to the continuum but is from the beginning also immanent to it. Zen is immanent-transcendent to the continuum.

The immanent character of Zen with respect to the continuum can be shown in various phases. First, it can be shown in absolute solitude. The old ninth-century Chinese Zen-master Chao-Chou (Johshu in Japanese) said, "Under heaven, in heaven, only I alone!"[18] An old Zen poem expresses it thus: "Between heaven and earth we stand alone, not knowing the limit of the universe."[19] A proverb from the Tao period (the ninth century) of China says:

> What is to be avoided most
> is to seek "It" outside of myself
> Then "It" is distanced from me more and more
>
> Now I just go alone
> So look! everywhere I encounter "It."[20]

Here "It" will be understood as the true self of the ego. It is clear that this ego is regarded as absolutely solitary.

Second, the spatio-temporal modality of Zen-consciousness possesses a character that is very similar to that of the continuum. An old Zen-master said, "The clear, pure, distinguished I is mountain, river, and earth; sun, moon, and stars."[21] Another Zen-master said, "The whole cosmos is true human bodily-flesh."[22] A third said, "Under every individual consciousness lies a cosmic unconsciousness as its ground."[23] These words could be understood as the expression of the inner ontological correlation between the ego and the world, as is found in the continuum.

Furthermore, according to the modern Japanese Zen-master Suzuki, time is not to be regarded as linear but rather as circular, where past, present, and future occur simultaneously and together for an absolute present. According to Dogen, the great Japanese Zen-master of the thirteenth century, time does not pass but rather sets up an absolute eternal present in every moment that penetrates each other. For example, a time when I climb a mountain and a time when I wade in a river involve in themselves the time when I reside in a palace, and they cast it forward at the same time. If time passes away there will be a void, but the beings of the entire world are connected continuously and always live in an absolute present, said Dogen.[24] A certain modern master also said, "If we reside in the present, forgetting ourselves, the eternal past becomes the present and the infinite world becomes the present. The quintessence of Zen consists in the very experience of the present."[25]

This remarkable emphasis on the present that does not flow reminds us of the temporal character of the continuum. It is still more surprising, however, when we hear Suzuki say that time and space are not separable but should be regarded as time-space, space-time; a hyphen should be set between both, and they are to be taken for one, for in the absolute present time as well as space is included.[26] We cannot regard the resemblance of Zen to the continuum of life as contingent any longer. However we must not forget that the immanent relation of Zen to the continuum is only one side of it. Zen still has another side: transcendence toward the continuum of life.

This becomes clear when we read in the Kegon (Gadavyuha)-sutra that infinite time is a moment, and a moment is infinite time; likewise a point is infinite space and infinite space is a point.[27] Still more concretely: the whole universe is included in the tip of a paintbrush, or when we lift one of our fingers, we can cover the whole universe with it.[28] Here we can see that immanence to the monadic continuum and transcendence of it onto the objective world are united. In other words, here the monadic ego identifies itself with a thing in the objective world. I am a corporeal thing and at the same time a monad. We must still pay attention to the fact that all things in the world are also granted their own monads. Absolute individuality is guaranteed to all things, not only to the human being. When a pupil asked Chao-Chou what the quintessence of Zen was, he answered "An oak tree in the garden."[29] An oak tree is now no longer a tree, but the amazing unity of a thing and the cosmic monad. Through its transcendence to the objective world the absolute solitude of the ego is brought to solidarity with the community of everyday life. To drink tea with a guest, to greet him, and to wash plates can be at the same time the revelation of cosmic, ultimate truth.

The anti-teleology of Zen acquires a quite peculiar character in everyday life. Not only the human, but also all things become the ultimate aim, for all of them, too, involve the monad, that is, the whole universe in themselves. But how can we act practically without any means? Only as nature does. When the wind blows, the wind chimes tinkle. When spring comes, the plum tree blossoms. In the same way, we handle like a thing, like the whole of nature, but for that we are clearly aware of what and how we are doing it. In other words, we do not use a thing merely as a tool, but we have always already known through inner contact with it what it wills. We only do what a thing wills and what the whole of nature wills. In the East we burn tools that were used in mourning because they are not mere instruments but also dissolved parts of our bodily flesh; even more, they are monads like our bodies. In Zen, it is said that all things illuminate us with the light of Buddha.

Such a paradoxical unity of thing and monad was brought to universal formulation through the paradoxical logic of the Prajna-Paramita sutra in ancient India. Here it is asserted that A is not A, therefore A is A. It might be interesting to compare this logic with Heidegger's thoughts on the identity and difference of Being, but I will not address this problem here. We must satisfy ourselves with the discovery that the continuum of life as the dimension of religiousness also constitutes a moment of Zen Buddhism.

I would like to end with a question: What would a religiousness be like that transcends the immanence of the continuum not onto the thing in general but onto the human, who, unlike the thing, casts a free gaze from out of itself? It seems to me that a genuine dialogical religiousness might emerge from this.

Chapter Six

The Monad and the Poem

Toward a Phenomenological Analysis
of the Japanese Haiku

THE THEME OF THIS CHAPTER is to clarify the spiritual and creative aspect of "phenomenological monadology." The confusing equivocation with regard to the concept of the life-world as the foundation of all cultural activities seems to come mainly from the indefinite nature of the concept of the "monad" in the Husserlian as well as the post-Husserlian sense.

In this respect we might say that Existential philosophy was a new attempt at monadology after Husserl. Heidegger's "Dasein," Sartre's *"être-pour-soi,"* and even Jasper's *"Umgreifende"* are to be understood as modifications of the idea of the monad. Their common inclination toward individuality or *"Je-meinigkeit"* and their common turning-away from the subject-object schema unmistakably suggest the monadological character of these concepts. At the same time the remarkable role of the imagination within all of them, which reaches its highest expression in the fundamental concept of "project," is also revealed. The tendency of the Existential philosophers toward monadology was only halfhearted, however, as can be seen in the fact that the word "monadology" was never seriously accepted by any of them. For example, Sartre said, "On the level of concrete experience the monadological description shows itself to be unsatisfactory," because the monad has no door and no window.[1] Whether the monad has in general no door and no window is, however, a question that cannot be answered easily. Particularly if the monad in its entirety and the core of the monad are somehow distinguished, this problem will need to be readdressed.

TO BEGIN WITH, let us return to Husserl's definition of the monad. Husserl had already used the word "monad" in his article "Philosophy as a Rigorous Science" (1911), where he wrote, "The psychical is divided (metaphorically and not metaphysically speaking) into monads that have no windows and only communicate through empathy."[2] Here we also find the expressions "a 'monadic' unity of the consciousness" and "an unlimited flow of phenomena in two directions."[3] This definition of the monad is still distinct from that of the *Cartesian Meditations* (1929) because of the qualification of metaphoricity. Husserl's monadology in the *Cartesian Meditations* is, however, still incomplete and even misleading. In the Fifth Meditation, section 44, he writes about the primordial reduction to the monad, that "we *disregard all the constitutive workings of the intentionality which immediately or mediately relate to foreign subjectivity*, and we first circumscribe the whole nexus of intentionality, actual and potential, in which the ego constitutes itself in its ownness *(Eigenheit)* and in which it constitutes the synthetic unities that are *inseparable* from its ownness."[4] Further, in section 45, he writes, "What . . . the transcendental ego constitutes in that first stratum as the not-foreign (as its own) belongs . . . to it as components of its own concrete essence, . . . it is *inseparable* from its *concrete* Being" (emphasis added).[5] Again, in section 47, "Where and insofar as the constituted unity is *inseparable* from the original constitution itself in the manner of immediate *concrete* union, there, the perceived being, as well as the constituting perception, belongs to my *concrete* self-ownness" (all emphases added).[6] Therefore we become aware that in many places that concern the owning *(eigenheitlich)* reduction, which Husserl takes for the necessary precondition of the coming-into-Being of the monad, the adjectives "concrete" and "inseparable" appear very often. As a further example, we might draw upon the following passage, where Husserl tried for the first time to define the monad conceptually: "We distinguish the ego in its full *concreteness* (which we want to name with the Leibnizian word 'monad') from the I as identical pole and as the substratum of habituality, in that we add that without which the I cannot be *concrete*" (emphases added).[7] Concreteness here means, it seems, that something that originally was inseparable from the monadic ego is now added to it. But what, then, is this "inseparability"? Is this merely the designation of the relation between intentionality and its correlate? Is my perceptive consciousness in its own peculiar perspective, only added to its perceived object, already a monad? Then we wonder, what is the difference between the perspectivity and the monadicity of consciousness from Husserl's standpoint?

On the other hand, it is remarkable that Husserl's ego as monad already possesses its body: "When I [primordially] reduce myself as human, I get my body and my soul, or myself as psycho-physical unity; in this unity my personal I, which operates in the external world in this body and by means of it."[8] Moreover, my body should be the center of the whole correlation of my monad: "My living body *(körperlicher Leib)* has its form of givenness as the central *Here* while reflexively related back to itself."[9] Furthermore, "Thereby in my primordial sphere the one spatial nature is constituted by a change of orientation, and indeed constituted in an intentional relation to my perceptually functioning bodily Being."[10] Of course, the proximity and the distance of the correlates would be involved in this correlation. Therefore the inseparable correlation of the natural surrounding world to my central bodily flesh seems to possess here not only a cognitive, but also a practical, ontological character, which should not be unidirectional, but rather reciprocal.

The ambiguity of the fundamental character of the Husserlian monad will, however, never be dissipated. Its meaning oscillates between the mere perspectival nature of the consciousness and the ontologico-practical intimacy of corporeality.

Indeed, although Husserl says that every monad is immanently *(reel)* an absolutely closed unity, and that monads of others are immanently *(reel)* separated from mine, nevertheless he follows at once with this: "On the other hand the original community is not a nothingness. . . . A being is with beings in an intentional community. It is an in principle unique solidarity, a real community, and precisely that community that makes the Being of one world, a world of humans and things, possible."[11]

Is this community, then, the genuine community of the monads? Is it not rather the result of a leveling and decentering of the genuine monad? This doubt is strengthened by the phraseology that precedes the sentences quoted above: "[To the immanent *(reel)* non-connectedness of the monads] corresponds the very real separation . . . of my psychophysical Dasein from that of others, who present themselves as spatial on behalf of the spatiality of the objective body."[12] If the ontological separation of the monads is once reduced to a spatial separation between objective bodies as the cores of monads, it would be easy to confuse the genuine community of monads with mere common perspectivity.

In reality, as we have attempted to show elsewhere,[13] Husserl's monadology is conditioned unexpectedly from the beginning by interperspectivity (interintentionality). Here I will refer to it only briefly. According to Husserl's theory of the appresentation of the alter ego, "The corporeal *(Körper)* body (afterwards of the other), which belongs to my primordial surrounding world, is a body in the mode of *There* for me. Its way of appearing . . . awakens a similar phenomenon reproductively that belongs to the constitutive system of my bodily flesh as a body in space. It reminds me of the way my body would look *if I were there*."[14] But we must ask the question, how can I understand the way I would look standing There without the cooperation of the intentionality of the alter ego, which, as if from Here out, objectifies me There? For I see myself from the outside only insofar as I have thrown myself into the foreign perspective, which functions as if it has its zero point in the Here. Therefore it becomes necessarily clear that Husserl's primordial monad is already penetrated by the perspective of the other and consequently by the interperspectivity of my ego and the other ego. This means, however, that Husserl fails in fundamental supposition of the constitution of the other through my transcendental ego alone. Rather, the precondition of the appresentative constitution of the other itself manifests the cooperation of my intentionality and other perspectival intentionalities, or, in other words, the interperspectivity, which reciprocally relativizes Here and There into Here = There, and establishes at last a common, decentered space.

Husserl's monadology is primarily based on the primordiality that guarantees the ego as Here an illusional priority vis-à-vis the alter ego as There. Together with the collapse of this priority, however, Husserl's monad reveals its own groundlessness. We might say that Husserl's monad is an envelope from which the previously hidden presupposition (namely interperspectivity) emerges. Or we might say that Husserl so to speak conjures the alter ego out of the shell of my ego, and then seeks to clothe both egos in a common shell. This new shell is in reality, however, nothing other than the former shell.

Yet Husserl continues to develop his theory toward a supposed intersubjectivity as before: "As a further consequence an empathy of the definite contents of the higher psychical sphere . . . arises."[15] The alter ego, which was found through the appresentation of other bodies, now supposedly will be given its monadic content through empathy. What it has done in reality, however, is only to affirm the exchangeability of perspectives between the asserted monads. Others are "monads, being for themselves exactly as I am for myself; however, also in communion, therefore . . . in connection with me, as concrete ego, as monad."[16] Furthermore, "In the meaning of a human community and of a person who already as an individual bears the meaning of community member . . . lies reciprocal Being-for-another, which contains in itself an objectifying equalization of my Dasein with that of all others."[17] Husserl continues, "Of course to this community corresponds . . . an open monad-community, which we call transcendental intersubjectivity," and this intersubjectivity is "constituted as necessarily bearing in itself the same objective world."[18] He asks, "Is it thinkable . . . that several separated monad-groups coexist . . . therefore two infinitely separated worlds, two infinite spaces and space-times? Clearly this is . . . pure nonsense,"[19] for "two intersubjectivities do not subsist in midair *(in der Luft stehen)*."[20]

What Husserl acquired in this way is in reality nothing other than the hidden precondition of his theory of appresentation of the alter ego, namely, the interperspectivity of the perceptive consciousness of every ego. In such a way the pendulum of Husserlian thought oscillates back to the mere perspectivity of perception from vague primordial monadology.

WAS HUSSERL'S THEORY OF APPRESENTATION then merely a superfluous trial in the constitution of the other? The presupposed mode of perceptive consciousness "as if he/she (the alter ego) were Here" as the foundation of this theory already contains within itself what it is aiming for, namely "he/she (the alter ego) is There" (in exactly the same way as the mode "as if I were There" is founded by the fundamental fact that "I am Here"). Indeed, if the subject of perceptive consciousness is immediately the subject of bodily apperception, Husserl's theory of the appresentation of the alter ego is certainly superfluous, for it grounds a fact on the very same fact. However, we have no reason to simply identify both subjects with each other, namely, the subject of perspectival perceptive consciousness (the transcendental ego) and that of bodily apperception. According to their manner of appearance, they are quite different. The former is the consciousness that objectifies everything and encounters me from the outside as a gaze in the mode of "he/she is There," while entering into me appears in the mode of "as if he/she were Here." The latter, on the contrary, is the subject of the "I can" and "I am Here," which can never be separated from my nonobjectifiable bodily-fleshly Being, and which therefore can be given in the external world only through appresentation in the mode "as if I were There."

Looking around in this way, it is clear that in terms of the Here, we must not simply identify the mode "I am Here" with the mode "as if he/she were Here," and in terms of the There, we must not identify the mode "he/she is There" with the mode "as if I were There." Rather, I believe that they can only be occasionally and dialectically reconciled with each other. Husserl's theory is, in fact, insufficient, insofar as it does not distinguish two subjects and immediately identifies these two modes of There by tacitly employing the identity of the two modes of Here. However, his theory of foreign-constitution remains useful insofar as it hints at how the monadic way in which the bodily-fleshly subject appears is distinct from that of the perceptive subject, which is originally intersubjective, even though he still greatly confused the two and consequently abolished the genuine inner totality of the monad that is originally proper to the bodily-fleshly subject.

I call this bodily-fleshly subject that has already passively accepted the perceptive subject, as Husserl virtually admitted, the naked core of the monad, because it is divided from the geuine monad as the totality of all possible correlations. The naked core is another name for the somatic ego—the *Leib-Körper*—which we treated in section 1.

Before we embark upon the structure of the genuine monad itself, we must add something to the meaning of appresentation. We must always pay attention to the difference between appresentation and image representation. The other bodily-fleshly subject itself is not represented as an image by bodily appresentation, but rather is only grasped thetically in the mode "as if I were There." This means that always already "I am Here and not There." The actual Being of the other bodily-fleshly subject is not the image or the shadow of my actual Being. The analogy of "as if . . . were" is concerned only with the mode of Being of the other bodily-fleshly subject, but not with its actual Being itself (not "as if he/she were There"). This is just like the fact that we do not represent the back of a thing in an image or color "as if it were the back," but rather appresent it in the mode "as if it were the front." Therefore, the other bodily-fleshly subject is always equally original with my bodily-fleshly subject, as the back of a thing is with the front. I can never produce the other bodily-fleshly subject himself or herself, either through the imagination or through empathy, or through a sliding of meaning. "He" or "she" (the other bodily-fleshly subject) is already There in reality. We can only subsequently imagine the contents or the how of his or her Being in the form of empathy.

We still must ask, however, then why and how is it possible? The answer is because the appresentation of the other bodily-fleshly subject already has an ontological foundation in my somatic ego as the naked core of the monad. Through the separation from the monadic totality itself and the acceptance of the objectifiable body, the Being of its core (my somatic ego) is thrown into groundlessness and suffers an inner self-negation that brings forth ontological relativization and scattering (pluralizing) of the absolute Here into outside Theres. In other words, the absolute Here becomes the relative Here and recognizes the same relative Hereness in every There as potentiality. To call this phenomenon "empathy" in the usual sense is not appropriate, because this is not a one-sided projection of my absolute Being into others. On the contrary, my ego itself is already passively relativized and altered. Therefore there is already no longer an absolute Here surrounded by Theres, but rather a relative Here (Here = There) surrounded by equally relative Heres (Here = Theres). Thus my somatic ego deprived of the monad always already anticipates in primal belief the Being of others outside it. I do not introject my absolute Being into other bodies, but rather I rediscover an already anticipated alter ego in other bodies. Thus the analogical appresentation of the alter ego introduced by Husserl is only the occasional concretion and reconfirmation of this ontological anticipation.

Through this ontologico-analogical capacity of the naked core of the monad the existence of another core (somatic alter ego) is originally given to it. We are always already living together upon interperspectival, decentered, common ground as naked cores. The other monad (ego) as a totality is never given in such a way, however, for the absolute Hereness of a monad does not lie in its naked core, which is only the already half-relativized Here. What distinguishes the absolute Here from Here = There is the inner totality of the monad, the monadic spatio-temporal continuum. Without this total structure, the absoluteness of Here is not definable, as is the case with Husserl. In the public, interperspectival, common space, on the contrary, the human exists as alienated monad like the nucleus of an atom that has been robbed of its electron shell. It exists there as distorted, as spontaneous indeed, but restricted in its freedom. Heidegger called just this way of Being "thrownness."

The monad in its totality should now be shown to be the ontological structure of the imagination. We find an important suggestion of the correlation between the imagination and the monad in Kant's *Critique of Judgment*. We read there: "We can describe the sublime in the following way: it is an object (of nature) the representation of which determines the mind to think the inaccessibility of nature as a description of rational ideas."[21] This nature as a description of rational ideas is also called "nature itself in its totality."[22] Kant says further, "This rational idea of the supersensible, however, which we cannot indeed determine further, and consequently as whose description we cannot *recognize* nature, but can only think, is awakened in us through an object whose aesthetic judgment expands the imagination to its limit, whether it be the limit of the expansion (mathematical) or of the power over the mind (dynamic)."[23] According to Kant, therefore, the imagination is stretched out to the limit of expansion toward the totality of nature through the sublime object. Kant's opinion seems to confirm that the imagination in its total extension has a monadic structure, even if it now has something to do with the supersensible idea "individuality of the being."

Of course, if the imagination constitutes a monad, what emerges in it is not a thing but an image. However, here an image means not only a fantasy or reproduction of the original perception. It also contains the profiling phase of a thing, which might be called its "physiognomy." When we stand, filled with the feeling of the sublime, before a massive mountain towering up to the sky, the mountain is no longer a thing, but an image that shows us the sublime physiognomy of this material mass.

Husserl used the word "image" in *Experience and Judgment* in almost the same sense. He writes, "When we speak about the image we get from a matter, then just the manner is thought, how we see it, how it shows itself to us. In this sense, every object of external perception is given in an image, and this object is constituted in the synthetic transition from image to image."[24] He also uses the word "perception-image" *(Wahrnehmungsbild)*[25] in this sense.

In the monad of the imagination, therefore, the perception-image, but never the thing itself, emerges along with fantasy and reproduction. Herein we can discover the decisive feature of the difference between the monad and mere perspective. A thing always comes into perceptual perspective along with its appresented reverse side; on the contrary, an image in the monad never carries its reverse side with it. Is it then two-dimensional? As the image of a thing in the monad usually has a relieflike upraised surface *(Gestalt)*, it will be better to call it "quasi-three-dimensional."

THE DEFINITION OF THE ontological state of the monad contains a difficulty that may not be solved without a thorough revision of Husserl's ontology. The question to be confronted is the nature of the ontological relationship between the positional character of perception and its neutrality modification. Husserl writes, "In the sphere observed up to this point that which appears perceptually or in being remembered had the character of simple being 'in reality' — of being 'certain.'"[26] But once neutralized, its "positional character" has "become weak ... the simple being is ... consciously there, not in the manner of 'real,' but rather as 'something merely thought,' as a 'mere opinion.' Everything gets the modifying 'bracketing.'"[27] In other words, the image is not real, but only "real, as it were."[28]

Does this express anything that is ontologically meaningful? Hardly! We must rather begin with the character of the Being of the monad's Hereness itself. The monad originally has absolute Hereness. The ego as the core of the monad can stand within the whole monad only in the mode of Here and not of There. This means that the core of the monad (the ego) not only stands at the center, but also everywhere in the whole region of the monad simultaneously. It does not and need not wander within the monad, for any movement of the ego already presupposes the difference between Here and There. The ego as Here is now the whole monad itself, including all Theres. Only this simultaneous Being-everywhere of the monad guarantees its absolute Hereness. In this sense the whole monad is filled with the continuous Being of the ego. This is not an empty space or nothingness, but a fullness of my Being.

But how is it possible that an ego with a body can be every-where in the monad simultaneously, even where an image floats? This question can only be answered when we take the Being of the monad (and the ego) not for real Being, but for potential Being. The real Being of the naked core is now neutralized to the *potential* Being of the imagination in the monad, and pure (bodily) flesh *(Leib)* without the physical body *(Körper)* possesses only po-tential Being as the subject of the imagination. Only this potential Being makes it thinkable that the ego is everywhere in the monad simultaneously. When the ego represents an image, it is already positioned potentially at this image. The ego of bodily flesh and the image are ontologically one in the monad. This ontological solidarity consequently founds the appresentation of other bodily flesh in the mode of "as if were There" through self-negating plu-ralization. Therefore the monad is full of my continuous potential Being. According to potential Being the core and the entirety of the monad are continuous and simultaneous. This simultaneity gives them the temporal character of the absolute present that never flows. The absolute Hereness of the monad is accompanied necessarily by the absolute standing-present with its thickness. Im-ages in the monad are governed by the self-identity of the ego, and their Being is intimately and continuously connected to it. Only the naked core, which is thrown as physical bodily flesh *(Leib-Körper)* and robbed of the all of its monad seeks it in the fu-ture by projecting it as an image.

In practical life the potential Being of the monad as continuous absolute Hereness is the necessary spatial foundation of the "distanc-ing" *(Entfernung)* of a place (There) from the ego (Here) in objective empty space; it is, as the thickness of the absolute present, also the necessary temporal foundation of the "duration" *(Dauer)* of a phe-nomenon, between now and then, in objective flowing time. There-fore in kinesthetic praxis spatial distance and temporal duration are often interchangeable (e.g., it is five minutes away, or it is a thousand-meter walk).

HERE MIGHT BE A PROPER PLACE to touch upon the phenomenon of "mood." Mood is always mine *(je-meinig)* but is also intersubjective at the same time. This fundamental character of mood shows it to belong not only to the monad but also to the naked core of the monad. Mood arises between the *Jemeinigkeit* of the monad and the interperspectival co-Being of the core of the monad. The naked core stands on common, interperspectival ground together with others, and feels the attunement (accessibility) or inattunement (inaccessibility) of his absent monad as mood. When my monad and those of others are given through the detour of appresentation onto kinesthetic bodies, they are already nuanced by moods. For example, I feel the mood of anxiety as the appresentation of the Being of my monad sliding away from me. Therefore, mood is the inner relation of one's appresented monad to its core (somatic ego), reflecting the attunement or accessibility of the former to the latter. Needless to say, in order to access its absent monad each ego must project it as an image *(worumwillen),* but there are various obstacles or aids to this projection. Mood represents this accessibility or inaccessibility to one's own monad, which is a priori absent in the objective common world.

We assume at least three kinds of Being: the probable Being of the object of perception, the potential Being of the image or the monad-all, and the real Being of things or the naked core of the monad. The third kind of Being is established only on the ground of the unity of the two former kinds of Being; for example, the core of the monad is real only in the flesh-physical body *(Leib-Körper)* unity, and a thing is real only in the unity of Being-ready-to-hand *(Zu-handensein)* and Being-present-at-hand *(Vorhandensein)*.[29]

In *Being and Time,* Heidegger writes, "The state of mood in which one may be found *(Befindlichkeit)* opens up Dasein in its thrownness."[30] This indicates that he rightly connects mood to the reality of the naked core of the monad. The analogizing, appresenting coexistence of naked cores, which he called "fallenness" *(Verfallen-heit),* is established when they are fulfilled by mood. In addition, "the question of the original wholeness of Dasein"[31] treated there will encounter the necessary intention of the naked core of the monad toward the monad-all. However, the ontological indefiniteness of Heideggerian Dasein will be able to grasp the monad only by means of anxiety as nothingness, but not as (potential) Being itself. In this connection, Heidegger's distinction between "the whole of beings" *(das Ganze des Seienden)* and "beings as a whole" *(das Seiende im Ganze)* in his "What Is Metaphysics?" is quite remarkable.[32] The former is the quantitative summation of beings, which is thinkable only on the plane of objective space. The latter is on the contrary a wholeness that is opened up only in mood; it is a wholeness that surrounds me in boredom and slides away from me in anxiety. Heidegger's sense of beings as a whole seems very near to my monad, but its definition remains ontologically ambiguous, or is still blind to the difference between real and potential Being. Although Heidegger paid extraordinary attention to the imagination in many places (especially in *Kant and the Problem of Metaphysics),* he did not reach the monad as the potential Being of images.

Perhaps the abyss of the phenomenological reduction lies in the difference between real Being and potential Being, or between the naked core of the monad and the monad-all. But the attitude of the indifferent onlooker, often emphasized by the later Husserl, is also possible on the ground of the potential Being of the monad. Also on the ground of potential Being we can remain indifferent to all the interests of real Being while keeping a distance from them. The reduction to the monad is one to the potential Being of a human ego, which makes a phenomenological insight into factic reality possible, as well as the Husserlian reduction to the probable Being of perception for its part.

It will be obvious that the identification of the phenomenological reduction and the transformation of real Being into potential Being gives rise to an opposition, because for Husserl the reduction and neutralization are not the same thing. I cannot discuss this difficult problem here. I will refer only briefly to the fact that insofar as the reduction means bracketing or switching off the general thesis, and as this thesis means the real Being of things in general, there is no problem with including neutralization in the reduction in a broader sense as one of its indispensable parts. Rather, it seems to me that this is the only way to understand the Cartesian method and the new way to the phenomenological reduction in continuity and unity. For even after Husserl's bracketing of real Being (thetic Being), potential Being (pre-thetic Being) still remains, which is valid as the passively pregiven world where his expanded concept of image predominates. In spite of all of Husserl's attempts to differentiate the phenomenological reduction and neutralization, they increasingly show themselves to be in principle connected, while the Husserlian insistence on the apodictic intuition of essence without any monadological foundation becomes less and less valid.

As is evident from what we have mentioned above, the community of the naked cores of monads is the life-world, but no static community of total monads that topologically arranges plural monads in itself is thinkable. This is because every monad is in itself an exclusive whole that allows no common horizon in which monads will lie parallel to each other side by side. Rather, the true community should possess a dynamic structure in which monads do not lie parallel, but in which each monad constitutes with every other a kind of complex in which they are also kinesthetically mediated (in this case, what is most important is their mediator, which we cannot, however, touch upon until the end of this book). In any case, the result is not a static fusion of monads, but rather a dynamic complex of monads where every single monad, instead of losing its ownness, makes up a community with every other by altering itself from the inside and by bringing other monads into itself under tension, while this monad itself is being brought into other monads under tension. Here a kind of reciprocal enveloping paradoxically occurs: my monad is in another monad, while at the same time another monad is in my monad. In other words, two absolute Heres are coupled without losing their absoluteness and without being relativized into a There.

However, as a matter of fact these Heres are not connected directly as Here = Here, but are necessarily mediated by Here = There (kinesthetic body), or by There (thing) in the manner: Here−Here = There−There−Here = There−Here. This mediation comprises the whole secret of human cultural activities, and I will attempt to clarify the true mediator by investigating the second-person dimension in the following chapters. I cannot, however, enter into this problem just yet.

Here in the community of monads as a complex, my and the other's commonly projected monadic Being beyond a thing is modified into universal linguistic meaning by connecting it (Being) with the all-temporal and all-local phonetic kinesthetic pattern of my body *(Körper),* which is now under the control of impersonal universal transcendental subjectivity. Husserl's idea of eidetic intuition through free variation means the process of this universalization of monadic Being into eidetic meaning. In our daily life, this origin of the essence is usually forgotten as in the idealistic phenomenology of Husserl, but in poetic language the intuition of this monadic origin of the meaning of words barely remains. As an example, I will introduce the Japanese traditional short poem, the haiku, in the next subsection.

Through the universalization of meaning into all-temporality and all-locality, monads are able to communicate with each other by way of everything in the world more easily, but are simultaneously threatened by the concealment of the monadic dimension and their genuine identity.

In order to prepare the way toward the haiku, I must here refer to an example of the extraordinary structure of the monadic complex. Ordinarily the communal complex consists of two equal monads enveloping each other, but sometimes one monad not only inwardly negates its own identity but also quits its own monad-all and keeps only the formal core of its monad. In this way, it is totally absorbed or enveloped into another monad, which appears to it as complete other-Being or Nothingness. In this Nothingness it encounters the various phenomena of the other monad passively. This is the extraordinary style of the monadic community, which is also capable of being mediated by an anonymous mediator. When the other monad is considered to be all of Nature *(physis),* or the Nature-monad, it constitutes the stage in which traditional Japanese art, including the haiku, is created.

In this way, the community of monads is revealed to be the necessary condition of human cultural creation. It is the place of encounter of my monad and another monad; my projection and another's projection are made common through mediation and pro-

duce a common meaningfulness. It is therefore the place of the genesis of meaningfulness in general, as well as of language.

As we are still at the stage where the name and the character
of the true mediator of the community of monads remains
unknown, we cannot enter into a detailed analysis of the community of monads itself here. Rather, we must satisfy ourselves with the
analysis of the Japanese seventeen-syllable short poem, the haiku,[33]
as illustrating one of the typical phenomena that occurs only in the
community of monads. It seems that here monadic intuition is
combined in a very specific way with linguistic meaning, and also
with the practical activity of a trip. Through this trinity a fundamental view toward the human being is also expressed in the haiku, a
kind of poem that is deeply affected by the peculiar monadic structure of Japanese art and artists. Indeed, every artistic relation has
essentially to do with the monad of the artist as the origin of the
imagination. However, in Japan some artists have actively refused to
see the monad as belonging to themselves. They become only the
(phantom) core of their monads, but in resignation remain alien to
their monads, which are not now to be called the ego, but rather
the concentrated Being of everything not their own, including their
former Being: the Nature-monad. Between the artist and the
Nature-monad Nothingness emerges as the sign of radical self-
negation that veils the latter monad and at the same time becomes
the stage of the occurrence of Nature. The Nature-monad produces everything as its image or phenomenon into the Nothingness
that these artists then observe and describe passively and nonarbi-
trarily. These Nature-artists therefore do not create by themselves,
but rather let Nature imagine freely through them. Even such a
specific kind of creation, however, can be performed only under
the control of the mediator of the community of monads, which
alone makes intuitable that all the phenomena in Nothingness ultimately come from the Nature-monad.

    As a typical example of such Japanese Nature-artists, let us
consider Basho Matsuo (1644–94). He was one of the world's
most important poets in the modern age, and the greatest haiku
master in history. Basho originated from the Samurai class and

studied Chinese literature and the Chinese philosophy of Lao-tse, as well as Zen Buddhism, all his life. He lived in Edo (old Tokyo) and made many trips throughout Japan. He kept many excellent records of his travels, which also contain many haiku. His most famous record is the *Oku-no-hosomichi (Path into the Deep),* which describes his five-month trip in northeastern Japan in 1689.

Basho liberated the haiku poem from its popular naive form and raised it to the standard of a genuine poetic art. Some of his poems may be used to illustrate the self-phenomenalization of the Nature-monad.

> Lush bushes in a summer field
> Trail of vain dreams
> Cherished by dead warriors
>
> (1689)

In this verse, which was sung on an old battlefield, the bushes and the vanished dreams are contrasted to each other. The bush in a summer field is not a mere thing, but a phenomenon in which the Nature-monad appears seasonally each year. In contrast, the dreams of warriors who struggled there once for their lives and killed each other indicates the monad of each, which was projected toward its own goal. Now these dreams, of both winners and losers, have gone, and the only trace that remains is the bush in the summer field. It is as if victory and defeat, life and death, the rise and fall of human history, are also one of the seasonal phenomena of Nature. Only the Nature-monad appears regularly and recurrently, and in this way it far outlasts the unstable, transient human monads.

> Calmness prevails
> Deep into the cliff-rock
> Cicada voices penetrate
>
> (1689)

This verse, which Basho created on the occasion of a visit to the Risshyakuji-temple near Sendai, excellently expresses the coincidence of silence and the occurrence of the Nature-monad. Calmness fills the temple on the mountain. This, for Basho, was nothing other than the silence of Nature itself. Into this calmness broke the sudden voices of the cicadas, or rather, the silence itself broke out as the voices of the cicadas; silent Nature itself occurred in this form. Just as beforehand silence prevailed on the surfaces of the surrounding cliff-rock, now voices press from all directions onto them, as if they were the appearance of silence itself. Just as the calmness had penetrated deeply into Basho's Being and had purified him, now the voices penetrate into all the surfaces of the cliff-rock, which is the pairing partner of his body. Here on the cliff-rock, which is also a part of the natural world, the Nature-monad itself encountered Basho in the forms of silence and occurrence (the cicada voices) simultaneously. The Nature-monad, the rock, and the poet stand there inwardly connected, while they are all deeply penetrated by the same voices of cicadas.

> Across the raging north sea
> Over beyond Sado Island
> Lies the Milky Way
>
> (1698)

Looking out across the Sea of Japan toward the island of Sado, which lies about forty kilometers from the coast, the poet sang this verse on a summer evening. At that time, when the sea raged no ferry boat could go to the island, which was originally a place of exile. People who dwelled on both sides of the canal thus necessarily lost their contact and communication with each other. But the Nature-monad, which figures itself in the Milky Way, embraces all of these in itself. Just like a floating bridge the Milky Way stretches itself toward Sado. When looked at from this bridge, the raging sea, as well as the life of the human beings on both coasts, seem only to be various occurrences of the one Nature. It is as if they were all occurrences of one cosmos, whether in harmony with each other or not. Over the black stormy ocean, without any lights of ships, only the great beam of the heavenly dome glimmers.

> On all this path
> No one is seen wandering
> Deep fall dusks
>
> (1694)

Here the Nature-monad reveals itself, on the one hand in the mode of "deep fall at dusk" as seasonally very solitary in mood, but on the other hand more intensely in the form of "no one." In the absence of any wanderers, in this emptiness, the cosmos occurs as the nothingness of beings. But this path that remains empty clearly reflects the presence of the poet, who must now wander upon it alone and in solitude. We see the lonely Being of Basho stretching infinitely forth on an empty track into the nothingness deeply veiling the Nature-monad itself.

> By an old pond
> Hark! a sound of water
> Of jumping frog
>
> (1686)

In this verse the cardinal point is the sound of water. It alone occurs as a phenomenon to the poet. Though the sound was probably caused by the jump of a small creature, Basho did not witness it with his eyes. But since this sound is the occurrence of the Nature-monad, it implicates everything in itself: the immeasurable age of the pond, the life of its small inhabitants, the smell of the thick old moss, and the prevailing calmness of the region. These are all embraced and represented by the sound of water. It is truly the product of the Nature-monad itself.

> Lying ill on a trip
> My dream rushes round and round
> Amidst the barren fields
>
> (1694)

Basho wrote this poem several days before his death, in the winter of 1694. Here he is not steadfastly devoted to the Nature-monad as he was before. His own monad, which he called a dream, roams uneasily in the winter field. The great Nature-poet sought his true home in Nature itself until the end. But all-embracing Nature now seems to him a barren field that will offer no one a place of rest. We might call this verse either tragic or genuinely itinerant. We can find in it, however, the fundamental ontological truth that the human Being with its monad cannot enter the Nature-monad as its home, that only as the resigned formal core of its own monad can it do so, even though it cannot help sometimes feeling alien to the fact. Herein lies the greatness and perhaps also the limit of this genius of Nature-poetry.

CHAPTER SEVEN

The Monad and Others

The Fundamental Congruency of Leib *and* Körper

IN THIS CHAPTER WE WILL DISCUSS the concept of monad, especially in relation to the intersubjectivity and the intrasubjectivity of the somatic ego, starting from the Husserlian idea of monad and intersubjectivity and deepening it phenomenologically.

THE PHENOMENOLOGICAL REDUCTION AND THE MONAD

In Husserl's later thought, the phenomenological reduction was consistently the reduction to a monad. Generally speaking, it does not seem that sufficient attention has been paid to this fact. For example, it is well known that in the second part of *First Philosophy* (a lecture of 1923-24), Husserl discussed the "psychologist's way" of performing the phenomenological reduction, based upon reflection on the experience of the world, instead of the "Cartesian way of phenomenological reduction," which appeared in the *Ideas* (1913) and which was based upon the proof of the possibility of the nonexistence of the world. The former way of reduction came to be called the "universal *epoché*" through the expansion of its application to the entire sphere of transcendental experiences beyond a correlation with particular objects. It literally makes possible the "universe of the transcendental subject."[1] It seems clear that this "universe," which is also held to be a unit of an aggregate, means nothing other than the "monad," because Husserl finished his lecture with the words "thus phenomenology is guided to a monadology, which is anticipated by the insight of the genius Leibniz."[2]

Moreover, in the *Cartesian Meditations* (1929), Husserl began with the *epoché* of the Being of the objective world but materially came to the same thing as the universal *epoché* of *First Philosophy*, namely, a reflection on "the infinite sphere of conscious life" by the transcendental ego as a "disinterested observer." Here, however, the monad is defined more clearly through the introduction of the "own-ness *(eigenheitliche)* reduction" or the "primordial reduction," and is distinguished from the simple "universe of the transcendental subject." To be precise, while this universe is separated into the "own sphere" that belongs to my constituted body and mind and the "foreign sphere" that does not belong to me through the ownness reduction, the transcendental ego, which constituted them, then unifies itself with the former sphere through "worldifying apperception."[3] As soon as the transcendental ego unifies itself in such a way with the "psycho-physical ego" constituted by itself, the "ego grasped in its full concreteness," namely, the *monad,* simultaneously arises. Therefore, a monad is, so to speak, the incarnation of the transcendental ego in its body, and hence we can understand why the body is called the "absolute Here" and occupies the functional center of the monad. The monad is not only something constituted, but also incarnated transcendental intentionality itself, which functions reflectively = nonreflectively and passively = actively. Its ambiguity is not contingent but is deeply rooted in its Being itself. Husserl closes his *Cartesian Meditations* with this sentence: "The necessary way to . . . philosophical recognition is that of universal self-recognition, first monadic, then inter-monadic."[4]

In Husserl's last book, *The Crisis of the European Sciences and Transcendental Philosophy* (1935–36), too, the discussion in the *Cartesian Meditations* is continued insofar as the reduction is concerned. Indeed, Husserl starts here from the *"epoché* of the objective sciences," but the "life-world" toward which this *epoché* is performed is the totality or the horizon of daily experiences appearing to the conscious life of a reflective subject, reductively changed from its natural attitude, and so it might well be identified with the above-mentioned "universe of the transcendental subject." In fact, alongside the usual term "transcendental *epoché,*" Husserl also uses the terms "universal *epoché*" and "universe of the purely subjective" as the goals of the *epoché.* When the "aporia of the human subject" between the "all-constituting transcendental ego" and the constituted "human" ego in the world inevitably emerges, Husserl declares the "self-objectification" (or the flowing-in) of the former ego into the latter one as the solution, and finishes by postulating the "reduction to the ultimately functioning, absolutely solitary ego."[5] Husserl writes, "In any case, not only with methodological reason, but also with the deepest philosophical reason, which we cannot enter into further here, sufficient consideration must be paid to the absolute solitude of the ego and its central position for all constitution."[6] It will be undeniable that this points to the incarnation of the transcendental ego in the solitary human ego or the ownness reduction to the monad[7]—though of course a question still remains: Why does Husserl never use the word "monad" in the *Crisis*?

As mentioned above, for more than ten years in Husserl's later life, when the phenomenological reduction began to follow a "new way" and its goal changed from "pure consciousness" to the "life-world," it always meant a reduction to a monad, that is, to the "sphere peculiar to myself" or to the "sphere in which I am full of concreteness in myself." To once pass through such a "solipsistic" and apodictic area is thought to be necessary in order to secure the evidence of the phenomenological constitution of the life-world. Husserl is not here concerned with methodology alone, however. On the one hand, he holds my concrete Being as monad to have an "in myself and for myself enclosed ownness *(Eigenheit)*,"[8] but on the other hand, he states, "Only the one monadic aggregation, or only the community of all coexisting monads, really exists."[9] We see, thus, that Husserl was strongly concerned about the "individuality" of beings as well as the "preestablished harmony" between them, both of which are problems he inherited from Leibniz. Now the first question that must necessarily be raised is this: Does Husserl deepen Leibniz's classical idea of the monad to a level of "existential" individuality in the modern sense? The second question is, How can a communication (communion) between such monads be secured without the mediation of God? These questions will be addressed in the following sections.

THE STRUCTURE OF THE MONAD IN HUSSERL

EVEN THOUGH HUSSERL GAVE THE IDEA of the monad such an important position, as we have discussed above, the Husserlian monad is today still plagued by ambiguities concerning individuality, which directly and indirectly have given rise to the equivocation surrounding the concept of "life-world."

Let us again take up the monadology of the *Cartesian Meditations* as representative of Husserl's later views. In section 33, Husserl writes, "We distinguish the ego grasped in its full concreteness (we will call it the monad from Leibniz's word) from the ego as the pole of identity or as the substratum of habituality. This is performed by the addition of something without which the ego can never be concrete. Namely, the ego can only be concrete when it is amidst the streaming multiplicity of its intentional life and among objects noticed or sometimes constituted by him as a being for that life."[10]

It is clear that this monad expresses an aggregate of the constituting and the constituted, a communion of subject and its objects around it. Now what kind of self-completeness or self-enclosedness does this monad, which is also called the ownmost sphere, have? In section 55 of the *Crisis* Husserl writes, "The world that is persistently pregiven and indubitable through the conviction of Being and the self-demonstration exists previously. Even when I do not presume it as a ground, the world is valid to me, to the I of the cogito, through constant self-demonstration. . . . There can be no stronger realism than when this word means 'I am certain that I am a human being living in this world; I do not doubt it at all.' But to understand this 'self-evidence' is a big problem."[11] Here the world is treated as an "indubitable" passive pregivenness. Regrettably, however, Husserl finished the argument by leaving the essential relation between this "pregiven" world and the monad unclarified. Nevertheless, it is clear that the monad itself as the peculiar ownmost sphere is also based upon a "pregiven" world.[12] In my opinion, this becomes true by virtue of the fact that the nonobjectifiable side of the body (the bodily flesh, or *Leib*), which is to be penetrated afterward by the transcendental subjectivity, is already the center of the pregiven world, unlike the always intentionally constituted, objectifiable "physical body" *(Körper)*. The reciprocal self-reflectivity (intentional arc) of the body occurs not only in the dimension of kinesthesis as generally thought. The pure *Leib* as the basis of the *Leib-Körper* connects itself ontologically with the pre-thetic surrounding world and shares the same (potential) Being with the surrounding objects beyond the subject-object schema.[13] Based upon such an ontological structure, the monad has the character of a closed "openness" *(Da)* inside this self-sufficient Being. Insofar as the monad centers upon the pregiven *Leib*, it conversely reflects upon this center from the Being of the surrounding world and is essentially closed in on itself.

Although Husserl discovered the dimension of the pregiven world, he could not clarify the ontological, or the so-called existential relationship of the three elements, namely monad, *Leib*, and the pregiven world, because he did not understand the inner relation between the body and the world. By contrast, if the *Leib* is recognized as the unconstituted (pre-thetic) entity pregiven together with the Being of the surrounding world prior to any thesis given through the transcendental ego, as I suggested, would Husserl's transcendental ego not lose its appealing title as the "absolutely unique subjectivity constituting everything"? In this sense, to "understand the self-evidence of world-Being" must indeed have been a "big problem" for Husserl.

I have pointed out that if the *Leib* is something pregiven that occupies "the absolute unique center" of the monad, as Husserl says, the monad must have a kind of ontological enclosedness or completeness in itself. The meaning of this nature of the monad becomes more important when we think of the relation of my monad to the other monad.

According to the *Cartesian Meditations,* Husserl's notion of the monad includes an intentionality toward others as well as every other kind of intentionality. However, at first, for the sake of methodological reason, Husserl would exclude the synthetic act of intentionality toward others (the reality of others to me) thematically: "By this special [residual] intentionality a new meaning of Being, which oversteps my monadic ego in its ownness constitutes itself, and an ego, which is not I myself, but reflects my ego or my monad, constitutes itself."[14] He says, further, "[This] other is a reflection of my self, and yet not the original reflection; an analogon of my self, yet not the analogon in the ordinary sense."[15] These words will mean that the egoicity of others but not their alterity itself, may be constituted from the reflection or the analogon of my self. Husserl seems to have graspsed this alterity of others as the "new meaning of Being" that oversteps me, although it is intentionally immanent to my monad.

It was Iso Kern who recognized that the monad intentionally includes alterity as constituted meaning that oversteps me, and who criticized the ambiguity of Husserl's monadology from this standpoint. He discusses the Fifth Meditation of the *Cartesian Meditations* in the introduction to the *Husserliana*, volume 15. Although this passage is very long, I will quote it completely because of its contextual importance:

> This ambiguity is most clearly seen in the relation of the idea of "self-ownness" or "primordiality" developed in this meditation to "alterity": *On the one hand,* the Fifth Meditation inquires into the relation between primordial and potential experiences given in apodictic self-perception . . . as well as the synthesis that is originally and inseparably constituted with them in it . . . and other monads that are never given originally, but only in representation *(Vergegenwärtigung).* This question is put forth under the guidance of the Cartesian idea of the foundation of apodictic, philosophical recognition and within the horizon of the problematic of the distinction of my monad from other monads. In the treatment of these questions, of course, the experience of other, insofar as it is my *own* experience, belongs to the ground-sphere (primordial sphere), while the ontic correlate of this experience, namely the other, remains excluded from it. In fact, Husserl says clearly in several places in this meditation that the experiences of the other belong to the proper sphere or the primordial sphere. But, *on the other hand,* in the Fifth Meditation the relation between my own (or the primordial) and the other also remains under the guidance of the problematic of the motivation of the experiences of the other. Moreover, it falls not under the guidance of *philosophical* motivation, but under the guidance of a "series of motivations" of *natural* empathy itself: "How is the natural experience of the other (empathy) motivated?" What motivates, or "the ground of motivation," is here the primordial or myself, and what is motivated is the other. From this point of view, to calculate my experience of the other itself—as its very motivation is questioned—into the ground of motivation or into the primordial, will be paradoxical. In fact, Husserl will, in several places, take this experience to be excluded from the primordial sphere gained by abstraction. What is shown herewith is not only the ambiguity of the "primordial" or the fundamental sphere to which primordial abstraction leads, namely that on the one hand it is the

sphere of my own monad experienced apodictically and primordially in philosophical reflection (the first in the order of grounding of philosophical reflection), and on the other hand it is the ground of the motivation of the natural experiences of the other (the first in the order of motivation of natural empathy), but also thereby the ambiguity of the whole process of thought in the Fifth Meditation is shown. Is the reflective, philosophical founding (grounding) of transcendental others and the transcendental relation between my monad and other monads questioned here, *or* rather the constitutive analysis of "natural," "worldly" empathy? In the reduction to primordiality, is it a matter of a limitation of the properly functioning life of the transcendental ego, to which its proper empathy also belongs, *or* rather of the constitutive dissolution of the world into the area where the transcendental [worldly?] ego can perform without the intervention of the alter ego, namely the dissolution of the higher intersubjective layer of constitution and its limitation to a lower constitutive stage? That restriction and this dissolution fall under completely different points of view.

In the first case, it is the transcendental-reductive method to determine my monad in reference to the determination of transcendental others, and in the second case the method of the constitutive analysis of the natural experiences of worldly others. The Fifth Meditation confuses these two lines of thought. At the beginning of the meditation the idea of the philosophical foundation of transcendental others comes to the fore, but soon after empathy is constitutively analyzed in accordance with the natural, ontic givenness of others, in order to conclude by saying: "Through this interpretation, which I perform as the transcendental ego under the transcendental reduction, it becomes simultaneously clear that I can necessarily reach others as *transcendental others*." That Husserl believed he had already gained transcendental others methodically merely by way of the transcendental-constitutive analysis of the natural experiences of others—and precisely by way of it—became possible only by way of that confusion.[16]

Now Kern's critique is irrelevant from our standpoint, since we know already that the monad is the sphere of the incarnation of the transcendental ego and is the result of its flowing into the "natural" world. What Husserl intended in the Fifth Meditation was to find the motivation of the "natural" experiences of others in the transcendental ontic meaning of others overstepping my monad. In other words, the problem was how to fulfill others as transcendental intentional meaning with concrete sensuous contents. Therefore, the fact that the "transcendental other" as intentional meaning is involved in the monad as "the foundation of the motivation" of the "natural" experiences of others is never paradoxical at all, contrary to Kern's argument. Rather, here the latter motivation has need of the guidance of the former intentional meaning. As already stated, Husserl's monad as the primordial sphere has the unity of a double character: originally transcendental as well as natural. This double character implies no defect. Kern's misunderstanding seems to come from his failure to adequately grasp the meaning of the self-objectification or the incarnation of the transcendental ego in the primordial sphere.

The same refutation is valid for Kern's critique of the whole process of the Fifth Meditation. The restriction of the execution of the transcendental ego to its self-ownness and the dissolution of the intersubjective world-layer do not fall under "completely different points of view," as he says, but on the contrary, they are both phases of one and the same fact to Husserl; Husserl does not confuse these "two series of thought" but rather wants to "combine" them intentionally through the "worldifying" apperception.

This issue does not conclude with the exposure of Kern's misunderstanding, however. No matter what Husserl's intention was, whether he really succeeded in combining the natural recognition of others and the transcendental meaning of others through the concept of "appresentation" (rather than that of empathy) is another problem. The problem is no longer whether he confused the doublesidedness proper to my monad, but rather whether he could methodically synthesize this recognized double-sidedness not only in relation to my ego but also to the alter ego.

However, after a careful investigation of sections 50–54 of the Fifth Meditation, which treat the problem of recognition of the other, we regrettably cannot help reaching a negative conclusion with regard to this point. Here Husserl has a good command of the concept of "appresentation" as a major tool, which is itself founded by the concept of "coupling" *(Paarung):* "Coupling is an originary form of the passive synthesis called association in contrast to the passive synthesis of identification."[17] First, he asserts the emergence of the phenomenal relation of coupling between my original body and a thing resembling my body that appears in my primordial sphere. He would have done better to argue for a transcendental coupling between my transcendental ego and that of others (associated intentionality), far beyond the sensuous, analogical coupling between both bodies. In other words, he should have combined the intentional, ontic meaning of transcendental others with the principle of "coupling" in some way. However, by virtue of the fact that he could not accomplish this, and instead regarded coupling only as the principle of passive synthesis valid for my transcendental ego alone, the appresentation thus founded does not reach transcendental others, but only makes the removal of my transcendental ego from "here" to "there" possible. Indeed Husserl's theoretical recognition of others, which uses the tools of "coupling" and "appresentation," lacks an adequate delineation of the meaning of transcendental others, contrary to his intention and assertion. Therefore, the others who appear in Husserl's monad are others only insofar as simply adding a difference of spatial positions in the monad to my transcendental ego, and they do not yet have transcendental alterity in a genuine sense.

Therefore, although there is no reason to think that Husserl should have attempted an intentional analysis of simple, natural empathy in order to constitute the monad of others, if we consider the transcendental definition of the concept of monad, still, in reality, he performed something very close to it, namely, the foundation of empathy virtually by way of my transcendental ego alone. This miscarriage must not be considered to be merely a simple confusion of essentially different methods, as Kern thought, but rather a methodological deficiency caused by an insufficient grasp of the transcendental meaning of others. The possibility of compensating for and developing the Husserlian method by deepening our grasp of the meaning of the transcendental ego still remains.

THE ONTIC MEANING OF THE TRANSCENDENTAL OTHER
AND ITS EMERGENCE

As mentioned above, Husserl's monad has its ownness in the fact
that although it is "an absolutely closed immanent *(reel)* unity,"[18] it
intentionally involves the transcendental other as meaning in itself.
This meaning, however, seems to have been only inadequately
employed in the critical stage of the recognition of the other. This
inadequacy is also evident in the very imperfect analogy between
the "past-constitution" in my present consciousness and the "other-
constitution" in my monad described by Husserl in section 52 of
the *Cartesian Meditations*.[19] What is the reason for this inadequacy in
Husserl's treatment of the other?

In the first place, is there a problem in grasping the other as the
intentional object of my transcendental ego, or, consequently, as its
noematic meaning? Why does Husserl grasp the body of the other in
the analogical coupling with my body but not try to grasp the intentionality of the transcendental other in the coupling with my intentionality? Insofar as the other is a transcendental subject as well, it
will be active intentionality and its unifying pole, just as my ego is. Is
it not erroneous to take the transcendental other for a passive, static
object with its meaning intended unidirectionally by my ego?

Of course, in the natural world the intentionality of the other is
made anonymous in many cases, and it is even less likely to appear as
pure immanence in the monad like the body of the other did. However, as a matter of fact, in order to make the intentionality of the
other emerge in its proper mode, precisely the ownness reduction to
my primordial sphere is indispensable. Then the monad is completely closed to the intentionality of the other except in its ontic meaning, insofar as, and only insofar as, the monad is the pregiven world
centered on the *Leib* (and not on the *Leib-Körper*). Against this closedness of the monad the intentionality of the other appears, not simply
as intentionally transcendent meaning, but rather as something
breaking through its closedness, or as the penetration from transcendence into immanence. This is the phenomenon called the "look."
The look is the emergence of the intentionality of the other itself by
way of its meaning, as is recognized most evidently in the case of penetration into my monad.

I think that the original intention of Husserl, who regarded the

primordial reduction as the indispensable path to the phenomenological analysis of the intersubjective life-world, would be better realized by the introduction of the emergence of the intentionality of the
transcendental other (the look) than by his own method. This is because he himself uses the result of the execution of the look of the
other without being aware of it, in the analysis of the recognition of
the other, as we have already suggested in the previous chapter.

About the process of "association" constituting coupling, Husserl says, "A thing belonging to my primordial surrounding-world is
for me a thing in the mode of 'There'. . . . The way it emerges . . . reproductively reminds me of a similar emergence belonging to the
constitutive system of my bodily flesh *(Leib)* as a body *(Körper)* in
space. It reminds me of the appearance of my body *(Körper), as if I
were there.*"[20] I would ask him in return, How can I originally attain the
appearance of myself posited "There" without the cooperation of the
intentionality (look) of the other objectifying me, as if I were not
"Here," but "There"? I see myself from the outside only insofar as I
have thrown myself into the perspective of the other. Therefore the
representation of my bodily ego in the mode of "as if I were There"
presupposes the emergence of my transcendental ego (as well as that
of the other) in the mode of "as if he/she (the transcendental other's ego) were "Here."[21] This is to say that only when my intentionality accepts the intentionality of the other (the look) in itself according
to the association of intentionalities, and alienates itself reflectively,
then, and only then, the objectification of my self emerges. In this
way the constitution of the other through my primordiality and that
of myself (my *Körper*) through the "look" of the other are connected
inseparably to each other. In other words, my bodily mode of "as if I
were There" and my mode of consciousness "as if he/she (the transcendental other) were Here" form a pair that originally defines "appresentation" as the possibility of the constitution of the other. This
is to say that when my alienated *Körper,* which is in the Here in the
mode of "as if I were *There,*" reincarnates the similarly alienated transcendental ego in the mode of "as if *he/she* were Here" and becomes
body-surface consciousness (consciousness of *Leib-Körper*), then correspondingly the similar *Körper* of the other in the mode of "as if *I*
were There" immediately incarnates the transcendental other as the
"look" coming from There in the mode of "as if he/she were *Here,*" in
order to bring about the appresentative "coupling" of the body-surface

ego and the body-surface other. In this way only through the introduction of the "look" as the ontic meaning of the other are the transcendental dimension of myself and the other inwardly connected. This was what Husserl originally intended, although in vain. Still, such an attempt to immanently overcome Husserl's thought will necessitate an important revision of his fundamental project; his fundamental plan for "the constitution of the other ego solely by my transcendental ego" fails. In order to accomplish the constitution of a concrete coupling between myself and the other, the emergence and the cooperation of the equally original and intentionally associative transcendental other ego in the form of the look are necessary.

We can immediately anticipate an attempt to refute the transcendental foundation of coupling mentioned above in the following way: For the positioning of my own *Körper* the presupposition of the emergence of the look of the other is not always necessary, for it is already possible through the reflection and the self-objectification of my transcendental ego alone. Those who object in such a way must recognize that the reflection of my self is always motivated by the emergence of a perspective other than my own, no matter whether or not it is perceived to be the look of any particular person. Therefore my reflective perspective always includes, even if only potentially, other perspectives that reflect from the same point of view. In other words, since the reflection and the self-objectification of my self is always intentionally associative and interintentional, reflection by my solipsistic consciousness alone is in principle impossible. Moreover, if the thesis of my *Körper* and another *Körper* were possible through the act of my transcendental ego alone, the existence of the transcendental other's ego would become contingent after all, and would remain the object of a kind of empirical analogical apperception, as Husserl indicated. In this case my ego and the other ego would never have equal originality *(Gleichursprünglichkeit)* in the transcendental dimension and the solipsistic situation would continue forever on principle.

THE TRANSCENDENTAL CONSCIOUSNESS AND
A DEEPENED CONCEPTION OF THE MONAD

If we believe that my transcendental consciousness is immediately in associative connection with the other transcendental consciousness, which emerges as the look, and that the bodies *(Leib-Körper)* of myself and others in the sole objective world surrounding them (the correlate of associative transcendental consciousness) appear precisely as their incarnation, the relationship of transcendental consciousness and the monad cannot but change and be deepened as well, compared with before. Transcendental consciousness cannot enter and be confined in my monad without windows, contrary to the traditional opinion of Leibniz and Husserl, insofar as transcendental consciousness is essentially intersubjective (or intentionally associative) and open to the other. In other words, my "universe of the transcendental subject" is penetrated everywhere by the intentionalities of other transcendental subjects, which are a priori equally original with me. For example, even when, through the en-worlding (incarnation) of my self, my subject settles into the central Here and unifies itself with the perspectival consciousness of perception, it already potentially involves the other perspectival transcendental consciousness in the form of the appresentation of the "invisible reverse side" of the objects presented to me, as I argued in chapter 1. Therefore, in order to perform the ownness reduction and realize the enclosed monad, it is necessary not only to exclude the entire intentionality of the other ego and the other ego as transcendence, but also to constitute the "world without unseen sides" through suspending my own transcendental consciousness itself and realizing the quasi two-dimensional or so-called relieflike perceptive (perceptive-image) consciousness that is particular to me. Only such a pre-positional "image" consciousness peculiar to me can illuminate the monad from the inside as the "opening" in the closed, pregiven surrounding world centering upon the pre-positional *Leib*. This fact shows that the agent who performs the "ownness reduction" and constitutes the monad as the primordial sphere is not the transcendental consciousness any longer, but rather the pregiven *Leib* with its own consciousness. In other words, the reflective transcendental consciousness indeed has the ability to constitute the *Körper*, but never the *Leib* itself. Rather, the *Leib* is given from the anonymous bottom, as the core of the pregiven primordial world or the monad. The fact that this pregiven primordial surrounding-world as the monad corresponds consciously to the dimension of the "imagination" neutralized from perspectival perception has already been pointed out and discussed in other places in this book. In this way, it now becomes clear that the self-sufficient monad lies in the dimension of the pure imaginative life, and not, as Leibniz and Husserl thought, in that of the perspectival perceptive consciousness. Because every perceptive perspective involves other perspectives in itself potentially, it will essentially have an incomplete, "open horizon" insofar as it is the enworlding of the associative transcendental consciousness.

Furthermore, we must think that insofar as *neither* the transcendental consciousness that constitutes the *Körper nor* the imaginative life that constitutes the *Leib* could constitute the other from another, a third agent, the "somatic ego," will be necessary to unite them kinesthetically as the *Leib-Körper* from the outside, so to speak.

Now the transcendental other emerges as the "look" to my deepened monad as the genuine primordial sphere; it breaks through the completeness of my monad from the outside. Immediately corresponding to it, my transcendental consciousness breaks through the wall of the monad from the inside, mediated by my somatic ego, which had been dormant in the monad, holding the ontic meaning of the other, and posits the *Körper* of myself and others upon the There in cooperation with the invading transcendental others in order to establish the common objective world. At this point everything is objectified in the open horizon and even my monad disappears and appears only appresentatively as mood.[22]

But when the transcendental consciousness, once it has overflown the open world, redescends unreflectively onto the surface of the *Körper* constituted by it and is incarnated, then the transcendental other is also incarnated by the surface of its proper *Körper* according to the transcendental principle of coupling. At the same time the *Leib* as the core of my monad, which has once become anonymous, reappears as potential Being fulfilling the incarnated *Körper* (bodysurface-subject) from the inside and dispersing itself from the Here into plural Theres. This is the phenomenon that is usually called "empathy."[23] In this way two constituting principles from the top and the bottom—that is, the intersubjectivity of the transcendental consciousness and the self-dispersion of the monadic imagination—meet on my *Leib-Körper* or on that of others as a contact point, and are unified preliminarily by the somatic ego, forming the central stratum of the kinesthetic practical life-world. We can here see the essential dualunity that is proper to the life-world. We must not forget, however, that in this life-world the pregiven Being of the surrounding world as well as that of the *Leib* is dispersed into each inner-worldly object, and the monad appears only in the appresentative form of the "mood," which is, so to speak, the veil of my Being. This means that the Husserlian life-world, which may surely be full of moods, remains essentially in the forgetfulness of pregiven Being and is in no way conceivable as a community of monads in the genuine sense.

The sole, intersubjective-objective world that Husserl intended above all in the *Cartesian Meditations* does not emerge as a result of the so-called communalization of the monad or more correctly the "communalization of the perspectives of myself and others" claimed by Husserl, but on the contrary this communalization itself is performed under the tacit presupposition of that sole objective world that is the correlate of the associative transcendental consciousness. The world at which Husserl really arrived—the kinesthetic practical community of the *Leib-Körper* (body-surface-consciousness) of myself and others—could come into view only through the processes of "self-objectification," "coupling," "kinesthetic removal," and "empathy" upon the ground of the above-mentioned "sole interintentional-objective world." When we call this community of *Leib-Körper* the "life-world," with reason, it is naturally not simply the static world conceived geometrically, but rather the dimension of the imperfect "interpenetration" of transcendental subjectivity and monadic individuality and that of the dynamic community of the *Leib-Körper* egos that perceive, imagine, and act.[24]

However, as already suggested we must not think that in such a life-world a proper community of monads is already realized, because here the realization of community is limited to the kinesthetic dimension without monads, while in the deeper hidden dimension of one's project, which is essential to the *Leib* (Existence), the exclusive domination of monadic individuality continues. That is, before projecting its own possible Being into the future, my *Leib* must again concentrate all the potential Being *(Leib)* of others scattered in "Theres" upon itself as its own Being, and regain the primordial monad, which is essentially exclusive of others, as the possible Being for the project. Insofar as the *Leib* or the somatic ego projects its own future, it must necessarily return to the solipsistic monad as before.[25]

Some kinds of the phenomenon "mood" seem to have much to do with the modes of this concentration of potential Being upon my monad. At the very least, the passively abandoned, scattered Being around my *Leib* in the life-world will cause the moods of boredom and diversion, while the scattered Being that obstinately resists my efforts at concentration will cause the mood of irritation. My already concentrated Being will also cause various moods through its appresentation into the life-world in accordance with its accessibility to a certain projection over and beyond the sole objective world (e.g., melancholia, anxiety, gaiety, tranquility, etc.).

Therefore, transcendental intersubjectivity (with its sole objective world) and monadic individuality are not completely mediated by the *Leib-Körper* ego. Rather, these two strata embrace and influence the somatic ego from top and bottom respectively, so to speak, in an immanent-transcendent way. Thus the life-world is not the simple field of the incarnation or the self-realization of transcendental reason, as Husserl thought. No light of reason could illuminate the very depths of monadic individuality. The dark foundation that supports the life-world from the bottom allows no simple rationalization. The life-world, or the somatic ego inhabiting it, is nothing other than the "contact point" of rationality and irrationality, as well as the "field of struggle" of both.

We can see an aspect of this situation in the relationship between modern science and scientific technology. Science is a product of transcendental associative subjectivity, or rationality aiming at the rationalization of the life-world; it aims to flatten the life-world into the sole objective world. This rational objective recognition of science, however, falls into the hands of huge opposing political powers or big industrial capital, and converted into more or less irrational projects for the sake of war or economic competition, and have become scientific technology, in this way, ever since the time of the Industrial Revolution of the nineteenth century. In this way, the rational flattening of the life-world proceeds hand in hand with an irrational abysmal deepening; each complements and promotes the other. A crisis in which this unstable expanding equilibrium will bring about the total collapse of the life-world seems quite possible.[26]

If, no matter what its procedure, the phenomenological reduction is nothing other than the making-valid of myself and the life-world as phenomena and the halting of the natural attitude, which regards everything as "things," it must, from the point of view of the "disinterested spectator," necessarily bring to the light of day both the perspectival "look" that emerges from the whole surface of the

Körper, and the imaginative life *(Leib),* which fulfills the *Körper* from the inside and disperses itself everywhere. In other words, it must disclose "incarnated intentionality."

This world phenomenon of *Leib-Körper* as the preliminary unification of "Here" and "There" will temporarily appear as the essential ambiguity of the "living present." On the one hand, the extensionality of things corresponding to my *Körper* incessantly flows away through the "standing present" in the perspective of the associate-subjects. On the other hand, the impression-data corresponding to my *Leib* as monadic center never flows, but incessantly sediments itself as "image" into the same present. For example, a desk as transparent extension with a reverse side incessantly flows away from the present that just profiles it as a voluminous extension (not as *hyle*),[27] while the visual impression of the front of the desk (a phenomenally given profile or a perceptive image) and the kinesthetic impression (e.g., of pulling out its drawer) do not flow away but are sedimented into the standing present of my monadic imagination. Once it becomes sedimentation, the impression is to be revived repeatedly. The true dimension of the "future" as different from the mere extension of the past is opened only through the combination of the project with the revived value-sedimentation, and of the protention with the revived kinesthetic sedimentation.

While the sole objective world with its various *Körper* flows from the present to the past and so belongs to the present-past axis, the monad of my self belongs to the present-future axis. The latter does not flow passively from future to present (there is no such flow at all), but rather springs forth actively from the standing present to the future. Because a human is the associative transcendental consciousness accompanied by its factic *Körper* intentionally correlating to the common objective world, and it is, at the same time, the *Leib* as the projecting center of the monad, that is, because a human is the so to speak incomplete self-identity of "the *Leib-Körper,*" the time flowing from the present to the past and the time springing from the present to the future can be connected to each other in order to make "history" possible. Because the life-world is not yet the true community of monads, however, human history cannot be harmonious, but rather is full of contradictions between monadic projections.

CONCLUSION

In this chapter it has become clear that Husserl's monad is a mixed concept in a far graver sense than Kern pointed out, and that in this concept the open perspectivty of transcendental consciousness and the enclosed monadicity of the existential imaginative life coexist. The consequences of the former perspectivity are, for example, differentiating the inside of a monad into the central "Here" and peripheral "Theres," recognizing orientation and perspectivity between them,[28] allowing the forms of time and space to intervene in the monad, letting "things" and "psycho-physical egos" coexist "side by side" in it,[29] and admitting the open coexistence of many monads. On the contrary, the consequences of the latter monadicity include calling my body "the zero point on the absolute 'Here,'"[30] stating that "every monad is immanently an absolute complete unity" and "the monad of the other is separated from my monad immanently."[31] The appresentative "coupling" between my body and those of others insisted on by Husserl is possible only in the former dimension, where my *Körper* and those of others are grasped "side by side," namely in the perspective of the transcendental consciousness, where, moreover, the perspective of others as the "look" already immanently intervenes, as we have discussed before. Such a coupling never occurs in the latter dimension, that of the windowless imaginative monad, where no "side by side" of images is allowed. Therefore, Husserl's "coupling between *Körper*" can never be a complete mediating principle between the dimension of pure *Leib* of each one, which we call the deepened monad. In other words, "the coupling" might be the mediation between one "'Here' already partially becoming There" or "Here = There" *(Leib-Körper)* and the other, but can never be the mediation between one "absolute Here" (the pure *Leib*) and the other, which are subjects of projection.

Thus I distinguish and clearly separate two areas that are mixed in the Husserlian idea of monad, namely, the area of the a priori associative transcendental perceptive consciousness and that of the existentially pregiven imaginative life. In addition, I must make it clear that both of these areas are incompletely mediated by our somatic ego. In this way, the problem of the constitution of authentic intersubjectivity no longer takes the form of correlating the simple ego and the simple alter ego with each other, but rather takes the form of correlating the unity of the above-mentioned two original areas inside my somatic ego with the same unity inside the somatic alter ego: namely, the correlation of double unities with each other or the mediation of double mediations. The question is, what ultimately mediates these double mediations?

SECTION III

CHAPTER EIGHT

Review of Modern Philosophical Theories of the Body

WHAT DOES IT MEAN TO DISCUSS the body from a philosophical standpoint? At the risk of stating a conclusion in advance, I will say that it is to clarify the figure of the living body or the "somatic ego," which is never to be grasped from the natural scientific standpoint.

In Occidental philosophy the body has long been accorded a comparatively inferior position and has never been a central issue of philosophy. This is remarkably different from Oriental philosophy, particularly Buddhist philosophy as well as Jewish mystic philosophy. From ancient Greece through medieval Europe the body was considered merely the animal side of the human being and no essential difference was recognized between the human body and the bodies of animals.[1] The sensuous soul, the *eidos* of animals, was considered to dwell within the body, and in humans it was lodged in the heart, the center of the human body. This Aristotelian-Thomistic idea of the body, which takes the human being to be a combination of superior "Reason" and inferior "body," strongly influenced modern thought even after the seventeenth century. For example, although Descartes introduced a substantial dualism rather than the Aristotelian principles of Matter and Form, and endeavored to distinguish Reason and the body more clearly and more distinctly, he too considered the human body to be the same as the animal body, this time both higher automatons.[2] Compared with the preceding age, although the body changed from an organic to a mechanical being, it was still regarded as an inferior being subject to Reason, just as before.

Descartes was still far from the idea that the body also possesses a kind of ego in itself.

To recognize an original subjectivity in a body, one must be freed in the first place from the illusion that "Reason = ego," but the idealistic tradition of Occidental philosophy was too strong to allow such a move. In fact, not a single philosopher who protested against this thesis appeared before Ludwig Feuerbach, in the nineteenth century. Therefore, he deserves the title of the founder of modern philosophical anthropology. Whoever is really freed from the illusion that Reason is ego can genuinely ask the question "What is man?" anew, and this question also contains a question about the body within it.

As a matter of fact, however, we can even find in Descartes's famous methodological doubt the beginnings of the anthropological problematic. As is well known, Descartes successively doubted the certainty of (1) the senses from the outside, (2) the senses from within, and (3) abstract ideas represented by number, and the genuine conclusion of this doubt was the discovery that I cannot doubt that I am doubting.[3] Therefore, the sole definitive conclusion drawn from methodological doubt must be the thesis "I doubt, therefore I am." The agent of doubt itself was, according to Descartes's own statement, not Reason, but Will, so the ego that he found must be not Reason, but Will. If we take the self-consciousness of Will for imagination, then the ego found by Descartes must have been an imaginative Will. In fact, because the function of doubt is to offer another possibility concerning a given judgment of fact, its agent should indeed be the imagination.[4] But Descartes argues that to doubt is to think doubtfully, therefore instead of "I doubt, therefore I am," he proposes "I think, therefore I am" as the sole true conclusion of his doubt. Next he immediately involves "understanding," "affirming," "negating," and so forth in this thinking *(cogito)*. The common view that the ego discovered by Descartes belongs to Reason has its ground solely in this, Descartes's own unjustifiably broad interpretation.[5] Such an interpretation is so violent that it almost invalidates the meaning of methodological doubt, but it is more surprising that the result of such a crude interpretation has been accepted by Occidental philosophy ever since. The strength of the Reason = ego thesis in the idealistic tradition of Occidental thought is undeniable.

If Descartes had not twisted the result of his doubt and had accorded the imagination the central role of ego, the history of Occidental philosophy would have been considerably transformed. In addition, as I will discuss later, because the imagination constitutes one of the main functions of the human body, the idea of the "somatic ego" would have already emerged. If this had happened, the real agent of scientific technology born of Occidental philosophy would have revealed itself to be the somatic ego rather than the rational ego.[6] As it turned out, however, the Occidental modern age never recognized the essence of scientific technology and left it free to do whatever it liked. One could say that the fictitious rational ego was attacked at its weakest point.

The leader of serious reflection upon this point, which finally began in the nineteenth century, was Feuerbach, as already mentioned. His book *Fundamental Theses of the Philosophy of the Future* (1843) is epoch-making in this sense. His standpoint can be seen clearly in the following statement: "If older philosophy began from the thesis 'I am an abstract, merely thinking being and the body does not belong to my essence,' the new philosophy begins, on the contrary, from the thesis 'I am a real, sensuous being. The body belongs to my essence; yes, the body as a whole is my ego, my essence itself.'"[7] He called this new philosophy "Anthropology." If we follow the self-reflective movement of Occidental philosophy from the beginning of the nineteenth century along this anthropological direction in a broader sense, we will find three fundamental movements: (1) materialistic philosophy originating with Marx, (2) the philosophy of life, originating with Schopenhauer and Nietzsche and developed by Dilthey, Bergson, and Scheler, and (3) existential philosophy, originating with Kierkegaard and developed by Heidegger, Sartre, and Merleau-Ponty, who absorbed the phenomenological method in the twentieth century. I will follow the development of thought critically in these three directions, focusing upon the problem of body, or somatic ego.

MATERIALISTIC PHILOSOPHY: FEUERBACH AND MARX

It is well known that the philosopher who was most directly and most strongly influenced by Feuerbach was Marx, and that Marx regarded himself as the successor of Feuerbach. Both thinkers believed that the human being as a sensuous, bodily individual is endowed with

species being *(Gattungswesen)*. However, there is a remarkable difference in their views of what *Gattungswesen* is. For Feuerbach, this word
signifies the "ability to objectify its own species or its own essential-
ity,"[8] and for Marx, too, it is the "ability to objectify its own species, as
well as that of others,"[9] but while for the former this species refers to
the trinity of "Reason, Will, and Love,"[10] for the latter it means nothing other than "the totality of social relationships."[11]

In general this difference has been explained as the development
of Marx's thought as he extended the self-alienation of the human
into social activity, while Feuerbach grasped self-alienation only in the
religious dimension. Is this difference only a matter of an extension of
the dimension of recognition? Or does it not rather reflect a difference in their views of what a sensuous, concrete person is itself?

In the first place, we can find a difference in the two thinkers'
views in the way they combine the species being and the individual
ego. While Marx shows no hesitation in immediately uniting the species and the individual, Feuerbach repeatedly expresses that "the
species being is the unity of I and Thou."[12] For example, when he
says, "Neither an ego, nor Reason thinks, but a human thinks,"[13] he
denies not only the thesis "Reason = ego" but also that the somatic
ego thinks solipsistically, because who thinks as a human being is the
specific cosubject "I and Thou" in Feuerbach's sense.

In contrast, Marx expresses the immediate unity of individual
and species with this definition: "The human being is a species being."[14] For Marx, spiritual as well as practical activity (labor) is species
life. Labor that is performed by a somatic ego in the course of a persistent material interchange with its "inorganic body" (nature) is also
the objectification of its species life. Therefore a human produces independently of his or her physical needs and reproduces the whole
of nature universally, unlike animals. The human being "intuits himself in the created world."[15] Furthermore, Marx writes, "The individual is a social being,"[16] because "the individual life and the species life
of a person are not different,"[17] and "A person as consciousness of
species only ascertains his real social life and repeats his real Existence in his thought."[18]

In this way we see that for Marx the somatic ego as the agent
of labor together with the whole of nature as its inorganic body is
at the same time a species being that directly accepts the totality
of social relationships in itself. Marx also writes, "Thinking and

Being are indeed distinguished, but are in unity with each other at the same time."[19] Marx's assertion has a very subtle but unmistakable difference from Feuerbach's statement that the "Ego does not think." According to the latter, a somatic ego as the center of nature can indeed take social relations as a superstructure upon itself, but cannot perform any rational thinking by itself. This is because the subject of rational thinking would not be a single somatic ego but rather the cosubject "I-Thou," which is a specific dialogical relationship and can never be deduced from any social relations of plural somatic egos.

Thus when Marx inherited the concept of *Gattungswesen* from Feuerbach and added to it the new meanings of "a free, universal reproduction of the whole of nature" and "a totality of social relationships," he did away with the absolute transcendental meaning of "The unity of Reason, Will, and Love" given it by Feuerbach. Coincidentally, an inconspicuous but decisive discrepancy emerged between their views of the sensuous, real person. The dimension of the cosubject "I-Thou" that Feuerbach anticipated and strove to establish was lost in the hands of Marx. This is not simply a change from sensuous passivity to practical activity, as is generally thought.

Of course, Marx succeeded in grasping the structure of the somatic ego more concretely. His well-known example in *Capital* shows that he grasped the function of the imagination in the somatic ego exactly:

> A spider performs an operation like that of the weaver and a bee humiliates many human architects by the structure of its waxed cell. But the reason why even the worst architect surpasses the best bee is that the former has already drawn the waxed cell in its head before it constructs it with wax. At the end of the labor process the result emerges that already existed at the beginning in the image of the laborer, therefore already as idea.[20]

However, it is not clear how such a function of the imagination, which objectifies (projects) itself in reproducing the whole of nature freely, connects itself to the consciousness of species that concerns the universal social relationship, also carried by the somatic ego. The relation of freedom (imagination) and universality (associate perspectives) and the problem of the cosubject that mediates them still remain unresolved in materialistic philosophy.

LIFE PHILOSOPHY

In life philosophy, instead of the material nature *(natura)* of material-istic philosophy, the universal will to live, the world-will, or their immanent form, the continuous flow of life-consciousness, emerges.

Schopenhauer's statement in *The World as Will and Representation* (1818) that the body is given to the subject of recognition in two completely different ways: "Once as representation in sensuous intu-ition, an object among objects which is subject to their laws, but then, at the same time, in a completely different manner, namely, as some-thing immediately known to everyone which the word 'Will' desig-nates,"[21] expresses the fundamentally double aspect of the body with classical brevity.

Through the pioneering works of Schopenhauer and Nietzsche, a common characteristic of the life philosophers' views of the ego as Will can already be seen. They are very romantic and subjectively metaphysical, that is, there is some slighting of the objective (spatial) aspect of the somatic ego.

Bergson

In the period approaching the twentieth century, Bergson appeared and conducted a more structural inquiry into the body. His book *Matter and Memory* (1896) is considered the classic study of the mind-body problem from the standpoint of life philosophy.

Bergson starts from the "image," which precedes the distinction into material things and perceptive presentation: "I find myself in the midst of many images. . . . But among these images there is one which is particularly to be distinguished from all other images at the point where I know it not only from the outside by perception, but also from the inside by emotion. This is my body."[22] From these words we see that what Bergson calls the image is not the objective of the imagination, but something we could call spatial extension, akin to Descartes's *res extensa*. Remarkably enough, Bergson reduces this perceptive consciousness of the image to a kind of physiologico-physical reflection instead of positing it as a subjective intentional act. Namely, the emotion in a body is the expression of a "delay" or "selection" or "interruption" between stimuli from the outside and the reaction of a body to them, and in this sense the body as image is "the center of indefiniteness"[23] in the universe. While this center has centripetal nerves that communicate outer effects from an enormous number of other images to the brain and centrifugal nerves that transmit stimuli starting from the brain to the periphery in order to move a part or the whole of the image (body), the brain does not transmit all the outer effects to peripheral nerves immediately but selects only those that have an interest in it, even suspending for a while its own reaction. The images surrounding this body emboss only those aspects that have interests in the body, as the reflection of possible reactions of the body. This is called the genesis of "perception." It is "a kind of mirror-reflection."[24] Therefore the function of the brain is only "that of the central telephone switchboard"; perceptive presentation is not in the brain, but in outer images. The difference between the material world as the whole of images and perceptive presentation is only one of whole to its parts.

Thus the spatial perceptive consciousness seems to vanish and perception is reduced to a physiologico-physical reflexive relation between the brain as image and other images. However, this is only Bergson's strategy to confine consciousness to temporality in order to be faithful to the dogma of life philosophy and to exclude all spatiality from consciousness. In fact, as he himself admitted, the "memory" already implicitly intervenes into the selection of external effects by the brain, so the acts of any perspective conscious subject which would generate memory must already be given together with the perceptive body. Therefore what Bergson called physiologico-physical reflection must be renamed the "intentionality" of consciousness. The selective reaction of the body against external effects should be a free intentional act of consciousness before any effect (physical bodily action) occurs, and the presence of a pure spatial extension called an "image" to a perspectively conscious bodily subject should be perception itself. Needless to say a perceptive presentation presents itself in a spatial perspective and not in a brain. This perspective is not a part of the material world as Bergson thought, but a partner of it, an always reducible dimension of consciousness in a phenomenological sense (it will be meaningless to fix this subject of perceptive consciousness in any portion of the body, e.g., in the brain, because it is to be able to move freely, sometimes to a spot outside of the body, sometimes at the origin of the eye's line of vision, sometimes on the whole surface of the body).

Now let us turn to Bergson's theory of memory, which is

inseparable from his theory of the body. He distinguishes fundamentally between two types of memory:

1. Imaginative memory: This "records all the events of daily life
   in the form of representation following the order of their occurrence."[25]
2. Repetitive memory: This is a memory "planted into the
   body," through the repetition of an exercise as in the case of
   text-recitation: "It is not representation any longer, but action."[26] It has no sign indicating its origin and its belonging to
   the past. Like my walking or the stroke of my pen, it has become a part of my present: "This is a memory which is fundamentally different from the former memory; it is always
   inclined to action, putting its foot on the present and looking
   forward to the future."[27]

Indeed Bergson is noted for having involved such kinesthetic
sedimentation in memory. The question it raises, however, concerns
how one connects both kinds of memory. He writes, "The body is the
proceeding border between the future and the past and is the tip
which is promoted by the past into the future,"[28] and also that our
body is posited "just on the point where my past is about to change
into action, once considered in the flowing (= duration) of time."[29]
Therefore repetitive memory as kinesthetic structure constitutes the
tip where all consciousness (which for Bergson means all imaginative
memory) contacts the body (especially the brain) as the central image and penetrates it from the past. The world of images centering
upon my body is only a section of the flow of time at the present.
Thus, while lower animals react to external stimuli more directly, the
human of good sense selects suitable images form the imaginative
memory of the past according to the request of the kinesthetic repetitive memory of the present. By projecting these images upon external images that resemble it, he or she produces attentive perception
and flexible attitudes toward the surrounding situation. Therefore,
"in ordinary life these two memories are fused with each other and
lose some of their original purity."[30]

In Bergson's former argument we first of all become aware that
there is no room for the generation of the imaginative memory. This
memory would be born where the perceptive presentation—be it
generated by a kind of mirror-reflection or not—is grasped passively

by a consciousness contacting it in the present, but in Bergson there is no consciousness acting passively in the present. He says that consciousness acting in the present is fundamentally disposed to action in a utilitarian way and is oriented from the present into the future. As already mentioned, it will become clear that the lack of an original perceptive consciousness and of a conscious stream flowing from the present to the past brings about this difficulty. Only through the return of imaginative memory to perspectival horizontal intentionality and of repetitive memory to the vertical temporal intentionality will this difficulty be resolved. Moreover, this will mean that the spatiality of the body is not only a present section of life-time, but also a historical embodiment of life into a definite form through the intersubjective coupling *(Paarung)* of vertical intentionalities.

Scheler

We take up Max Scheler, the next philosopher of life, as one who indeed employs the phenomenological method, but who regards it as a mere procedure of "sufficiently utilizing the impact of the thought of Nietzsche, Dilthey, and Bergson."[31]

In order to clarify the position of the body in Scheler's system of thought with its multiple strata, I present a diagram (see figure 8.1) according to his *Formalism in Ethics and Material Value-Ethics [Der Formalismus in der Ethik und die materielle Wertethik]* (1916).[32]

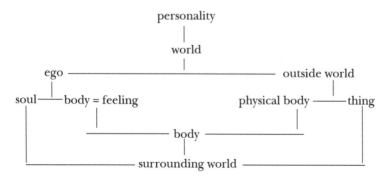

Figure 8.1

As shown in figure 8.1, the body constitutes a peculiar middle area that bridges the inner-perceptive (psychological) area where the ego presides and the outer-perceptive (physical) area called the outside world. The body is regarded not as a unity of soul and physical body but as psychologically and physically neutral.

Scheler summarizes the errors of traditional philosophical theories of the body as follows:[33]

1. It is false to take inner body-consciousness for a mere collection of sense perceptions.
2. It is false to say that the difference between the so-called *Leib*-sensation and the sensation of sense organs is only one of gradation, and that the *Leib*-sensation differs only in degree and content from sensations like sound, color, taste, and smell.
3. It is false to say that the living body *(Körperleib)* is to be found as originally as other things.
4. It is false to say that bodily feeling is a psychological phenomenon.
5. It is false to say that inner body-consciousness is originally not articulated and is articulated only through the parts of the physical body that are secondarily connected to it.
6. It is false to say that the contents of inner body-consciousness are originally nonextensive.

These represent, in a negative form, Scheler's opinion that the body or somatic ego belongs neither to the physical world nor to the psychological realm.

For Scheler, the sensation proper to the body is different from external perceptions, which, as external to each other appear to be parallel to each other in space and successive in time. The sensation proper to the body is also different, however, from inner perceptions (e.g., sorrow), which are perfectly immanent to each other and nonextensive. The sensations of the body such as pain, hunger, fatigue, and itchiness, are external to each other and extensive (e.g., a pain spreads down one's back), but nonspatial, nontemporal, and never calculable. Moreover, "that vague whole of the body"[34] (body-feeling) is always given as the background of these sensations and is always being intended.

Scheler says that such corporeity is given independently of the psychological ego, while we need not pass through any bodily givenness to grasp such an ego for its part: "For example, the manner in which I am sad is essentially different from the manner in which I am tired or hungry."[35] Furthermore, the relationship between a psychological ego and body-feeling is regarded as being that between "concentration" and "relaxation." In a "concentrated Being in one's self," or when we live deep within ourselves, our whole psychological life seems to be summarized as the "one" including the past, and seems to act as the "one": "It is a rare moment—for example, a moment of confronting a big decision or a big action."[36] In this occasion of concentrated Being the body is included as a partial moment and is subject to it. On the contrary, when we live "in the body," for example, when we are deeply fatigued or relaxed, or by contrast when we are involved in empty diversion, "the once fulfilled place now becomes empty" and we live in fragmentary moments according to the degree to which we live in the body. Now the body seems definitively to be our self, and psychological occurrences "flow away vainly by our side."[37]

However, insofar as Scheler takes the ego to be a mere center of a psychological area, somewhat like Bergson, and neutralizes the physical area completely from the control of the ego (see figure 8.1), he encounters difficulties in grasping the body (and the somatic ego) as the dimension of the historical interchange between a psychological area and a physical area. We may see here a limitation of life philosophy for the early Scheler. Indeed, this relation between the psychological ego of life and the body gradually changed in his thought. In a later book, *Die Stellung des Menschen im Kosmos [Man's Place in the Universe]* (1927), he writes: "The opinions of philosophers, medics, and natural researchers who are engaged in the problem of body and soul are converging to an ever greater extent into a unified, fundamental view. According to this view, the same life takes a psychological shape in its internal Existence and a corporeal shape in its Existence to others."[38] In addition, he says, "What we call the physiological and the psychological are only two sides of an observation of the same process of life."[39] Here, in his later thought, that which represents life and its ultimate ground, namely, *Drang* (impulse), is no longer a psychological ego, but a psycho-physical somatic ego. This somatic ego corresponds to the act-center (called the Person) of another transcendental ground of the human, *Geist* (spirit), and both together, body and Person, constitute a human being ("Person" is also a psychologically and physically neutral entity). Together they make it possible for the *Geist* to suppress the *Drang* of life and to transform or sublimate its impulsive energy into spiritual energy. Moreover, this process is given a metaphysical meaning, namely, that a hidden *Gott* with two attributes, *Geist* and *Drang*, realizes itself there through the human being and its history.

Although in the later Scheler we can thus discern a reconsideration of his excessive foray into the psychologism of life philosophy, this reconsideration does not go nearly far enough. Even though the body, which was at first called "psychologically and physically neutral," is now called "psycho-physical," it is difficult to call it an essential change, insofar as it is no longer evident what mediates between the body and the physical area. Scheler's attempt in his later period to deduce objective space and time (space = an emptiness of the psychic) from a kind of protention of a preconscious impulse appears as a kind of fairy tale.[40]

It seems that no other way remains than to regard the entire area of external perception, including space and time, as the intentional correlate of the intersubjective, perspectival consciousness. A part of my non-thetical amorphous vital-psychological area (body-feeling) is objectified through the reflective mediation of this consciousness as an external extensive physical body among innumerable thing-objects in space (e.g., in a mirror). When this physical body is moved by my Will, then a kind of kinesthetic sedimentation necessarily occurs in the remaining vital-psychological area. The more concentrated the reflective consciousness of my moving physical body is on objects of intended action, the smaller the reflective gap between my physical body and my remaining vital area, until both coincide and the former is put on to the latter like clothes. This is not a simple return to the prereflective stage of my vital psychological area. Rather, through the objectification by the reflective consciousness my vague body-feeling is dialectically articulated into a new structural synthesis: the incarnated body *(Leib-Körper)*. Then my extensive body is no longer a posited object but rather a restricting surface enveloping my vital area in itself and dividing and limiting it from the external world. Because the conscious subject for its part can no longer stand apart from this surface in its former reflective stance, when the intentional distance has thus become zero, it will be scattered all over the surface of my articulated body and will necessarily become the body-surface-consciousness.

The body-surface-consciousness, which spreads all over the surface of my body as the clothing of my life, looks around the world through the whole surface of my body (including the back or the tips of the toes) as a horizon-intentionality, and looks at the object "by becoming the thing" (Nishida), grasping the whole surface of a thing with the corresponding whole surface of my body as an object-intentionality. In other words, my perceptive consciousness looks at the world or objects only through and in accordance with my physical body, which my life wears as its nonpositional clothing. In addition, the same surface-consciousness, as incarnated by life *(Leib)*, gives an ambiguous character to all the kinesthetic sensations of my body, which are extensive and external to each other, though not posited in space and time, as Max Scheler has shown. This consciousness can also be aptly called "the kinesthetic body-apperception."

In this way, when we are freed from the prejudice of life philosophy, *there emerges before us at last the figure of a somatic ego that consists of a double subjectivity: a perceptive body-surface-consciousness and a self-projective imaginative Will to live.*

EXISTENTIAL PHILOSOPHY

Existential philosophy, which originates with Søren Kierkegaard, is to be taken as the first step toward the recognition of the double-subjective structure of the body.

Heidegger

In contrast to life philosophy, which grasps the ego simply as a vital phenomenon as a result of its inclination toward the dimension of life, existential philosophy clearly anticipates the irreducibly double structure of the body. Unfortunately, however, it divides this duality into two independent moments and allots each of them two different ways of human life. We already find in Kierkegaard's scheme of the "mass" and "the single" (*der Einzelne*) the predecessor of this division, but in Heidegger's dichotomy of "authentic" and "inauthentic," or of "anticipatory resoluteness"[41] and "*das Man*"[42] we find its epitome. Here, two subjectivities that originally belong to a single body appear as centers of two separate incompatible areas. Of course both areas have a common structure, *Sorge* (Care) or "already being in the world in advance of oneself,"[43] but even this takes, in the inauthentic life, the form of "presencing (*gegenwärtigen*) while looking forward (*gewärtigen*),"[44] and so the center of gravity moves from the future to the present, allowing the commonality of both areas to wane. In other words, "ecstatic horizonal" temporality predominates in the authentic realm, while vulgar temporality as the succession of "nows" characterizes the inauthentic (daily) realm. In the same way, with respect to spatiality, in the authentic area "exclusion of distance" (*Ent-fernung*) and "orientation" (*Ausrichtung*) emerge[45] on the ground of world-projection and the tool-nexus, while in the inauthentic daily area invalidation and the isolation of tools as mere things emerge as a result of forgetful expectation. To call the latter a degenerate form of the former, according to Heidegger, would be nonsense. Rather, we should think that both areas together simultaneously constitute the dual aspect of a human somatic ego as its respectively proper constituents.

To explain this more clearly we will see how Heidegger's *das Man* correlates with our body-surface-consciousness. According to Heidegger, the other in daily life encounters us "from out of the world in which concernful, circumspect Being-there *(Dasein)*"[46] is settled. When we walk along a field, it appears as anyone's field, and as well or poorly cultivated by someone. A book before me appears as having been bought in a certain shop or presented by someone. A boat tied up to a bank appears as belonging to an acquaintance or to a stranger.[47] These appearances do not emerge from my own world-projection, as Heidegger suggests, but rather are read upon the surfaces of things confronted by my body-surface-consciousness as the analogical reflection of my own kinesthetic sedimentaion in vertical intentionality. This is not simply to be called empathy but rather a fundamental coupling between my body-surface-consciousness and the surfaces of things. I see the trace of the other body-surface-consciousness with a living Will through the analogical understanding of kinesthetic-projective sedimentation engraved upon the surfaces of things, as on a stone implement found in the earth. The temporality in which such a finding of others occurs is not an anticipating, forgetful presentification (Heidegger) but a "thick present," which gathers up the standing present of the encounter between obverse surfaces and the already-flowed-away presents of kinesthetic processing by others. The imaginative subjectivity, another pole of my somatic ego, lives generally in such a present before the transcendence to the future. Perhaps Heidegger's *Gewesenheit* would be very close to such a thick present.

Thus it has become clear that even in the dimension of daily life the double subjectivity, body-surface-consciousness and imagination, already cooperate with each other. The distancing, leveling, and standardizing that Heidegger points to as dominating *das Man* are indeed to be regarded as founded upon the coupling between body-surface subjects, but the dimension of body-surface subject not only has such negative characteristics but also founds the exchange and sharing of our various social roles. A social role is nothing other than schematically defined body-surface subjectivity coupled with its proper kinesthetic sedimentation.

In the same way in the dimension of so-called authentic life we also find the hidden cooperation of double subjectivity. Heidegger argues that only through the world project of Dasein is "the total relevance *(Bewandtnisganzheit)*"[48] of the tool-nexus, in which a tool is for the first time discovered as a tool, disclosed. Insofar as a being is given to such a concern, "it is from the beginning a tool of the surrounding world, and is never a world-material existing for the time being as a thing."[49] However, except in the case of habitually repeated projection, the constitution of a total relevance *(Bewandtnisganzheit)* of tools requires an offering of objective data concerning things beforehand by a perceptive body-surface subject (or by its reflective synthetic stance). Not only the applicability of particular things but also the causal relations between physical phenomena and the social relations between various roles must be known in advance. For example, when we want to project a trip abroad, a lot of objective knowledge about various things and matters is necessary (e.g., the weight of a bag is its objective attribute, but if it exceeds twenty kilograms, it will lose its utility as a bag to be checked on to an airplane). Therefore, objective characteristics of beings in the world are not the simple privation of their tool-characteristics, but their *conditio sine qua non*. In general, the projection that neglects objective data would not be able to realize itself because of the incompleteness of total relevance and would thus be condemned to failure. We must not overlook the indispensable role that perceptive body-surface subjectivity plays in the world projection of imaginative subjectivity, as Heidegger regrettably did.

Sartre

Sartre's consideration of the body is distorted by his introduction of the nonphenomenological, metaphysical substance of *"l'être-en-soi,"*[50] in spite of the sharpness of the phenomenological analysis found in various places. Insofar as the body is considered to be one of the *être-en-soi,* it must be transcendent to every consciousness. Sartre states that the imagination is the consciousness of the absent *être-en-soi,* so the consciousness of the body in presence must be a perceptive consciousness, but a non-thetical one. Sartre uses the literary expression "nausea"[51] to designate this bodily consciousness. However, it is a priori doubtful whether any "inner" perception of the pure material being, which is the body in Sartre, will be possible, for this would precisely be the consciousness of one's own corpse.[52] Even if it were possible, we could never reach Sartre's *"l'être-pour-soi"*[53] from this *"l'être-en-soi,"* because, while the former is introduced where the non-thetical consciousness of one's body rediscovers its own Being in the Being of the object previously posited by the thetic consciousness, there is in fact no similarity or continuity between *l'être-en-soi* of my body and that of the objective being, if any metaphysical assumption of the totality of *l'être-en-soi* is not introduced in advance. The situation is exactly the same as the relation between the material Being of a desk and that of a word processor upon it. They are definitely circumscribed and completely external to each other. If anyone says, with Sartre, that the "thetical consciousness of an object is always a non-thetical consciousness of one's own body,"[54] presumably the imagination—which is now, however, not the consciousness of the absence of Being, but of possible or potential Being as constitutive of life—must already be acting in common in these consciousnesses.[55]

Non-thetically my body appears to me through the double aspects of the outer perception of my body-surface and the inner feeling of imaginative will (the pure inner sensation—mood, fatigue, pain—can be called an "image" insofar as it originally has no fixed position in space and time. For example, I feel my own pain on any wounded part of the body of the other. The phenomenon of the "phantom limb" will be explained from such a localization of my image). Thetically the consciousness of the distanced similarity (intimacy) of Beings (and then Sartre's *l'être-pour-soi*) emerges only through the expansion of the potential Being of my imaginative Will into the object through the coupling of my body-surface and a surface of the object. Moreover, insofar as Sartre argues for the utility *(utensilité)* of posited objects, a suspicion remains that Sartre introduces the imaginative Being of kinesthetic sedimentation in secret from behind, while formally excluding the imagination as a nothingness from the seamless Being of objects. In any case, the human being as *l'être-pour-soi* is never founded by the non-thetically perceived material body, but rather by the indivisible combination of the imagination with the non-thetically perceived body-surface. (The relation between the body-surface and the imaginative Will is to be roughly modeled on the movable, flexible hull and its fulfilling and flooding content. Of course what unifies them—the somatic ego—will also be necessary.)

Merleau-Ponty

It is somewhat problematic to include Merleau-Ponty with the existential philosophers, since his primary concern was to overcome the schism between the two subjectivities, perception and imagination, which is evident in Heidegger's and Sartre's thought. The fact that he sought a solution to this question in the discovery of a new figure of the body that has a kind of double structure shows the affinity of his standpoint with mine. For Merleau-Ponty a body is "Existence incarnated in the world."[56] The world in this case is, like Husserl's natural world, an object of primal belief and a world of the anonymous *"on"* (one),[57] defined as intersubjective a priori. When human Existence anchors itself in the world, inhabits it, and becomes "visible" as well as "invisible" through a chiasm, Existence becomes a body. At that point the body is not only in external space but also has its own proper spatiality; namely, it is connected with objects by an invisible "intentional arc."[58] What corresponds to such a duality (ambiguity) of space on the side of the body is "the corporeal schema,"[59] a kind of dual bodily structure. It is, like the repetitive memory of Bergson, a sedimentation of kinesthetic patterns or a dynamic *Gestalt,* which is proper to a certain individual body, but it can nevertheless be imitated or learned from. We can find in this idea of "corporeal schema" something like the unity of objectivity and subjectivity, or of the body-surface-subjectivity and imagination, or in a sense of the *"das Man"* and Existence in Heidegger. Merleau-Ponty also calls it "generalized Existence."[60]

Indeed, I find in Merleau-Ponty's view of the body the closest affinity to my view, but the two are not identical. I have doubts about his view of the subject to the world. The intersubjective world, which he calls "the antepredicative world," has no definite subject except an anonymous subject called the "one" *(on)*. But "the one" or *"das Man"* cannot be combined directly with a particular body in which Existence will be incarnated, because, as mentioned above, a subject that is combined with a body must indeed necessarily become a body-surface subject, which is a priori intersubjective through coupling, but it is nevertheless "my" subject, not an anonymous general subject ("one").

Because it lacks a proper subject to the world, Merleau-Ponty's body loses the solid structure of double subjectivity and does not possess a proper stance from which to objectify itself in the world, and therefore it cannot demonstrate the process of acquiring new corporeal schemata. The historico-cultural sedimentation of the human body becomes possible only through the dialectical process of "primal synthesis," "reflection," and "re-synthesis" between the perceptive self-consciousness and its clothed body. This will become clear when we think about the process of mastering a special professional technique in a sport or musical performance. In particular, the necessity of this process will become more evident when we must be incarnated into the modern technological world. On account of this, not "one" but "my" body-surface subject becomes necessary. Only when my body-surface subject, which had reflected upon itself beforehand, has resynthesized itself, can my imaginative Will (Existence) be incarnated in it completely. The peculiarity of the body-surface subject is that, once synthesized, it is essentially "doubly sensuous," namely, "the view and the visible," "the tangent and the tangible" coincide completely between the perceptive consciousness and the body-surface. Contrary to the common view, not only tangibility but also visibility is doubly sensuous on the body-surface. Therefore, the more objective it becomes by reflection, the more it is able to be subjective by synthesis. Merleau-Ponty seems to have closed the door on the body-surface subject, at least in *The Phenomenology of Perception* (1943), by denying the double sensuousness of visibility.[61]

Indeed, Merleau-Ponty introduced the idea of the "reversibility" of the view and the visible in his later thought, but this reversibility still seems somewhat different from my idea of the coincidence of both. He writes in *The Visible and the Invisible* (1964), "The body always presents itself 'from the same side' — (by principle; for this is apparently contrary to reversibility). The reversibility is not an actual identity of the touching and the touched. It is their identity by principle (always abortive) — yet it is not ideality, for the body is not simply a de facto visible among the visibles, it is visible-seeing, or look. In other words, a fabric of possibilities that closes the exterior visible in *(referme)* upon the seeing body maintains between them a certain divergence."[62] Thus it is clear that he still admits to some divergence or gap *(écart)* between the perceiver and the perceived, which I take to be already overcome by the completely nonreflective body-surface-consciousness.

I must refrain from giving any conclusion here to the interesting problem of the comparative study of Merleau-Ponty's later idea of *chair* (flesh)[63] with my idea of the potential living Being of the imaginative dimension.

CHAPTER NINE

On the Relation between Science and Technology

CONSIDERED FROM A PHILOSOPHICAL standpoint the inner relation between "natural science" and "modern technology" is by no means a problem that has already been successfully elucidated. Rather, it is a question with urgent significance, a question that has an essential relation to a much wider problematic concerning the very nature of our civilization.

It has been said that especially through and after World War II science and technology began to become more and more closely interrelated, establishing a new epoch in the modern history of civilization that is symbolized by the development of nuclear and genetic technology.[1] It is not so surprising, therefore, that some philosophers, notably Heidegger, already discerned not only the same root but a common essence of science and technology. Heidegger writes:

> It remains true, nonetheless, that humans in the technical era are provoked into disclosing *(Entbergen)* in an especially striking way. This disclosing first of all concerns nature as a main reserve of energy. Correspondingly, the ordering *(bestellend)* behavior of humans is revealed at first in the rise of modern exact natural science. Its way of presentation *(Vorstellung)* pursues nature as a calculable power source. . . . But mathematical natural science arose about two centuries before modern technology. How could it already have been in service to modern technology at that time? The facts rather speak to the contrary. Modern tech-

nology began only when it could support itself on the ground of the exact natural sciences. Chronologically calculated, this remains correct. Thought historically *(geschichtlich)*, this does not capture the truth.

The modern physical theory of nature prepares the way not only for technology, but also for the essence of modern technology. For the provoking gathering *(Versammeln)* into ordering disclosure already holds sway in physics. But it does not properly come to appearance therein. Modern physics is still the forerunner of Enframing *(Ge-stell)*, a forerunner whose origin remains unknown. . . .[2]

That which begins early shows itself to the human being only at the end. . . . Modern technology, which is later for chronological calculation, is, from the point of view of the dominating essence, historically earlier.[3]

Thus Heidegger concludes: "Because the essence of modern technology lies in Enframing *(Gestell)*, it must apply the exact natural science. Thereby, the deceptive illusion arises that modern technology is an applied natural science. This appearance can be maintained only insofar as neither the essential origin of modern science nor the essence of modern technology is sufficiently inquired into."[4]

In this way, Heidegger argues for the common essence of "Enframing" for modern technology and the natural sciences. His argument, however, cannot avoid the criticism that it is oversimplified, for it neither explains why the natural sciences arose two centuries earlier than modern technology, nor does it clarify the fundamental difference in the characteristics of the two domains. For example, it is generally recognized that one of the fundamental characteristics of modern scientific investigation is value neutrality *(Wertfreiheit)*, or the exclusion of teleology, while no technology proceeds without values (in the form of projected ends, purposes, or the efficiency of instruments, etc.), or teleology in a broader sense.

In my opinion, the inner relation between these two domains should be sought first of all through the recognition of the essential differences between them. Therefore, our investigation will begin from the dawn of the modern age (the seventeenth century) and will roughly follow the chronological order of events, while still thinking "historically" *(geschictlich)* in a Heideggerian sense.

LET US BEGIN WITH THE INVESTIGATION of the birth of the idealistic epistemological theory of science, which for a long time concealed the true nature of science. In this sense, it will be worthwhile to ask why René Descartes persistently adhered to the absolute distinction between mind and body, as the full title of his *Meditations* suggests.[5] This evidences the great impact that the novel concept of the universe as *infinite* space had during that period. Blaise Pascal's well-known passage, "The eternal silence of these infinite spaces terrifies me," is another indication of this impact. We know that Pascal held that "Man is a thinking reed" in order to overcome this terror. Apparently both Descartes and Pascal were compelled by an anthropological motivation to protect human autonomy and dignity against the "clockwork" of the universe, and against the human body, which, as a thing, must be subject to this mechanism. Thus it is obvious that the modern notion of *cogito*, which tries to strictly detach itself from all material things, including the human body, was motivated by the dread and detestation of unrestricted "objectification" that the emergence of the notion of the infinite universe had made possible.

A *pseudodualism* in our sense appears when this "modern (self-) consciousness" attains the status of the "epistemological subject" of natural science, which intends to recognize the world of things.

Modern self-consciousness is a "pure consciousness" deprived of all corporeal or spatial aspects, because it is a result of an escape from or an evacuation of the threatening infinite universe. Obviously, herein lies the historical origin of "Modern Idealism." However, whether this "idealistic subject" can also be the epistemological subject of natural science is not so obvious. In other words, a purified subject without objective corporeity faces an aporia: how does it subsequently relate to the objective world? The difficulty is essentially the same as that which Descartes encountered in his mind-body problem. Just as a mind strictly distinguished from its body cannot reunite itself with the body, it seems that a pure consciousness that has once rejected spatial properties can no longer have any relations with extended things. Therefore, it will also be impossible for a pure consciousness to perceive any external things in natural scientific observation.

Accordingly, it is not surprising that the idealistic mainstream of modern philosophy since the time of Descartes has been able neither to solve the mind-body problem nor to work out a successful epistemology. The same pseudodualism between "pure consciousness" and "extended things" (bodies) fatally underlies both problems.

Let us now see how representative modern idealists trapped in this fictitious pseudodualism sought in vain to find an epistemology, as if trapped in a hole from which there is no exit. For Descartes, extension is primarily an "idea" that exists within consciousness as an object of pure mathematics. Whether an extended thing that corresponds to a "clear and distinct" idea "really exists" in space is by no means obvious, for we only "seem to clearly see that the idea of mat-ter comes from external things, which it perfectly represents."[6] That this "seeming" is not an illusion is only assured by "the veracity of God," for which a medieval type of proof was necessary. In short, the only ground for Descartes's argument was that "God cannot be a deceiver."

Even after the existence of corporeal things had been assured by means of this roundabout argument, Descartes still had a deep distrust of "sensation," because he thought that "the perceptions of our senses pertain only to this union of a human body with a mind," and that they are by nature merely confused, accidental cognitions. Hence, he came up with the conclusion that we should reject prejudices arising from sensations and should depend solely on the understanding, even in order to recognize the nature of external things. Indeed, Descartes declares, "I do not accept or desire in physics any other principles than there are in geometry or abstract mathematics."[7] He also writes, "Nothing concerning these [divisions, shapes, and movements of material substance] can be accepted as true unless it is deduced from common notions, whose truth we cannot doubt, with such certainty that it must be considered to be a mathematical demonstration."[8]

As is now well known, this underestimation of sensation, or adherence to deductionism, is responsible for the dogmatic misconceptions of physics and dynamics that Descartes held.[9]

Descartes, who lived in the seventeenth century, could still resort to "God" for the mediation between "pure consciousness" and "extended things," but a century later Kant could no longer use the notion of "God" and was forced to rely on "transcendental apperception" instead. Kant seems to have successfully shown that this reflective self, which is the center of consciousness in general and which includes extensional space (and time) in itself as a priori forms of intuition, can bridge the epistemological gap between particular empirical consciousnesses and extended substances. However, this success costs him the dissolution of corporeal things into "unknowable things-in-themselves" and "sensuous manifolds without unity."

We can thus see that Kant's so-called Copernican turn was nothing but an attempt to overcome pseudodualism, that is, the antithesis between "pure consciousness" and "extended things." Kant deprives the latter of extension in order to change them into the sensuous manifold (and things-in-themselves), and then restores extension to them through a priori forms of intuition and categorial synthesis. In other words, extended things forsake their extensionality only to re-attain it (or something similar) by a surprisingly circuitous route.

However, the residuum of this process, the things-in-themselves, must be regarded as evidence that the mediating transcendental apperception failed to perfectly regain the lost extension of the object, which should be strictly transcendent to it, and further, that (as Kant himself admits), the space confined to the intuition of finite consciousness could no longer serve as a form of genuine reality, which must be infinitely deep.

Kant's remarkable feat, moreover, lost most of its epistemological significance when the laws of physical science turned out not to be results of a priori synthetic judgments, as Kant thought they were, but only of a kind of highly probable relation. In order to know nature, scientists today no longer have to seek the circuitous route that transcendental apperception was expected to provide, because our consciousness is already in the midst of space as its constituent.

Husserl provides another example of the unhappy efforts to bridge consciousness and the world. In his theory, the mediator between pure consciousness and extended things is "intentionality," which means the act in which consciousness transcends itself. This notion is manifested in his basic thesis that "consciousness is consciousness of something." The operation called the "phenomenological reduction" reveals how the mediation takes place. In his *Ideas Pertaining to a Pure Phenomenology and to a Phenomenological Philosophy,* Husserl defined this operation as a "bracketing" of beliefs generally held in the natural attitude,[10] and thought that he could obtain "transcendental pure consciousness" as a phenomenological residuum of this reduction. This consciousness differs from Kant's "consciousness in general," because it is not transindividual, nor does it include space within it. However, they are similar in that both are supposed to "constitute the world as an intentional object." A corporeal object is first dissolved into an "intentional object x" and its continuous appearance, that is, a flow of *hyle* (which exists within consciousness), by the phenomenological reduction. The *hyle* is activated by the sense-giving act (noesis) of pure consciousness, and is formed into an intentional unity. Thus it provides those features that are to fill the transcendental objective meaning (noema) attached to object x. In this way, a corporeal object is constituted as a noematic object that is correlative to pure consciousness. Here Husserl seems to take the extension of the objects to be one of the idealistic (eidetic) features prescribed by the regional category proper to the pregiven intentional object x. Thus, in the same manner as Kant, Husserl at first deprives an extended thing of extension by dissolving it into an "intentional object x," which has no features other than self-identity, and a *hyle* in a current of consciousness. Then, after a long detour through the intentional working of pure consciousness, he seems to restore extension by constituting a noematic "extended" object.[11]

We must ask, however, in what direction we should point empty intentionality in order to reach the identical object x. Where is that unifying center amid the ever-changing phenomena, a center that alone, according to Husserl, categorically gives extension to these appearances? Is it possible to intend this ideal object without the previous aid of an extension that would prescribe the horizonal modality for moving appearances? Epistemologically, this will prove impossible, because, on the contrary, we can empirically reach the object only by way of such proper extensionality (*Gestalt* or formal structure), and not vice versa. This is to say that Husserl's idealistic empty intentionality by itself does not have sufficient capacity to restore the spatial unity of a once-dissolved extended object, since it is not accompanied by the spatio-temporal dimension distinguished from the category, unlike Kantian apperception, and the extensionality of the object must necessarily be pregiven from other sources. In this way, the epistemologically pretentious character of the noematic object x becomes evident. The final attempt of modern idealism to

overcome the pseudodualism of pure consciousness and extended things has also failed.

IN THE PREVIOUS SECTION we hastily examined the development of
the philosophical epistemology of science during the three hundred
years from Descartes to Husserl. This too-brief description has, I
hope, revealed that transcendental philosophy was the result of
pseudodualism, or the fiction of pure consciousness, which had to be
provided as an escape from an impending and threatening
objectification into infinite space. It should also be clear that transcendental idealism failed to provide an epistemology capable of
explaining cognition in natural science, because a purified consciousness could hardly secure any real contact with extended
things.[12]

I must now explain why the antithesis between pure consciousness and extended things is a pseudodualism. There are two reasons.
First, these two correlates do not constitute a genuine antithesis. Second, a genuine antithesis characterizing the modern age already exists, but it consists of a different pair of correlates. I shall start by
elaborating on the first reason.

Our perspectival consciousness is not a pure consciousness,
which, having no extensionality, is opposed to extended things. *Such
a pure cogito does not exist.* The truth is that a perceptive consciousness
is always a kind of "bodily consciousness" united with an extended
body. More precisely, a perceptive consciousness is united with an *apperceptive body* (somatic ego), which formulates and controls particular extended *body phantoms.*[13] This concept of the schematic
apperceptive body resists our understanding because it is an unper-
ceivable body that never renders itself objective. Nevertheless, it is
certain that when we perceive a particular thing before us, our perceptive consciousness grasps this object through the working of our
apperceptive body. In a sense, one perceives things by analogy with
the body phantom of oneself. Our consciousness works not from a
view-point, but rather from a *view-body-surface.* One regards an object
as a branch, or as a modification of one's three-dimensional body
phantom. It is for this reason that an object of perception is given as
a whole as three-dimensional, together with its unseen and unobserv-

able reverse side, and further that we connect an object to our potential body-action by observing the object as our tool. For example, a book appears as to be opened; glasses as to be worn; an open window as to be shut; a bicycle as to be ridden. If our consciousness is pure from any extensionality and begins only from a point of view, how can we explain these phenomena? Furthermore, in our actions, tools and our body phantom are no longer separable for our consciousness: a ballpoint pen serves its purpose when it connects inseparably to one's hand and becomes its extension. To be a good driver, we have to make the body of the car an extended body phantom of ourselves. Thus, both our extended body phantom and things surrounding us are subject to the same bodily apperception. It is thus very understandable that in many European languages, the same word, such as corpus, or *Körper,* refers to both of them.

Without this apperceptive body there is no perceptive consciousness at all, and the extensionality formulated by the apperceptive body is neither an idea (Descartes) nor a form of intuition (Kant). Therefore the apparent dualism between pure consciousness and extended things never really exists. While the perceptive consciousness is an intentional subject inseparable from the apperceptive body, the latter involves a partly objectifiable moment (body phantom) through a reflection of the former, and can thus accept new extensions into it. Thus, when we acquire a movement pattern of a body-schema through repeated practice, including reflex actions, the pattern is "planted" into our apperceptive body as a nondated memory. Later, when we plunge into the water, for example, we can display a series of extensive bodily motions by recalling various patterns from the stock of planted memories.

However, as this example shows, during prereflective action the bodily extension (phantom) produced by the apperceptive body does not have any perceptual objectivity. It is considered to be an object only when perceptive consciousness takes a reflective stance. If perceptive consciousness in this reflective stance keeps an infinite distance from its body phantom as well as others' objectified bodies, and regards both of them as objects of the same kind, this consciousness becomes an intersubjective (or cosubjective) consciousness with an "infinite space" (nothingness) as its working schema.

Therefore, the emergence of infinite space that terrified Descartes and Pascal at the beginning of the modern age was nothing but the transition of human perceptive consciousness from its pre-reflective stage to the infinitely reflective stage. People in those days, not knowing the crucial role of the unobjectifiable apperceptive body in mediating reflective consciousness and objectifiable body phantoms even in infinite space, isolated the former as a transcendental subject in order to attain a complete separation. However, in truth a reflective consciousness is still united with objectified body phantoms in space by the mediation of the invisible apperceptive body (the origin of space), and infinite space is given as a common schema throughout various perspectives of our reflective intersubjective consciousness. This infinite space is the "universe" of the natural sciences, wherein reflective consciousness works as a cognitive subject with the apperceptive body. Thus the universe of cognition (consciousness) and the universe of existence (space) become one and the same. A change in the way of cognition means a change in the mode of existence. When we depart from sensuous cognition to attain a more abstract knowledge of nature, the mode of existence of subjects and objects will change accordingly.

The discovery of the apperceptive body thus abolished the dualism between pure consciousness and extended things, or between the subject and the object, which had long predominated in modern thinking. This turned out to be a pseudodualism based on a fictitious notion of consciousness. Let us now turn to the true nature of modern science. The apperceptive body tends to shrink to a "point" when it takes the stance of the infinite reflective consciousness and engages itself in rational abstraction. Accordingly, things shrink into points or sets of points through the similarly shrinking body phantom. Homogeneous properties such as "mass," "electric charge," and "velocity" are assigned to these points. Being homogeneous, they allow for measurement numerically in terms of standardized units. The cognitive universe of natural science is the universe of things rendered as "points" with measurable properties. This is exactly what we shall call *the decomposition of the world into elements*. Human creation is not *creation from nothing*, but rather *creation from elements* in the sense that we create a new set of points on the basis of laws that are found to hold among these abstract points with numerical properties. For instance, when we want to launch a satellite that orbits the earth, we first reduce the movements of heavenly bodies to those of points, then discover the law of celestial mechanics, and finally combine points (material constituents) in consulting mechanical laws. In a similar manner, we analyze a given material into molecules and atoms, reveal their structural correlations in numerical terms, and then create a new kind of compound by synthesis. Thus, these technological creations are possible only when we have the "cognitive universe of the sciences," which really has existed as a unique horizon beyond the pseudodualism of the modern age.

GENUINE MODERN DUALISM has finally reached maturity in our own age, when technological creation by humans has become a central issue of philosophy. This very real dualism consists of two moments of human creation that have replaced God's creation. These are the already mentioned moment of the "apperceptive body united with the infinite reflective consciousness" and another, new moment of "imaginative will to project the world via images." Both are also constitutive moments of the modern human personality *in concreto*, which has lately been sadly divided into two because of a self-contradiction due to the inability of the apperceptive body (somatic ego) to control the imaginative will. Indeed, the apperceptive body originally belongs to the region of the transcendental imagination in the Kantian sense, which, deriving from the imaginative will, controls and unifies perception, but as restricted to the kinesthetic and cognitive capacity it has no power to control the freedom of its own foundation.

The latter moment of human creation originates in the dimension of "matter," the basis of the world. Unlike its definition in materialism, however, here "matter" means a pure source of force, that is, *natura naturans*. It does not have a form *(eidos)*, but produces various forms (images). The will to life stands on this material ground. Life is a force immanently united with the will, that is, a force with a certain direction and preference. By nature it aims at the retention and expansion of force. Furthermore, in humans it is immanently united with "imagination" through the bodily flesh *(Leib)*. The working of the will of human life that aims at the retention and expansion of force is not based on mere impulses or conditional reflexes, as in animals. It is rather realized via the production of "images." Thus the will to life in humans formulates its desires as "projections" *(Entwürfe)* toward the future. Projection of purpose as a definite image enables us to find appropriate combinations of "means" for its attainment. Thus the material- or bodily-fleshly-moment of human technological creation is "projection" based on matter or life as bodily flesh. The "arrangement of means nexus" *(Bewandtnisganzheit)* is made possible only by the preceding projection. Imaginative projection aiming at the rention and expansion of force is in essence an attempt by the human being to return to the "source of force." Therefore, it is in a sense an attempt at a "reunification with the whole material world-basis." It is suggestive that Karl Marx wrote, "An animal produces only itself, while man reproduces the whole of nature."[14] We can say that human technological creation has its ultimate motivation in such a natural history.

Despite this motivation, the means for the realization of projects were barely available before the Industrial Revolution of the nineteenth century had begun. Until then, the motivation could express itself only imaginatively in myths and fairy tales. Only the "decomposition into material elements" of natural science from the beginning of the modern age on provided humans with the long-awaited means for its realization. In this sense, the decomposition of the world, which was made possible by the infinite reflective consciousness and by the typifying or synthesizing functions of the apperceptive body, can be called the form- or *Körper*-moment of human technological creation.

Owing to the discovery of causal laws governing things regarded as points with physical properties, we can now predict certain probable effects as well as mutual relations in numerical terms from certain causes, that is, in terms of differential equations.

Imagination, which plays a leading part in the material- or *Leib-*moment in technological creation, extrapolates these numerically expressed causal relations from presently existing space to an imagined future space. As a result, cause-effect relations turn into means-end relations. For example, a causal relation between the "rapid evaporation of a certain liquid" and the "absorption of heat" turns into a teleological relation between the "mechanism of an air-conditioner" and the "cooling of air." As this example indicates, a machine is generally a package containing a bundle of causal phenomena arranged in one direction for a certain purpose.

In this way, the human technological imagination reorganizes

the world decomposed by natural science into a bundle of causal relations, and builds up a "linkage of tools" for certain purposes.
Among these, those that will be repeatedly used are molded into
packages, that is, into *machines*. Thus, as a result of this effort over
two centuries, we now, at the beginning of the twenty-first century,
find ourselves in a world filled with a variety of machines and linkag-
es of tools. This is exactly what we meant by the human "creation
from elements."

This description might seem to lead to the view that the
Körper-moment (the body phantom with apperception) and the *Leib*-
moment (the imaginative will) of technological creation, are complementary without any dualistic antithesis between them. However,
as we have already said, the imaginative will originates on a sheerly
material basis and therefore is half-blind. It always insists on its principle, that is, on the retention and expansion of force, whatever contents an individual person's imaginative will might have. In history, it
is typically seen in the unrestrained development of capitalistic production. However, in this respect, the situation is essentially the same
as in socialist (or communist) economies, for although a socialist
economy places restrictions on private projections, the state as a
whole is engaged in a projection on the basis of the same principle:
"retention and expansion of production." The history of the modern
age shows that these half-blind monsters of projection have tried
hard to expand, competing with each other and sometimes even re-
sorting to a cruel war to defeat others. In the meantime the physical
body-moment seems to have been subject to the bodily flesh moment in serving as a "means" for the latter. However, its principle,
"the decomposition into elements," only displayed its nature fully for
the first time when nuclear weapons appeared (a development that
took place regardless of individual scientists' intentions). This was, in
a sense, the appearance of the "nothingness" that supports natural
science from behind. Nuclear weapons, the use of which decomposes
even the very will to life on earth into homogeneous elements,
threatens the very existence of the *Leib*-moment itself. The imaginative will now confronts the possibility of self-destruction by its own
technological creation. The radical and *genuine dualism* of the
modern age has now revealed itself. The physical body *(Körper)*
and the bodily flesh *(Leib)* of modern technology, that is, an ever-
decomposing natural science and a half-blind material production,

are no longer complementary, but are now in principle opposed to each other. This genuine dualism will soon be manifest in other fields, such as life-technology, too. We can foresee a new conflict between science, as it tries to carry on the decomposition of life into "homogeneous elements," on the one hand, and unknown phenomena of life, which by nature refuse decomposition, on the other, emerging inside and out of scientists themselves.

THE RELATION BETWEEN SCIENCE and technology is not as simple as Heidegger thought. In the modern age, this relation is conceivable only as a kind of incomplete mediation of the human internal schism, which began at the outset of our era and was only falsely symbolized by Cartesian dualism. The nonteleological character of modern science was made possible only through the methodological, and therefore temporal, exclusion of every teleological cogito of human life. In this sense, the value-neutrality of scientific knowledge is the result of a kind of "reduction," which might be called a "value-annihilation."[15] As soon as the "brackets" of reduction were deleted, and what was bracketed in them was opened toward the world two centuries after its birth, this accumulated value-neutral knowledge was immediately absorbed into the teleological vector of human projection and, in changing the direction of its coordinate axis from past-to-present into present-to-future, became modern technology in service to an enormous material production. Therefore, on the one hand science is certainly prior to technology, and technology is an applied science. On the other hand, however, technology is completely dominated by the teleology of human projection, and this domain of the imagining half-blind will to life originated in its potentiality precisely at the time when the value-annihilation of modern science began (i.e., the seventeenth century). These two domains, nonteleological knowledge and teleological willful projection, are twins born in polarity derived from the innermost part of modern human personality, that which originally was a physical body = bodily flesh *(Körper = Leib)* unity with proper consciousness.

In this sense science and technology have exactly the same root or origin (but not, as Heidegger said, the same essence) in the abysmal schism of the modern human. Science has its root in the pure physical body (the body phantom with the apperceptive body), and the teleology of technology has its root in the pure bodily flesh. The unprecedented complete separation of the person into these two inner regions at the beginning of the modern era, which was caused by the intrusion of the causal reduction of the cogito (the annihilation of value), also made the premise of the birth of modern economical production possible. The imagining half-blind will to life was then given its autonomy and set free from every reflection. The genuine dualism of the modern age was growing concealed behind the mask of Cartesian pseudodualism.

Modern technology comes up *in actu* as a kind of mediation between these two separated human regions: as a nonteleological cogito absorbed and transformed into its teleological counter-pole. This explains why technology emerged somewhat later than science from their common root. This mediation is, however, somewhat incomplete, because its ground of existence rests upon the very schism itself. It has no power to overcome the modern human internal schism or the genuine dualism itself. The fundamental danger of the technology of our time is rooted here.

CHAPTER TEN

The Phenomenological Ontology of Power

The Being of Things and the Being of the Fundamental Life-World (Monad)

THE MOST IMMEDIATE POINT where "phenomenology" touches "ontology in a genuine sense" (not as "the formal and regional eidetic science" in Husserl's sense, but as "the science of Being in general") apparently lies in the phenomenological reduction as phenomenology's cardinal method, for it is the way to bracket the Being of objects and that of the world in a single stroke. When Husserl discovered and established this method, however, did he know exactly what Being he was bracketing? It is evident that he did not know it philosophically or phenomenologically, but knew it only in a mundane and incomplete sense, because phenomenology begins only after this reduction and not before it.[1] In this chapter I will try to show that Husserl's treatment of Being in general was so insufficient that the essential difference between the Being of objects and that of the world, namely the genuine ontological difference, was overlooked, and hence the reduction remained invalid for the latter kind of Being, with the consequence that this Being of the world has remained veiled even to this day.

In *Ideas I*, Husserl still states of the world of the natural attitude, "An empty fog of obscure indeterminateness is populated with intuitive possibilities or presumptions, and only the 'form' of the world, precisely as 'world,' is traced out. Moreover the indeterminate surroundings are endless, that is, the nebulous and never fully definable horizon is necessarily there."[2] In this way he seemed aware of the world as horizon, but at the moment of reduction he treated it indiscriminately together with the sum total of objects, lumping them together as the "general thesis." After ten years, he differentiated more clearly in *First Philosophy* between the Being of objects and that of the world, applying the "phenomenological" reduction to the former and the "transcendental" reduction to the latter.[3] But the relationship between both kinds of Being still seems to be that of parts to whole, and Husserl still had no idea of the antagonism between them. According to Husserl's original intention, the Being that is bracketed is never lost, but is grasped solely under the new perspective of the phenomenon. In fact, he later tried to connect the *Urdoxa* of Being with the rational positional character of the constituted noema. For Husserl, to *be* truly and genuinely means to be posited rationally or by reason. For example, every thing-object in the world always appears with some unseen sides or indeterminate characteristics that will never be exhausted empirically, but insofar as it appears in accordance with the rational idea *(Idee)* "thing itself" in the Kantian sense, it is regarded as truly and genuinely being.[4]

Apart from the unmistakably artificial impression this idea gives us, we cannot help asking this question: if Being is essentially so rational, why must Husserl, as a transcendental idealist, bracket it in order to reach the "matter itself"?

When, in the *Crisis*, Husserl reached the idea of the *Lebenswelt* through the reduction of the scientific objective world, he went a step further toward an understanding of the ontological difference between objects and the world itself; however, he remained merely contemplative insofar as he could not grasp Being as force (or power). Being is, in my opinion, not only the object of belief, as many phenomenologists thought, but a force or power in an eminently practical sense.

In the *Ideas*, Husserl states that

> Reality, the reality of things taken singularly as well as the reality of the entire world, essentially lacks (in our strong sense) self-sufficiency. It is not something absolute in itself that binds itself to others in a secondary way, but it is, in an absolute sense, nothing at all, it has no 'absolute Being' *('Wesen')*, it has only the Being *(Wesenheit)* of something that is in principle *only* intentional, *only* something recognized or represented.[5]

However, after twenty-five years, in *Experience and Judgment,* Husserl writes,

> If I grasp in its particularity some object, for example, a book on a table, in my perceptive field, I grasp a being for me that was already "there" for me beforehand "in my study," even if I was not yet directed to it. . . . In this way every being that affects us, affects us on the ground of the world. It gives itself to us as a putative being.[6]

Therefore, we can conclude that here the Being of such a pregiven thing or world is no longer nothing at all in contrast to the act-intentional consciousness, but has some self-sufficiency. Nevertheless, one might ask again, "Is the Being of the world not still a correlate of some consciousness, namely a believing consciousness, and does it not still depend upon it?" We agree with the latter description, but only partially, because the ontological weight of the Being of the world seems to break through not only the idealistic preponderance of consciousness in the early Husserl, but also even the parallelism between consciousness and Being of the later Husserl. This is to say that a Being that an epistemological consciousness never expects springs out from the depths of the world in the practical dimension, a prerational teleological force of life, so-to-speak, and consciousness can only control the outcome of this power. *Consciousness does not know what this power is and where it comes from.* Indeed, it is my power on the one hand, but on the other it is a Being that is completely other than mine. Thus, as Heidegger suggested, the surrounding world *(Umwelt)* as such is neither the sum total of objects nor their mere horizon. It is horizonal Being, which is inseparable from my living somatic ego as its center, as well as the goal *(worumwillen)* of its project over and beyond surrounding objects, always supported and penetrated by the anonymous teleological force of life. We will call this primordial individual world "the fundamental life-world" or the "monad."

As is well known, Heidegger and Sartre understood the human being as "Being-in-the-world." However, life in general and the fundamental world (monad) are originally inseparable. In this sense, Husserl's term "life-world" is pregnant with significance. Viewed ontologically, it does not mean "the world of life," namely "the world belonging to life," but rather it means *"vita sive mundus,"* or *"mundus sive vita.* " The fundamental world is the horizonality of life and the Being of the world is the Being of life itself. By contrast, the alienated form of life is a body isolated from its world. The isolated body is always objectifiable in empty space, which is not the world. The Being of life as a teleological force, however, contains in itself the causal Being of the objective body as its lowest and instrumental element. Only the human body is a complex of both Beings, teleological and causal, and moves dialectically between them. The animal's body is more simple and does not contain the Being of the object; therefore, it cannot use any tools. Teleological Being must always fight against causal Being in order to assimilate and control it (the teleologization of causality). The stiffening of muscles without any specific purpose (clenching the fist, stiffening the shoulders, etc.) is already a kind of causal alienation or reification. Reification sometimes has a positive meaning, however, when it brings about an inner sense of fulfillment of power, for example, in the coupling confrontation with a huge rock or mountain, which is often found in primitive religion. This sense of power is inert, passive, nonteleological, and inwardly closed, however.

The Being of the causal object, by contrast, clearly exposes itself as it is only when it is about to be absorbed and assimilated into the Being of the teleological world as a resisting force against it. Not only does this force resist the Being of the world, but it also erodes it (tension, fatigue, sickness) and dissolves it (pain, death).

The Being of objects as such is neither "ready-to-hand" *(Zuhandensein)* as a part of the Being of the world nor "present-at-hand" *(Vorhandensein)* as its privation. Rather, as inert resistance and as the force of dissolving reification *(Verdinglichung)*, it is the extreme limit or border situation *(Grenzsituation)* of the teleological Being of the world of life. Life as the fundamental world (monad) absorbs and assimilates various objects passively through eating (mastication), drinking, and respiration, and actively through manufacturing labor and technological creation. However, objects resist even as they are absorbed and assimilated into the world of life, and thereby bring tension, fatigue, sickness, pain, anxiety, and even death into life. For example, in mastication we experience the resistance of objects to our teeth. We must overcome this resistance in order to change the object-food into nutrition and energy. In this process, however, our teeth must sometimes be motivated, by an inertial force, to a simple reaction to the resistance of the hard food-object, and in this way our teleological Being of life must inwardly contain in itself the causal Being of the object.

Death is the complete reification of the life-world into an objective space into which life is thrown. Objective space and time are originally the leeway *(Spielraum)* of the causal Being of objects, that is, the place of the dissolution and extinction of life.

The Being *(il y a)* of Emmanuel Levinas, a Being that is distinguished from any concrete being, is very close to our sense of the Being in general of things. It is anonymous and impersonal. It is regarded as the object of the never-sleeping "insomniac" consciousness. It is impossible for this Being to die, perhaps because it is already dead.[7] It signifies a Being that is intolerably and violently objectified in space by the primal transcendental subjectivity, which is originally impersonal and anonymous and is beyond any particular ego.

Sartre's idea of the *"pratico-inerte"* points out a dimension where objects assimilated into the world resist or even revolt against it and erode or dissolve the fundamental world (monad) into an isolated body, or even subordinate the world to the objects.[8] However, since Sartre's world is, as it were, an aggregate of materiality and nothingness, and not life, the way objects resist the world would differ from my depiction.

The teleological force of the life-world and the resisting causal force of objects can compete with each other quantitatively as physical action and reaction, but their qualities are completely different. The former is teleological and spontaneous, while the latter is causal and inert. The former is mediated by the imagination and the latter is blind. Max Scheler called the Being of the world *"Gefühlsdrang"* (feeling-impulse), and completely identified it qualitatively with the resistance of objects. He writes, "What gives us real Being is the experience of the resistance of the open world-sphere—and this resistance exists only for our instinctive life, for our central life-impulse."[9]

Since these two forces—that of the monadic life-world and that of things—are as Being totally and essentially different from each other, we must say that Scheler overlooked their ontological difference, although he must be noted for his recognition of the Being of objects as resistance.

Tools and machines are objects that are penetrated by and reorganized into the Being of the life-world, but they do not yet stop to resist life. To manage them always requires force and struggle, and whenever trouble occurs, they totally resist life.

On the contrary, fatigue and pain manifest the penetration of the Being of objects into the world of life. Here resistance occurs not outside, but inside the life-world, and if it increases and becomes impossible to overcome, then death takes over and the fundamental world is de-worldified and becomes a corpse, one of objects. Here all pouring-forth of teleological power ceases.

Maine de Biran correctly recognized an antagonism between two different powers, the active free force of the will and the resisting organism, within the human body. He called this inner conflict of forces the "effort," and found in it the origin of the individual ego. He unfortunately called the free will "hyperorganic," however, and deprived it of every organic characteristic.[10] I would ask of him where the hyperorganic force of will comes from and how the pure intellectual hyperorganic force can encounter the organic one. To the contrary, in my opinion, the Being of the life-world is a force of the totalized and totalizing organism, because the world is my secondary body that includes the primary one (my bodily flesh).

The mutual relationship between various species of life as fundamental life-worlds can be called the ecological or environmental problem. While each species is more or less grouped according to its peculiar mode of life-project, there are relationships of mutual assistance and mutual conflict between groups. While one group called the human species now assimilates and increasingly and to an enormous extent absorbs other groups of species as tools into its own world, or even extinguishes them as obstacles to its life-project, other groups resist it through their counter-projects (e.g., the generation of a new virus) or by promoting causal objectifying forces (e.g., global thermalization). Even if they are assimilated, they can in various ways cause the erosion or dissolution of human life-worlds from the inside (e.g., pollution by toxic agriculatural material).

THE PHENOMENON OF "POSSESSION" also describes the assimilation of objects into the world of life. An invisible force connects the object and its possessor, the somatic ego incarnated in bodily flesh, who is the center of the world. This ontological force works here in a way that is not only strongly individual but also egocentric and difficult to rationalize. Regarding it as immediately rationalizable or communizable may be the fundamental error of Marxist Communism. The most serious problem concerning the phenomenon of possession, however, would be, as Gabriel Marcel pointed out, that whatever I think I have has the tendency to suppress me as the possessor.[11] The possessed thing (even if it is an immaterial idea) may absorb the possessor himself, who imagines that he or she manages it freely, making him or her rather a possessed. This is not a simple reification, but rather the de-monadization of life and the monadization of things. It is the essence of Mammonism, which makes the original teleology of the life-world completely impossible. Such an alienating shift of the center of the monad from life to a thing must necessarily become an object of study for phenomenological ontology.

We cannot avoid confronting the problem of whether the Being of the fundamental life-world founds only the individual private phenomenon of possession or also the Being of the intersubjective social community. We cannot agree with Sartre's opinion that a we-subject of a project is essentially impossible.[12] I can plan for and engage in many projects at the same time, and I have as many derivative worlds as I project, among which there can be worlds projected by us, namely, by me together with other subject-I's. For example, I write a letter as a single agent, but at the same time I engage in a group project by establishing an academic association. As an author I am a single subject, but as a member of an establishing committee I am (one of) a we-subject. Therefore, I belong simultaneously to the derivative world of the individual subject and to that of intersubjectivity, each of which eliminates and organizes some appropriate objects as its tool-nexus from the common objective space for its respective goals. In this case, we cannot say that as these intersubjective derivative worlds of life are mediated by others they are ontologically more genuine and more rational than individual derivative worlds, because the teleological force or Being, which promotes these intersubjective projects, often loses its freedom and becomes causally restricted, in not coming directly from the fundamental life-world that is ontologically pre- or proto-rational. We must next examine the conditions under which the Being (power) of this fundamental world can be genuinely compatible with intersubjectivity in general and with reason.

We must pay special attention to the specific, teleological character of the pure power of life. Life itself does not know exactly what the *telos* of life is; nevertheless, it essentially appears as teleological and not causal. Consciousness in general is perhaps nothing other than the increasing self-awareness of the *telos* of life, beginning with the tropistic nature of primitive creatures and moving toward the reason of the human being. The rational consciousness of the human being seems to stand, so to speak, at the threshold of the complete self-awareness of the *telos* of life, but it is far from entering into it. Human reason therefore has its ontological ground in the teleological prerational power of the life-world as monad.

But the modern idea of rationality has lost sight of its roots. It has become *déraciné*, uprooted. The monad has been broken up into common, objective, infinite space. The source of the power of life, the absolute "Here," has been dispersed into plural "Theres" in this common, empty space, and has become relative "Here = Theres." The individual has been reduced to the collective human whose power is leveled through kinesthetic analogy and empathy. Thus the ego has lost its genuine freedom of decision and projection, just like Heidegger's *"das Man."* As the ego loses sight of the *telos* of life, its source of power is dried up, in the very way Freud described the suppression of the libido.

However, as Leibniz stated, the monad changes only through its own internal principle.[13] It needs no external cause to avoid solipsism and to establish coexistence with others. As I have already argued, the power of life is not always mine, and the *telos* of life is not always I myself. In a sense, indeed, life belongs to me and is entrusted to me, but I nevertheless do not know what life is and where it comes from. I also don't know when it will depart from me. In this sense, life is precisely other than mine and has a *telos* beyond me. *The power of life must thus be regarded as something contradictory: as mine and as other than mine at the same time.*

On this point, my view of life fundamentally differs from that of Nietzsche. For him, life is not only power but also the will to power. This means that for him, life is the power that seeks only to be itself. For Nietzsche's life, to be power means self-identity and self-purpose. Therefore, Nietzsche's will to power knows no contradiction in itself. It contains no other-element that denies its identity from the inside. Nietzsche's "eternal recurrence of the same," as the style of willing, proves this fact. However, our ring of eternal return would everywhere be cut by the inner contradiction of life. Concerning this point, Schopenhauer's view of life seems much more plausible. However, his insistence upon the self-identity of life is too weak to resist resignation and to keep inner contradiction, which is essential to life, alive.

What is necessary to save the fundamental life-world (monad) from the leveling invasion of modern infinite space is a confrontation with and reduction of this contradictory, teleological character of life. If, on account of its essential contradiction, life could have its center neither in the first person ("I") nor in the third person (the "Other"), that is, if it could be neither egocentric nor altercentric, then we might say that it must necessarily have its center in the second person ("Thou"), or must be "tu-centric." This is to say, my life and the Other's life are perpetually being presented by Thou and have their common ultimate aim *(telos)* in Thou, the second person. Moreover, I can encounter and be authentically copresent with the other ego only in and through the encounter with Thou.

The recentering of the monad from an egocentric structure to a tu-centric one corresponds to its qualitative change from pre-rationality to protorationality. We might call it another kind of phenomenological reduction (tu-logical reduction) applied to the Being of the fundamental life-world, which has long remained external to any reduction.

The teleological power of life appearing as "Thou" is the ontological foundation of dialogue, and thence of language, because the Thou intends Thyself as the ultimate *telos,* while acting through I and Others in the same monadic community. The Thou is originally the self-purposive phenomenon mediating I and Others kinesthetically and semantically.

In this sense, the Being of Thou is the completion of the teleology of the fundamental life-world. However, to grasp the second person as a mediating goal or center, the traditional view of Thou must first be transformed. I will discuss this Thou thematically in chapters 11 and 12, but here I will roughly circumscribe its fundamental characteristics. In the following chapters I will first distinguish between the possible Thou and the actual Thou. We will understand the partner in Buber's I-Thou relationship, who stands face to face with me and whom I call "you," to be a possible

Thou or another somatic I (= He, She), through whom the actual Thou will occur to me. I myself am also a possible Thou for another I, that is, the actual Thou will occur through me, too, toward another I. Therefore, those who encounter each other, to be precise, are not I and a possible Thou (= another I), but rather the actual Thou through the I and the same actual Thou through another I. The actual Thou once thus separated, for whatever reason, encounters Thyself through and between I and another I. In this way, the actual Thou mediates and embraces my somatic I and another somatic I who are standing face to face with each other.

This means that the second person lies dimensionally not on the same plane as the first and third person. The second personal dimension totally mediates and ontologically embraces the other two personal dimensions, including the assimilated Being of things in them. The teleological power of life becomes communicative through this tu-logical reduction. Here the dialogue between I and another occurs with true rationality, in that every *telos* of my (and the Other's) project over and beyond surrounding things defines the essence (*eidos*) of these things, once intentionally gathered upon the kinesthetically synthesized common standpoint of I and Others (copresence).[14] This kinesthetically common standpoint produces phonetic words (phonemes) as well as written letters (graphemes) as historically limited, all-temporal, and all-local phenomena.

I believe that linguistic signs as ideal entities must be not only all-temporal, as generally thought, but also all-local; that is, they must be found to be the same everywhere where the kinesthetic synthetic schema takes the same form—of course under a provision for local variety—and at the same time they are found nowhere in objective space, that is, without reference to the common project of life. Thus the linguistic sign as kinesthetic synthesis exists everywhere and nowhere, as Husserl said of ideal objects.[15]

This kinesthetic common standpoint of I and Others (copresence), which is only granted to the human being, is only possible on the ground of a Thou-centered community of monads (field of encounter), but has always been under the pressure of erroneous substantiation and has tended to be regarded as another independent "I" or a so-called transcendental ego. However, a relationality without a foundation in the Thou-centered community of monads is uprooted, just like an *eidos (Wesen)* without a foundation in the *telos* of the teleological projection of my (and the Other's) life.

The traditional epistemological attitude, as a typical example of "cultural" accomplishment, from the beginning abstracts from (instead of bracketing) the Being of the prerational force of life and the causal force of objects. Thus the ego becomes a pure consciousness and objects become *res extensae*. There is no contradiction or antagonism between consciousness and *res extensae,* unlike the relationship between life and things. What exists in the former relationship is a temporary peace that consists of sense-giving and sense, symbolizing the cessation of resistance on the part of the Being of objects against life and the establishment of an abstract territory for the present. Genuine ontology, on the contrary, stands on the ground of *praxis* and the contradiction of life. Being as "force" or "power," which is beyond mere *doxa* or belief, appears for the first time upon the ground of *praxis*. Thus, epistemology must return again and again to genuine ontology as its ground.

The history of phenomenology is the proof of this circular or dialectical relation between epistemology and ontology. Husserl begins his intentional epistemology through a tentative understanding of Being, which he nevertheless brackets. However, the development of his thought necessitates a new basic ground of intentionality, namely, the life-world (universe of transcendental experiences). This world produces genetic epistemology and a new theory of temporality, both of which, I believe, necessitate a renewal of an ontological understanding of the life-world. In my opinion, this is the phenomenological ontology of teleological power, which is contradictory in itself.

Contrary to Husserl's opinion in the *Crisis,* the ontology of the life-world does not always oppose transcendental analysis of the world taken in the broader sense.[16] Rather, the inner illumination of the Being of the fundamental world (not its abstraction) immediately brings about transcendental analysis of it in the broader sense. The tu-logical reduction of the Being of the world necessitates taking not only the teleological life-force of the fundamental life-world but also, through the kinesthetic sedimentation, impersonal transcendental subjectivity itself into consideration and illuminating them monado-logico-transcendentally by the light of the Thou.

The traditional analysis of the life-world, on the contrary, excluded or alienated this force from the beginning, and called this world merely "a universe of experience" or "a world of sensory intu-ition." If the natural attitude consists in open or tacit recognition of the Being of the fundamental life-world as teleological force, as well as in an actual hesitant avoidance of total confrontation with it, then Husserlian phenomenology itself still remains within the natural attitude. We must go one step further than he did through the *confrontational (tu-logical) reduction of the contradictory teleological force of life into Thou*. Through this new step phenomenology will become a genuine theory of "life." Then a phenomenologist will no longer be a "disinterested onlooker," but will rather become an "eminently self-aware performer."

SECTION IV

CHAPTER ELEVEN

Some Problems Concerning the I-Thou Relation

IN ORDER TO PROCEED to the investigation of the dimension of "Thou," who, as was suggested in the previous chapter, is the ultimate mediator of the inter- and intrasubjectivity of the somatic ego, I will address the dialogical thought of Martin Buber as the best guide.

BUBER'S BOOK *I and Thou (Ich und Du)* gained irrevocable fame as a classic of dialogical philosophy.[1] It is indeed rich in content, but at the same time not always easy to understand. Even after reading it many times, questions remain about those passages I feel I have understood only to some degree. I will here enumerate some of the main points from these passages.

(1) In Buber's thought, the I-Thou relation, which refers to the totality of human relations, and the I-It relation, which refers to, so to speak, to the kinesthetic relation of the somatic ego with another body (or thing), are regarded as completely independent and exclusive of each other. Yet is the I-Thou relation in our daily lives really so pure and autonomous? Is there no intermediate stage between them?

*

The following passages attest to the fact that Buber regarded these two relations to be independent and exclusive of each other: "The world becomes double toward the human according to the double attitude he takes."[2] Furthermore, "The primary word *(Grundwort)* I-Thou can only be spoken with the whole Being; the primary word I-It can never be spoken with the whole Being."[3] He further declares that knowledge, consciousness, image, will, feeling, and thought, together with their objects, found the world of "It," but "the realm of Thou has another ground."[4] By contrast, there are very few passages suggesting the intertwining or interpenetration of these two regions, such as this one: "'It' is a pupa and 'Thou' is a butterfly. But there are not only conditions where they are purely separated. Rather, phenomena in which they are deeply and dually entangled are often seen."[5] However, he says nothing more of these entangled phenomena, except in the last part of the book, where he refers to the "figure" *(Gestalt)* as the combination *(Mischung)* of Thou and It.[6] Rather, Buber usually emphasizes the alternation of Thou and It, as in the following passage: "The individual Thou must become an It at the end of the relation. The individual It can become Thou by entering into the relation."[7] For example, a tree is "It" for the one who analyzes and observes it, but it is "Thou" for the one who loves it as a whole. No intermediate stage seems to be allowed for between "It" and "Thou."

However, when we consider the experiences of our day-to-day lives, do we always call our partner "you" "with our whole Being"? Does even a swindler not call his or her victim "you"? Of course, Buber, too, says that "the shape of spoken words proves nothing. However many times Thou may be repeated, if its is spoken from habit and monotony, it is an 'It' as a consequence."[8] Is such a daily "Thou" always already an "It," then, as Buber says? Even a swindler, who is anxious to use and to deceive his or her partner, could not confuse the conversation partner with an objectified third person. Even if he or she speaks with a partner while casting furtive glances, the latter could not become "It" or "He or She" completely. Therefore, it would be excessive to immediately identify the so-called daily Thou, or Thou not spoken with the whole Being, with the third person, as Buber did. It will at most be an "alienated Thou," or "a He/She-like Thou," but no "He or She" as such. If such a point of view is recognized, we must now ask, how does the alienation of the Thou occur?

(2) In Buber, "I" in the I-Thou relation and "I" in the I-It relation are considered to be completely different. How are these two "I's" connected in an individual human being?

*

Buber writes, "The I of the primary word 'I-Thou' and the I of the primary word 'I-It' are different. The I of the primary word 'I-It' appears as an individual *(Eigenwesen)*, and is aware of itself as subject of experience and utilization. The I of the primary word 'I-Thou' appears as a personality *(Person)* and is aware of itself as subjectivity (without attaching the genitive)."[9] Furthermore, "the individual appears by contrasting himself to other individuals. Personality appears by entering into relation with other personalities."[10] Finally, "personality directly sees itself; the individual is concerned with its 'mine,' namely my style, my nation, my creation, my genius, and so on."[11] He continues describing the relation between the two I's:

> There are not two kinds of human. There are two poles of humanity. No one is a pure personality or a pure individual. . . . Everyone is living in two kinds of I. However there is a human called personality, because the tendency to personality is very strong, and there is another called individual, because the tendency to individual is very strong. The true history is decided between the former and the latter.[12]

According to these citations, the I of "I-Thou" and the I of "I-It" constitute a tensional polarity in a human being. A person or a situation affects the inclination toward this or that pole. To connect such qualitatively different I's in the form of "polarity" does not solve the problem at all, however, for the question necessarily arises: What is the third that connects these two poles to each other? Is it possible to explain it from Buber's standpoint, which allows only three categories, namely, I, Thou, and It?

Indeed, Buber's view of the "double pole of the I" or of the so-called impure personality warrants our attention, because it seems to tacitly suggest as its partner the "impure Thou" mentioned in (1). However, the answer to the question of how such an "intermediate stage" (alienation) could occur seems not to be given anywhere.

(3) According to Buber, Thou is not an object among objects but an

opposite face to face with me, who is completely exclusive of others. However, at the same time, Buber writes, "Without neighbors and without a seam is Thou and fulfills the heavenly sky. . . . All others are living in his light."[13] He continues, "Insofar as the heaven of Thou spreads over me. . . ."[14]

How can Thou as my opposite, so to speak, embrace every other in Thyself and extend Thyself over me?

*

Buber writes, "In the complete (I-Thou) relation my Thou embraces myself without being myself,"[15] and "Before which we live, in which we live, from and into which we live, the mystery (of Thou): it remains what it was."[16] Therefore, we must pay attention to the fact that the pure Thou not only stands opposite me, but also envelops and embraces me. This is, of course, impossible in ordinary space. Is it possible in the dimension of Thou, which has "nothing to do with Time and Space"?

(4) Since Descartes, Western philosophy has been consistently dominated by the opposing concepts "Consciousness" and "Being." How is the I-Thou relation to be expressed, if it is considered in using these concepts?

*

In my opinion, the fundamental opposing concepts of modern philosophy that correspond to the *eidos* and *hyle* of ancient philosophy as well as to the *essentia* and *existentia* of medieval philosophy are "Consciousness" and "Being." Not only the idealism and the materialism of the modern age, but also phenomenology and phenomenological ontology, which arise later, seem not to be able to get rid of this schema. Therefore, it will be significant to consider the I-Thou relation by using the opposing concepts "Consciousness" and "Being" in order to clarify its historical position.

Moreover, only by answering this last question (4), will we presumably be able to answer questions (1), (2), and (3) with any certain evidence. Therefore, we begin with the explication of the last question.

BEFORE ATTEMPTING TO DISCUSS the I-Thou relation by using the paired opposing concepts "Consciousness" and "Being," I will offer a seemingly bold proposal concerning the mutual relation between "Consciousness" and "Being."

I will express this in the following way: *Being appears in two completely different ways to the consciousness of the somatic ego, which confronts Being in the broadest sense.* The first of these ways is "Being seen from the outside" (so-called extended Being), while the second is "Being seen from the inside" (so-called living Being). The former indicates all Being in empty space and measurable time, to which my own body, too, belongs as *Körper,* insofar as it is seen from the outside. This Being is not only thought to be a perception or a representation but also presumed to exist transcendently to any consciousness. We must pay attention to the fact that Being in the memory, too, belongs to Being seen from the outside, insofar as it is intended in empty space and at a certain point in time. Physiological phenomena—for example, a stomachache, headache, or feeling of fatigue—which are intended "inside" of me, belong nevertheless to Being seen from the outside, insofar as my consciousness projects them into space and allots them portions of the "image" (or reflected expanse) of the body seen from the outside. Of course, these physiological phenomena can never be completely "spatialized," and so some residue always remains.

However, my body is also seen "from the inside," by the consciousness. Indeed, my body is seen from the outside as a *Körper* in space, but simultaneously as *Leib* from the inside in a completely different dimension called the "monad." As mentioned above, something heterogeneous to the spatialization of physiological phenomena concerning my body appears already before this operation and remains after it. For example, when I look at the image of a beating heart in an X-ray film, I judge it to be mine only by combining this image with something never to be spatialized, that can be seen only from the inside.

A certain vital psychological phenomenon (e.g., shock) is seen from the outside insofar as it is posited in a certain dated memory, but if I still feel some pain whenever I recollect it, it is also seen from the inside (at least partially).

Furthermore, when I fall asleep every night, ceasing the activity of my consciousness, the region to which I return will be precisely this "Being seen from the inside." Therefore every activity of consciousness that looks at Being "from the outside" disturbs sleeping. Strong sensory stimuli during waking hours as well as vital memory or emotion aroused by it can thereby prevent one from falling asleep. The only conscious activity compatible with sleep is imagination or dreaming, which are essentially akin to Being seen from the inside.

Now it is remarkable that our fundamental thesis that Being appears to consciousness in two completely different ways is also found in the thoughts of the philosophers Arthur Schopenhauer, Albert Schweitzer, and Henri Bergson.

Schopenhauer argues that our body seen from the outside belongs to the world as representation, but seen from inside it belongs to the world as "Will," namely, as the so-called thing-in-itself, and says "We already see here that the essence of things can never be got at from the outside: however much one might investigate, one comes up with nothing more than images and names. He is comparable to one who wanders around a castle seeking the entrance in vain and for the present sketching the facade."[17] However, Schopenhauer's opinion differs from mine in the following ways: (1) He regards the world of representation as that of illusion without any reality in itself, but I acknowledge that Being seen from the outside has a proper independence. (2) He calls the Will "a blind Will to live," whereas I do not identify the Being seen from the inside with a simple Will to live, but rather I regard it as also comprising an individual ego. (3) He generally recognizes the Being of Will as the thing-in-itself behind the world of representation, and recognizes a kind of Will even in a stone, but I will allow only an individual ego to occasionally expand its proper Being seen from the inside over and beyond the region of Being seen from the outside in general.

Albert Schweitzer writes in his book *Christianity and World Religions* (1925),

> The recognition of God according to nature is always incomplete and inadequate, for we see things of the world only from the outside. We see a tree grow, leaves become green, and flowers bloom. But the power which causes them is incomprehensible to me. The formative ability of this power is an enigma to me. But inside of me I recognize things from inside. The creative power that makes all Being occur and maintains it, appears in me in a form never recognizable in other cases, as an ethical Will, as something that will be creative in me. . . . My life is

defined completely by the mystery experienced in me, the mystery that God is manifested in me as an ethical Will, and will possess my life.[18]

Furthermore, he writes,

> Use of a metaphor might be permitted. There is an ocean. Cold water does not move. But in the ocean there is the Mexican Gulf Stream, water streaming from the equator to the pole. Among the waters of the ocean as between two banks of a river, hot water streams, moves in the unmoved water and is hot in the cold water. . . . Just like this, is the God of love in the God of world-power, one with it, but completely different from it.[19]

Indeed, Schweitzer's insistence directly concerns the recognition of God, the difference between a nonethical creative God found outside of me and the ethical God of love found inside of me. We realize that this difference in the recognition of God immediately reflects the difference in the recognition of Being in human consciousness when we hear him say that "the most immediate fact of human consciousness is 'I am life willing to live in the midst of lives willing to live,'"[20] but that the world before our eyes is only "the meaningless repetition of creation and destruction, reproduction and slaughter."[21]

Schweitzer's assertion differs from my proposal in the following ways: (1) Schweitzer calls the immediate inner givenness to consciousness "Will to live," or life, but for me every life also comprises "I" as a particular, individual Being. (2) Schweitzer regards the Will to live of others as an immediate givenness, but for me the other "I" in its totality is never immediately given. (3) For Schweitzer the universal Will that will harmonize and unite all given Will to live is the "God of love," but for me some other principle is necessary to harmonize and unite my "I" and the other (never immediately given) "I."

In *Essai sur les données immédiates de la conscience* (1888), Bergson writes,

> The life of consciousness appears under a double aspect according to whether man grasps it directly or in refraction through space. . . . Considered in itself, the condition of profound consciousness has nothing to do with quantity; it is pure quality. . . . To characterize these moments (of duration) by

saying that they erode each other will still be to distinguish them from each other. . . . But the more completely the condition of social life is established, the more accelerated is the flow that brings our condition of consciousness from the inside to the outside. . . . Thus a second I is formed which covers the first I, an I whose existence has distinct moments, whose conditions are separated from each other and are easily expressed by words.[22]

Furthermore, he writes,

Therefore there are two different I's as a result, one of which is, as it were, the outside projection of the other, its spatial and so to speak social representation. We reach the first I through a deepened reflection, which lets us grasp our inner conditions as living beings persistently on the way of formation, as the contrary condition to measurement that penetrate each other and whose succession has nothing in common with a juxtaposition in homogeneous space. But the moments where we grasp ourselves again in this way are rare, and this is why we are rarely free. Most of the time we live outside of ourselves; of our I we appercept only its distorted phantom, a shadow that pure duration projects in homogeneous space. Therefore our existence is developed in space rather than in time.[23]

It is evident here that the time Bergson refers to is not a measurable, spatialized time but the dimension of so-called pure duration.

In this way, we find here the difference between the Being of the spatialized ego which is, so to speak, seen from the outside, and the completely different Being of the ego, which is given immediately to consciousness, or, so to speak, seen from the inside. Bergson's standpoint differs from mine, however, with regard to the following points: (1) Bergson regards the domain of the genuine ego as pure duration, but I think that even pure duration is only a superficial layer of Being seen from the inside, and the genuine ego lies beyond every kind of time and space already known. (2) Bergson expands pure duration, which is first found inside the ego, toward the region of life in general, but I distinguish the ego, especially the personal ego, from life in general. (3) Bergson takes language to be something essentially spatial, but I believe that the origin of language also lies in the domain that is beyond any space or time.

As ALREADY MENTIONED in the preceding confrontation with three philosophers, I refer to "Being seen from the inside" as "the region of life and of an 'individual I'," and by contrast we call the "Being seen from the outside" the region of "It." The "I" belongs to Being seen from the inside, but through the so-called transcendental consciousness the "I" can also see Being from the outside. In other words, the "I" sees both kinds of Being at the same time. By way of this positioning the "I" sometimes assimilates Being seen from the outside into Being seen from the inside, and constitutes the *kinesthetic dimension* in a broader sense. Only through this kinesthetic dimension can the "I" find another "I," to be called "He" or "She," in the midst of Being seen from the outside. These names—that is, the individual I, He, She, and It—correspond to the same names in Buber's *I and Thou.*

It is worth noting that the dimension of "I" comprises the consciousness that sees Being from both sides, inside and outside, at the same time. This is the self-consciousness that mediates both sides of Being and that can be regarded as the complex of the transcendental consciousness and the imagination. It is also the consciousness of "I" (somatic ego), and not any impersonal consciousness. By contrast, in the dimension of "It" there is no consciousness except the impersonal consciousness of primordial transcendentality. The human consciousness of the "I" gradually absorbs this transcendental consciousness during its development. The self-awareness of the "I" itself seems to grow with this absorption. Therefore, in the region of Being seen from the inside, consciousness and Being are mediated by "I" (somatic ego) and make up a kind of unity, but in the region of Being seen from the outside, consciousness and Being are related only externally and make up no unity (e.g., as in the case of intentionality).

Buber does not differentiate between "It" and "He" or "She," but from our standpoint, they are to be distinguished above all as the difference between the nonliving being without an ego and the living being with an ego. When I see a seriously wounded man, I do not merely regard him as a higher form of automaton, as Descartes did, but rather as something very different. Not only do I see him from the outside, but I feel a kind of sympathy with his pain. What is this phenomenon, which is generally called "empathy"? It will be the location of the image of pain, namely, of a mode of Being seen from the inside, into the body-object of the wounded man. In other words, I will see him from the outside as well as from the inside as an extension of my body *(Leib)* simultaneously. Therefore, this is indeed the recognition of life other than mine, but not yet that of the other "I" (He or She). In other words, I will still be seeing the inside of my life through the refractive mediation of Being seen from the outside.

There is yet another case of empathy. When I see a human body moving somewhere, I do not merely feel it as an extension of my body, but rather "as if I were there," as Husserl pointed out. According to him, this feeling of "as if I were there" is founded by a kinesthetic coupling that occurs between my body here and another body there. Through the analogical mediation of the kinesthetic realm the "other I" (He or She) is given as an appresentation or as the analogical representation of my "I." It is worth noting that in this case the Being of my "I" is already passively spatialized through kinesthesis, and becomes alternative with that of the "other I" (He or She). This is the "I-He (or She)" relation (e.g., the social role-exchange relation) distinguished from the "I-It" relation, which is also founded by kinesthesis, but has no appresentation of the I.

However, since the Being of the I that founds the "I-He (She)" and "I-It" relations is defined and limited by kinesthesis, or by Being seen from the outside, these are not relations of the I in its (monadic) totality. At best I find here the analogy (the second) of my "I," which never genuinely exhibits the otherness of the other.[24]

There is another phenomenon that seems to appresent the existence of the "other I": the look *(Blick)*. As Sartre describes it in *Being and Nothingness,* the look, anonymous or not, appears from the midst of the outer world, evoking the transcendental consciousness in me and forcefully putting Being seen from the outside upon me. This phenomenon of the "look" teaches me that there are evidently other consciousnesses than mine that are also seeing Being from the outside, but I have no evidence that this consciousness, for its part, is also seeing Being from the inside at the same time.

Therefore, neither empathy mediated by kinesthetic movement nor the look representing the activity of the transcendental consciousness proves the existence of the "I" in its totality on the side of others.

Thus, the existence of another self-consciousness that sees Being from the inside without any restriction (existence of the other I in its totality) seems to have become, so to speak, the object of a kind of "wager."

This wager is somewhat different from one that would make the existence of life on Mars its object, however. Indeed, in both cases this existence has never been proved by any experience, but the belief in the existence of the other I, unlike that of the Martian, is founded by a kind of doxic (believing) relation with Me. My consciousness cannot posit any other I in its totality from the standpoint of a mere onlooker, but rather it can posit Him (or Her) only by wagering my total Being on the sight of him or her *coming from inside of Me*, or only by accepting my own "Being seen from the inside" as also *"the Being seen from the inside by the Other."*[25] My own total Being seen from the inside continues to be my own, but at the same time it is to be regarded as something seen from inside by the Other than me, too. Of course, this is not a straightforward negation of my Being, nor the establishment of the solitary nonego. Rather, I keep my identity while I feel this Being of the ego as also belonging to another ego simultaneously. Only by such an internal self-negation, only by wagering myself wholeheartedly on the sight of the "Other" inside of me, do I gain the Other in totality outside of me. Herein lies the paradoxical secret of human personality in general. An invisible doxic correlation holds between both total "I's": the complex of the monadic structure of both I's. Here the other I is neither the analogy (the second) of my I nor the result of the empathy on the part of my Being. He or she is an absolutely independent autonomous Being, the object of respect and trust.

Such a total relation between I and the "other I" seems at once to correspond to Buber's I-Thou relation, into which he said that anyone can enter only with his or her whole Being. However, an unexpected difficulty arises here. Both the I and the Thou of this relation gain their totality as monads only in once thoroughly eliminating the restrictive "Being seen from the outside" as the realm of kinesthesis from their "Being seen from the inside," so this relation must remain one of only tacit mutual recognition and of silent respect for the self-purposiveness of each. Without kinesthesis, however, both I and Thou have no means to act or to express themselves; they cannot even speak a word to each other. In fact, Buber's I-Thou relation, too, incomprehensibly yet undeniably exhibits such a tendency, and, in being a relation between pure subjectivities without any dependent genitives,[26] has its culmination in "silence."[27] The totality is necessary, but is not sufficient. Therefore, it seems better to call this relation of totality (including Buber's) only the potential relation of I-Thou, and to call this Thou a potential Thou.

To deepen our analysis of this difficulty, let us consider the problem of authentic language, which is generally and plausibly thought to be the most important phenomenon of the I-Thou relation. Language in general never rests on any ground that is proved by any experience in the area of the "It." Rather, it rests upon an unproved precondition supplemented only tentatively and practically by an occasional coincidence in the area of the "It." Modern linguistics, and especially semantics, can only address this coincidence. By contrast, linguistic analyses of the "I" area and, correspondingly, of the origin of meaning, usually lack any coincidence with each other to a remarkable degree.

The linguistic coincidence in the area of "It" is founded by the transcendentally analogical coupling of kinesthetic phenomena, which produces the phonetic scheme. The phonetic scheme is transmitted in a practical way from parents to children through mimesis from generation to generation. However, the transmission of "meaning" must, in turn, be founded only through the synthetic mediation between the "I" and "the other I" inside of Me, and, at the same time, by the same mediation between them outside of Me. In other words, not only the inner self-negating wager of my Being on the sight of the Other but also the internal synthetic mediation of "I" (Being seen from the inside) and "not-I" (Being seen from the inside by the Other, and Being seen from the outside) must make the commonalization and the phonetic articulation of my private meaning possible. At the same time, these must make the transmission of this meaning by way of phonetic kinesthesis to the external "other I" (potential Thou) possible. The internal mediator and the external mediator must, of course, be one and the same. Now, however, we unfortunately cannot further clarify what this mediation is with our categories "Consciousness" and "Being." This demands a new perspective, which will be addressed in the following chapter.

In short, in order to make language possible, the same mediator must stand between "I" and "the other I" in the inner and outer monadic dimensions, which are both quite different from the space-time of "It" yet embrace it. Such a double-unitary synthetic media-tion of Being is necessary in order to transform the potential relation of totality, the "I-Thou," into an actual, dialogical, practical relation.

There is no proof of this unity of inner and outer mediation in the "It" dimension. However, the fact that the external I-Thou rela-tion breaks whenever my internal unity is broken, and that when I am betrayed by any confident Thou, my internal unity also breaks, will support the above presumption.

Buber calls this dimension of a Third that mediates I and Thou the region of "Between" *(das Zwischen)* in a later period, but he does not sufficiently explicate it. This will truly be an important area with-out which even the human personality can hardly be thought in a genuine sense.

IN THE ABOVE SECTION, we have tried to explicate Buber's I-Thou relation by means of the pairing concepts "Consciousness" and "Being." This explication is not complete, of course, but it seems to have reached its limit. In the following, we will attempt to answer three questions that arose before from the standpoint we have attained.

(1) Concerning the alienation of Thou

From my standpoint, too, the I-Thou relation and the I-It relation are quite different from each other. This fact does not exclude the possi-bility that these two relations interpenetrate or intertwine with each other, however. For example, language has the I-Thou relation as its precondition, but the content of speech is usually a description of "He, She, It." In this case, I must also see Myself from the outside and posit my objectifiable Being in space together with He, She, It, except for the Being of my linguistic kinesthesis, which has already been completely synthesized with my Being seen from the inside. Moreover, the action of I toward Thou is always performed by means of "It." In this case, too, the relation of I to It becomes possible only by "seeing myself from the outside" and by assimilating this "Being seen from the outside" into "My Being seen from the inside" (the genesis of kinesthesis). Therefore, to the degree that I speak about He, She, It, or work on the other I practically, I must posit or involve the heterogeneous region of It in Myself, which amounts necessarily to the restriction of my entire Being. However, if I specifically want to speak the other I of a "He, She, It" with my whole Being, as Buber requires, not only the heterogeneous phonetic kinesthesis but also My objectifiable Being seen from the outside must necessarily be suspended and completely synthesized into my total speaking Being seen from the inside. When I succeed somehow or other in speaking in this way in my daily life, I feel that the one who mediates both heterogeneous Beings is not Myself but an anonymous Third. However, insofar as the Beings that are seen from both inside and outside are mediated by Myself alone, it is difficult to unify Myself and synthetically totalize Myself in this way completely. At this point the pollution (depurification) and alienation of my Being seen from the inside occurs. Even when I confront the other I, I cannot perfectly get rid of this attitude toward He, She, It (the objectification of Myself and the other I) anymore except for speaking kinesthesis. This is neither the I-Thou relation nor the I-He or I-She relation in Buber's sense, but an intermediate stage between them. A quasi I-Thou relation is realized only in the restricted region of speaking kinesthesis, but in the broader remaining region, an I-He (or -She or -It) is established. Thus, the possibility of the alienation of "Thou" becomes undeniable.

Such a quasi-I-Thou relation must be contained even in the dimension of the possible Thou (which will be addressed in the next chapter), although it is originally the third-person dimension (He, She, It) at the threshold of direct communication with Me, insofar as it is usually accompanied by a verbal appeal ("You!"). This is why I can occasionally say "You" without my whole Being. In this sense, it must be an unstable condition that could either proceed to a real encounter or return to the mere I-He (-She, -It) relation. However, a case might sometimes occur where the individual I would intentionally fix this unstable condition and use the quasi I-Thou relation as the instrument of the realization of some concealed I-He (-She, -It) relation. This is why even a swindler can say "You" to his or her victim.

It is true that the genuine I-Thou relation essentially concerns the dimension of purpose, and the I-He (-She, -It) relation concerns the dimension of means or instrument. In the alienation of Thou mentioned above, however, Thou as self-purposive could become the means to realize some I-He (-She, -It) relation, and, on the contrary, the I-He (-She, -It) as a means could become self-purposive in various ways and degrees, as can be generally seen in the life-world.

(2) Concerning the correlation between the I of the I-Thou relation and the I of the I-It relation

The correlation between these two I's has already been almost completely explicated in the answer to the first question raised above. The I of the I-Thou relation is, in its authentic form, total Being seen from the inside either purified from, or dialectically synthesized with, Being seen from the outside. On the contrary, the I of the I-It relation is the multiple complex of Being seen from the inside and Being seen from the outside. The former Being must necessarily assimilate the latter Being in order to be active, but this assimilation generally causes the alienation of the Being of the former's I—and accordingly the alienation of its partner, Thou—unless an authentic mediation between the two Beings occurs.

It is remarkable that the I of the I-Thou relation *(Person)* and the I of the I-It relation (*Eigenwesen*—somatic ego) do not essentially oppose each other on the same plane, contrary to Buber's description, but rather the former I is a dialectic synthesis of the complex moments (namely, "Being seen from the inside" and "Being seen from the outside") that are also constitutive of the latter I. However, this synthesis depends on a mediation far beyond the ability of any I, and hence often this synthesis is left unfinished or the authentic I *(Person)* is alienated as a result. Now we are aware that the situation is exactly the same as in the case of the Thou mentioned above, because it is exactly reciprocal with the case of Thou:

a. The completely mediated "I" corresponds to Thou.
b. The incompletely mediated "I" corresponds to the alienated Thou.
c. The unmediated complex "I" (somatic ego) corresponds to He, She, It.

d. The pure monadic "I" corresponds to the pure monadic He,
She, It as the potential Thou.

It becomes clear that the correlation of these I's is not a simple polarity, contrary to Buber's claim, but what the mediating Third of the authentic I is remains unclear.

(3) Concerning the way Thou appears to Me

How can Thou appear to me in two different ways: on the one hand, as an opposite face to face with Me, but on the other hand, and at the same time, as fulfilling the heavenly sky and spreading over Me?

I consider this somewhat enigmatic statement of Buber concerning Thou is explicable with reference to the monadic structure of I as well as that of the other I. In the true encounter, the I and the other I mediated in their totality by the unknown Third encounter each other. I in my totality and the other I in its totality can aptly be called "monads." Every monad has its intentional center in the body. Thus, in intending the body of the other I and achieving a kinesthetic coupling with it, I embrace the other I in my monad, while at the same time I am embraced into its monad. Buber privileges the Thou (the other I), but I myself also "fulfill" the aura and embrace the other. In short, I find the other I as Being seen from the outside (as body) and, at the same moment, as Being seen from the inside by Me (as my monad) as well as Being seen from the inside by Him/Her (as its monad), which embraces Me as if "fulfilling the heavenly sky" while "spreading over me."[28]

CHAPTER TWELVE

The Phenomenology of Thou

I HAVE TOUCHED ONLY very briefly (in chapter 10) on the tu-logical reduction, a reduction that will disclose the "Thou" who mediates among the community of monads or between the first-person dimension "I" and the third-person dimension "the Other" that are both immanent to life. In chapter 11, I attempted to methodically clarify the structure of Buber's so-called "I-Thou" relation, which might be the best guide for our investigation of true intersubjectivity, by restricting ourselves to the categorical concepts of "Consciousness" and "Being." I have indeed succeeded in disclosing some new aspects of this relation, but in the end I have failed to explicate the true mediator between Being seen from the inside ("I"), Being seen from the inside by the Other (He, She, It as the monad), and Being seen from the outside (He, She, It as phenomena). Without this mediator genuine human relations will be impossible. Therefore, I will investigate Buber's notion of "Thou" again, this time more directly, and I will try to assure the true mediator between I and the Other (He, She, It).

THE MOST DIFFICULT PROBLEM we encounter in Buber's thought is, as is well known, the *dichotomy between the I-Thou relation and the I-It relation.* It is quite remarkable that in the collection entitled *Martin Buber—Bilanz seines Denkens* (1983), at least four authors raise objections to Buber's dichotomy.[1]

Buber believes that our attitude toward the world is dual, reflecting this double relationship between I and the world.[2] The I-Thou relation can be established only with the whole Being of the I, while the I-It relation can never be established with the whole Being of the I. Therefore, these two I's are not the same. The I of the I-Thou relation is a personality *(Person)* who will encounter Thou, while the I of the I-It relation is an individual *(Eigenwesen)* who merely experiences and uses "It." On the other hand, He or She may be substituted for the It of the I-It relation, according to Buber.

In Buber's opinion, we oscillate between these two relations, namely between the two I's, and between Thou and He, She, It. The friend whom I encounter in my wholeness disappears after a while and inevitably becomes an object of observation or evaluation.

Buber writes, "'It' is a pupa. Thou is a butterfly."[3] Thou and It succeed each other alternately, one after the other: "That every Thou in the world must necessarily become 'It' is the sublime melancholia of our lot."[4] Therefore, I should like to ask Buber this question: What is the fundamental difference between Thou and He, She, and It, except for the wholeness and partiality of the Being with which I speak to Them?

Buber writes that Thou is "not an object among many objects,"[5] but that "Thou fulfills the heavenly sky"[6] with its presence: "Not as if there is nothing other than Thou, but everything lives in Thy light."[7] Soon after this, however, he adds, "I can take out the color of his hair, the tone of his speech, and the goodness of his nature . . . but then he is already not my Thou."[8] Thus I must ask him, why are hair color, tone of speech, and goodness of nature not in the light of Thou? It seems, then, as if my Thou can lose all kinds of sensual attributes. How, then, can I identify my Thou? Or is my Thou already not any individual, but rather a universal being? We might take, as another example, a pine tree in the garden, which Buber says is sometimes my Thou. It is no longer an object or a value, but a real presence to me. It has become a "spark of God"[9] in the Jewish mystical sense. However, I would also like to ask, when the pine tree becomes my Thou, should it stop being a pine tree?

If a pine tree and my Thou are related like a pupa and a butterfly, then a pine tree is not yet or no longer my Thou, and my Thou is no longer or not yet a pine tree. However, in our daily experience, the matter seems quite different. For example, when I encounter my friend Mr. A., and during our conversation I feel his real presence with my entire Being, even then he remains my friend A. He never becomes an anonymous Thou. Or, if I encounter a small and beautiful flower in my garden and I find in it Thou, it is nevertheless still a flower with its distinctive shape and color. At this point, I agree with Jochanan Bloch, a pupil of Buber whose book *Die Aporie des Du* makes a very important contribution to the discussion of this problematic. In Bloch's view, Thou is indeed not He, She, or It. However, this "not" is no negation of the dimension of He, She, It *(Es-nicht)*. Rather, it is *"Nichten"* and consequently *"Lichten"* (lighting, clearing) in the Heideggerian sense.[10]

Therefore, we can see that Buber's dichotomous view of the I-Thou and the I-It relation must give way to his other view: *everything lives in the light of Thou.* I will say more clearly that Thou always comes to us through the "He, She, It = World." My friend A. becomes Thou only by the presencing of the Thou through him, namely, through his words, his look, his gestures, his expressions, and so on. A pine tree and a small flower in my garden become Thou only through the presencing of the Thou from out of their shapes, textures, and colors. Even Buber himself says, "The tree itself encounters . . . me."[11] Mr. A. does not disappear when he becomes my Thou; he is still there. But everything he has now appears in a new light. They have become the phenomena of Thou. His words do not form a monologue, his gestures are not play, his look is not empty. All of them indicate something new in them: *my Thou!*

We must not misunderstand this Thou as his "I" or his alter ego. His I is, from my point of view, nothing other than He himself. Thou appears through or by way of his self. He himself is surely the unifying center of phenomena: his words, his gestures, his looks, his expressions, and so on. He himself as a total unity (monad) is therefore not on the same plane as the He known in those partial, dispersed, objectifiable phenomena that are not gathered into a unity. It is then not justifiable to absolutely deny the Being of the monadic whole (Being seen from inside by the Other) to He, She, and It, and to identify them simply with partial, objectifiable phenomena (Being seen from the outside), as Buber did. We must distinguish at least two dimensions here: The I-He (or -She, -It) relation as an intermonadic relation between whole Beings, and the I-He (or -She, -It) relation as my relation to partial Beings—to dispersed phenomena without totality (e.g., kinesthetic movement, color, shape, or sound). The latter dimension might also embrace within itself all kinds of social role exchanges.

However, my Thou necessarily and primarily appears through the former monadic dimension (He himself, She herself, and It itself) even though it must necessarily be accompanied by some phenomena. For example, if I as a teacher speak to students in the classroom, it is possible that my speech is a monologue, that students hear it just like the physical sound of a tape recorder. Even when some formal words are exchanged, there can hardly be any trace of Thou between I and a He or She in this case. Sometimes, though, by chance, a glance or a word from a student can break through this barrier—see! there my Thou happens through him or her.

It seems, then, that three dimensions should be distinguished: (1) The I-Thou relation, (2) the I-He (or -She, -It) relation as inter-monadic, and (3) the I-He (or -She, -It) relation as my relation to objectifiable, dispersed phenomena. However, this will not be the case, as will be shown in what follows.

If He (She, It) could change his (her, its) Being and could become the central route of the phenomenon of Thou, then what about the Being of my I? Could my I also change its Being on becoming the partner of Thou? Buber says that my Thou requires the wholeness of my Being. What does this mean?

When I confront the appearance of Thou in Him, it is evident that I never become a completely other I, as Buber suggests; I do not change from an individual into a personality. If He is still Himself, even upon becoming the phenomenon of Thou for me, and does not change into another He, why then should I change into another I that is completely different from the former, as Buber thought? Although I become aware of the appearance of Thou in Him, I still remain the same I of the I-He relationship (somatic ego = individual), just as He remains Himself. What is important is only that I become aware, just at the instant of encounter, that I am silently called "Thou" by the Thou in Him. Thus far, something new happens in my I, too. It is a very significant characteristic of the phenomenon of Thou that to be aware of Thou in his words, look, and so on is at the same time to be aware of the silent call from Him to Me as his "Thou"! Both kinds of awareness not only occur at the same time but are originally two aspects of one and the same fact.

In other words, in a genuine encounter the I-Thou relation is always and necessarily at the same time the Thou-I relation, and this reciprocity carries a grave importance in itself. This is to say that the

simple I-Thou relation must be duplicated in reverse to become the
Thou = I—I (He, She) = Thou relation.

There seems to be no room here to change into a completely
other I (personality) from the I of the I-He relationship (individual)
through the encounter with Thou. Rather, by virtue of the fact that,
in this encounter, He as monad is changed into the phenomenon of
Thou for Me, *I am also changed into Thou for Him,* while still keeping
my identity, or more exactly, I, too, become the phenomenon of
Thou for Him. In and through myself as monad his Thou toward
himself appears. I become *the individual who is at the same time person-*
ality (the synthetic unity of Being seen from the inside and Being
seen from the outside).

Thus it becomes clear that Thou does not occur only through
He (She, It) = world, but always from both sides, into the I-He (-She,
-It) relation (intermonadic relation) through both poles: I and He
(She, It). This is the fact that Buber expresses still very insufficiently
with the words: "Only with the wholeness of Being can the primary
word I-Thou be spoken."

Thus in reality those who meet here are not I and Thou, but my
Thou and his Thou through I and He, both as monad and as phenomena. We have no reason to essentially distinguish between these
two Thou's. Rather, we should think that the Thou who potentially
abides between I and He once separated into two directions and now
comes together again between us: I and He. Then it becomes clear
that Thou is not primarily my face-to-face partner. Rather, "He" is my
partner in the sense we have outlined. Once in and through his face,
look, or word the Thou appears together with Him, then I, too, inwardly become the passage of Thou, and now Thou and Thou encounter each other between us: I myself and He himself.

Hence the first dimension, to which the dimension of I-He (-She,
-It) as the intermonadic relation and the dimension of I-He (-She, -It)
as my relation to dispersed phenomena are to be added, is not I-Thou
but only the "Thou" who abides, happens, and encounters through
other dimensions. This is to say that only Thou art the true mediator of
I and He, She, It (or the Other) *in front of me,* while Thou simultaneously mediates I myself as monad and my objectifiable phenomena
inside of me.

The most serious error of all kinds of dialogical philosophy, including that of Buber, is to confuse the call to a partner (even in my

wholeness), or the discovery of the Other by the inner self-negation of my monadic I, with the core fact of the real, actual encounter itself. From this error arises the simple identification of the I-Thou relation with the encounter. However, my calling to others with the word "Thou," or discovering an absolutely independent ego in an external being, is a one-way act of the ego and not yet a real encounter, for the one whom I call to or acknowledge as Thou is still He (or She or It) as the possible *topos* of the appearance of the real Thou. Only once the real Thou appears in and through Him or Her does another Thou reciprocally and simultaneously occur through Me to be encountered. My word "Thou" or my inner acknowledgement as Thou does not yet signify a realized, occurring Thou. Rather, they are one-way relations between one possible Thou and another possible Thou. This forms at most the precondition for the realized reciprocal encounter itself.

BUBER WRITES THAT THOU CAN NEVER be (sensually) experienced.[12] However, the word Thou as the second-person pronoun is to be predicated with sensory qualities, just like He (She, It) is: For example, Thou art beautiful. This discrepancy reflects the above-mentioned difference between the possible Thou and the real, occurring Thou in the encounter. That which can never be (sensually) experienced is not the possible Thou, but the encountered Thou. When I really encounter my Thou, I do not, or need not, even say "Thou" anymore, for the realized Thou is not in front of me. I and He (She, It), both as possible Thou, are now embraced by and assimilated into the actual, realized Thou, although without losing their identity. As Buber says, in the very moment of encounter, the center of Being is in neither Me nor Him, but between Me and Him, namely in the realized Thou, which is never sensually predicated.

The limitation of the dialogical relation never lies in the fact that I must always speak to my Thou about something in the third person, namely, about He, She, It. All kinds of personal pronouns—I, Thou, He, She, and It—can signify the possible Thou, the *topos* of appearing of the real Thou. Indeed, from time to time the possible Thou limits or disturbs the realization of the occurring Thou, particularly by dispersing itself into external phenomena, but nevertheless the actually occurring Thou presences Thyself only through the possible Thou as monad and as phenomena. Thou Thyself never appears absolutely and independently. Thou always appears through I and He, She, It, as monads and as phenomena. Mr. A. can become an expression of Thou and a pine tree can, too. Thou Thyself, however, is invisible, intangible, and inaudible. Thou Thyself can only be believed in and waited for through the inner self-negation (as in a wager) of the monadic I by Nothingness, as the Japanese philosopher Nishida taught.[13] Thus Buber's view of the human Thou who must from time to time necessarily be transformed into He, She, It is not correct. Thou never "becomes" He, She, It, and He, She, It—or I—never "become" Thou. Thou only appears from time to time through I and He, She, It, and then disappears from Them. They are only the expression and the passages of Thou.

Consequently, the meaning and expression of Buber's distinction between the human Thou who from time to time becomes He, She, It as its destiny, and the eternal Thou (God) who never becomes He, She, It[14] must change. This is because it becomes clear that the real occurring Thou is essentially transcendent and eternal and never becomes He, She, It, which are only monadic and phenomenal passages of Thou. However, we often call them "Thou" in the sense of the *"possible Thou"*: Mr. A. is my possible Thou when he is called upon: "Mr. A, are you—?" He is not immediately the real Thou who will eventually appear in him. Therefore, instead of Buber's distinction between the human Thou and the eternal Thou, now a new difference, between the possible Thou as monad and phenomenon and the real, actual Thou who appears or occurs in and through the possible Thou, arises.

This new view of Thou coincides nicely in its characterization with Buber's view of the Spirit *(Geist)*. According to Buber, Spirit is something that abides and acts between I and (the possible) Thou. The chief works of the Spirit are language, love, and creation. Buber says, "Language is not inserted into us. Rather, we are in language, and speak out of it . . . so is all the word and all of Spirit. Spirit is between I and (the possible = H.K.) Thou."[15] Again, he writes, "The human dwells in his love. This is not a metaphor, but reality. Love exists between I and (the possible = H.K.) Thou."[16] He discusses further creative acts in the following way: "Creation as the result of spiritual activity is the response to the calling of an anonymous Thou. Here

Thou is speechless and imperceptible, but it calls me with an original idea or an invisible form. I respond to it with works of art or of the intellect, which are the realization of that idea or form."[17] However, insofar as this Thou is an opposite with respect to me, as Buber thought, how, as merely an opposite, can this speechless, imperceptible Thou perform the activity of the Spirit, which, according to Buber, abides not in Thou, but between I and Thou? If the calling of Thou necessarily awakens the I's response, as perhaps Buber would answer, then what is the difference between the I-Thou relation itself and Spirit? Is it necessary to introduce the concept of Spirit in addition to the I-Thou relation? It seems that Buber introduces the idea of Spirit in order to moderate his exaggerated dichotomy between the I-Thou relation and the I-It relation. In fact, the idea of Spirit seems to involve the transitional process from the I-It relation to the I-Thou relation, as, for example, the words "relational force" suggest. However, insofar as his Thou remains absolutely exclusive of He, She, It as before, Spirit's position in Buber's thought cannot avoid ambiguity. Only if, as I have described, this Thou occurs in and through I and He (She, It) and reencounters Thyself again between them, can Thou and Spirit be exactly identified.

Of course, even without any activity of the Spirit there will still be so-called language, so-called love, and so-called creative acts between I and the possible Thou (He, She, It). Without the function of the Spirit as the occurring Thou, however, they are all nothing but ruins . . . as computer language, marriage consultation by computer, and computer art often suggest!

Some philosophers, such as Franz Rosenzweig and Emmanuel Levinas, criticize Buber for his overestimation of the Thou and his underestimation of He, She, It.[18] They say that even in the Bible God is often called "He," and that, moreover, Buber himself is always forced to use the word "Thou" in the third person in his philosophical writings (e.g. "Thou is . . . "). This is certainly true. However, in reality, Buber's error lies not in the overestimation of the Thou. Rather, he did not sufficiently recognize the transcendence of Thou, because he saw it as essentially on the same plane as He, She, It. Therefore "They"—Thou and He, She, It—become successive to and exclusive of each other. As a matter of fact, however, They are not on the same plane. Rather, He, She, It—and I, too—are the only *topoi* where the real Thou appears. On account of this, They are to be called "Thou" in daily life only in the sense of the possible Thou. In this respect, we could say that Buber not only underestimated the real Thou, but also, in a sense, underestimated all the other personal pronouns in absolutely excluding them from any Thou-dimension.

In philosophical language, indeed, the real Thou can be expressed only in the third person, as is done here. This is nothing to be ashamed of; rather, it is the honor and glory of the third person that it becomes the expression and passage of the real Thou, who Thyself never becomes a first or third person. Even the genuine second-person pronoun—Thou or You—often designates not the real Thou, but only the possible Thou (I and He, She, It). In this sense, the second-person pronoun seemingly has no privilege with respect to other personal pronouns. This is not true, however. Indeed, the occurrence of Thou in the world is not identical with the use of the word "Thou," but such a revelation is expressed and appealed to most decisively by this pronoun "Thou." In other words, the pronoun Thou not only means the possible Thou, as do other pronouns, but can also, so to speak, conjure up Thou, whether in the second person as in an appeal, or in the third person, as a philosophical category.

In the same way, the Bible speaks of God as "I" or "He," because these pronouns symbolize the real occurring Thou who alone can fulfill the meaning of these words. This is to be compared with the manner of designating each other in our conversations, as possible Thou's. A possible Thou always calls himself or herself "I," on the one hand, and another possible Thou is often called by his proper noun (third person) on the other hand. In any case, these names remain empty without the occurrence of the real Thou Thyself!

According to the argument above, Emmanuel Levinas's designation of God as *"Ille"* (He) is quite questionable. He believes that the intimate word "Thou" (*Du* in German) allows us to all too easily to forget the infinite transcendence of the Holy, which separates us from Him. Therefore, "He" seems to be a better designation for God. Levinas refers only to the face of another person as "Thou." He writes, "The dimension of divinity is opened up from the face of the human,"[19] or "The face enters into our world from the sphere of absolute foreignness."[20] The face is the trace of the transcendent "He." In Levinas, therefore, the divine He appears only through the human Thou. For us, on the contrary, Thou appears only through (the human) Him as the possible Thou. For Levinas, the I-Thou relation is essentially "asymmetric" because "To say Thou already means to give and . . . separate from this giving . . . there is an ethereal friendship, purely spiritual, which is already fallen and can easily decompose, far distanced from the construction of an original phenomenon."[21] For him, "The Other is, as Other, poor and abandoned,"[22] and without showing solicitude for him, no dialogue is possible. In other words, within ethics is "the other at the same time higher and poorer than I."[23]

Therefore, for Levinas, the I- (possible) Thou relation is much narrower than for Buber, and pragmatically distorted through the former's tendency toward being a scribe. Levinas's letter to Buber of March 11, 1963, reveals that he did not, in the end, understand the difference Buber delineates between solicitude *(Fürsorge)* and the I-Thou relation in a genuine sense (= encounter),[24] namely, the fact that solicitude may remain in the I-He relation, which does not always develop into an encounter, but may also sometimes decompose into a vast hypocrisy such as that of the Pharisees. The asymmetry of the Levinasian I-Thou relation makes the Being-in-between of the occurring Thou between I and He, She, It impossible. Thence inevitably follows the absolute retreat of God from the world into transcendence. Levinas's God consistently remains a *Deus Absconditus.* For its part, Buber's dialogical philosophy of I-Thou can and must be transformed into *the phenomenology of Thou* who occurs in the world between I and He, She, It as somatic beings.

THE THOU WHO OCCURS into the region of the In-Between is no other than the true mediator whom we have been pursuing all along in this book. This Thou mediates the dimension of the first-person pronoun and that of the third-person pronoun inside of Me (as the monadic I and the objectifiable, kinesthetic I) as well as outside of Me (as I and He, She, It) at the same time. Since and insofar as we participate in this pure second-person dimension from time to time through inner preparation and destiny, we are worthy of being called personality.

To be perfectly truthful, this occurring Thou was not disclosed through ourselves or by our initiative. On the contrary, it came to us autonomously to reveal itself by itself, and it will always come to us in this way by itself. In this sense, our method cannot properly be called the "tu-logical reduction," because we have nothing to reduce in order to invite the Thou decisively. Will we invite misunderstanding by daring to call this a "tu-logical conjuration" because our theory is nothing more than our appeal and entreaty for Thou to come?

As Nishida taught,[25] the best stance to take in waiting for the coming of Thou is the negation of my self-identity and the acceptance of the Being of the Other in myself. The deepest paradox of human personality is expressed in the phrase "While keeping my identity, I can become the Other."

It is evident that Thou is the origin of every meaning, because meaning is the pre-thetic Being of the monad modified by Thou. Meaning is truly subjective-objective and acts as the mediator of the self and the Other, too. Meaning contributed by Thou comprises not only linguistic meaning but also practical meaning (value) and aesthetic meaning. Kant's categorical imperative can be better understood through the unconditional occurrence of ethical meaning through Thou, and the inspiration that makes every artistic creation possible can be regarded as the onslaught of aesthetic meaning through the occurring Thou.

It is remarkable that Thou brings forth not only meaning, but meaning always accompanied by the sign in a broad sense, which belongs to the third-person dimension (medium of expression). We call this fact the personification of the meaning. The unity of the meaning and the sign is constituted by the intentionality corresponding to the unity of the monad and the kinesthesis in the somatic ego under the mediation of Thou.

Now when we consider the broader implications of what we have just established, we will come to this question: Is reason, which according to Descartes is "distributed fairly and equally to everyone," not only "transcendental consciousness in general," but also the partial and restricted expression of this occurring Thou? Reason, too, is not originally in our possession or under our control, but rather it comes to us freely and occurs among us. The words "to be illuminated by the light of reason" express this fact. According to our analysis, reason must be the function of the nonobjectifiable apperceptive body *(Leib)*, which shrinks to a cognitive point,[26] and intends the significatively personified noematic sense in cooperation with the all-temporal and all-local kinesthesis produced by (impersonal) transcendental subjectivity in general.[27] As we have seen, noematic sense originates in the pre-thetic world (monad) whose Being is the goal of the occasional projection of the apperceptive body.[28] Since the mediation of the occurring Thou is the precondition of every synthetic cooperation of transcendental subjectivity and the apperceptive body as the pre-thetic self, which is necessary to the personification of meaning, reason, whose apperceptive body is now restricted to cognitive acts, must also be mediated by and involved in Thou. However, the Modern Age has lost sight of Thou and has too hastily identified reason with transcendental subjectivity. Moreover, it made the fatal error of regarding reason as a kind of "ego," whence the endless turmoil concerning the "impersonal" ego followed. Just as in the case of Thou, reason consists—though it is restricted to the modality of cognition—in negating itself toward the Other while keeping its identity. The mediating function of reason between I and the Other, as well as its universality, originates here. This simultaneously objective and subjective character of reason can be explained with the expression "Reason is a partial, restricted, occurrence of Thou."

Thou is, however, essentially much larger, much deeper, and much richer than reason. Therefore, we may call Thou the substratum of reason.

When we receive and accept the approaching Thou, becoming one with it, then and only then do we become personality. The German word *Vernunft (vernehmen)* expresses the passivity of the human being with respect to reason, as the partial phenomenon of Thou. The human also works actively, however, in receiving and accepting Thou, in being embraced, penetrated, and fulfilled with life by Thou. We cannot discriminate at this point between the activity of Thou and that of I. The relation between Thou and I is asymmetric in a different sense from Levinas's depiction of it. It is neither the relation of subject and object, nor of passivity and activity, nor of whole and part in the nonorganism. It will be most akin to the relation of whole and part in the organism, but while a part in the latter is not independent of the whole, I keep myself persistently independent of Thou. I accept Thou autonomously and obey it voluntarily. Therefore, I can also reject Thou on occasion, and evil, that is, "blasphemy to personality," which cannot be found in an organism, can thereby exist.

I owe my thought primarily to Buber. Without his dialogical thought there would not be a pure monistic thought of Thou. However, since Buber's thought lacks any analysis of the body, I must supplement it with the phenomenological method. As a consequence, Buber's thought itself undergoes a rather extensive revision, especially with respect to the dichotomy of the I-Thou relation and the I-It relation. I would like to believe, however, that this revision has made his original intention much clearer than before.

It was Buber himself who strongly insisted on the independence of I from Thou, especially in *I and Thou,* part 3.[29] In this relation he saw the essential difference between the dialogical relation and ecstatic mysticism. The same will be true for our relation between Thou and I. To forget myself and be immersed in Thou is a kind of mysticism, but not a personalism. Indeed, I might forget something when I am fulfilled by Thou, but I shall never forget that I am I. Rather, precisely in, and only in Thou can I live totally and concretely as a monad together with other I's as monads. This coexistence is no longer founded by any analogical relation, but is, so to speak, a paradox beyond all reasoning.

In this way, the occurring Thou reveals itself not only as the foundation of personality but also as the origin and source of the new "Second-Person Philosophy," which reaches far beyond the traditional antagonism of individualism and totalism, or of rationalism and irrationalism, and will also transcend all the differences of the subjectivism (first-personism) called idealism and the objectivism (third-personism) called realism.

SECTION V

CHAPTER THIRTEEN

The "I-Thou" Relationship in Modern Japanese Philosophy

JAPANESE PHILOSOPHY IN AN ACADEMIC SENSE, that is, as a system of thought organized around a strict logical method, began only at the end of the nineteenth century, several decades after the end of National Seclusion. Even the Japanese word for philosophy, *"Tetsugaku,"* was coined only in 1874 by the utilitarian philosopher Amane Nishi (1829-1891), who had studied at Leiden University in Holland from 1862 through 1865. Therefore, in a narrow sense, there is nothing but "modern" Japanese philosophy. The history of modern Japanese philosophy during the first half of what has been little more than a century, has consisted more or less of a constant struggle against, and often a setback in the face of, the absolutism of the imperial government, which was only somewhat enlightened. The pressure exerted by the patriarchal sovereignty of the emperor *(Tennoh)*, combined with the Shintoistic state religion, both explicitly and implicitly disturbed the freedom of thought and the dignity of individuals. However, this is not only the story of the past. Even today, when the deification of the emperor has long since been denied, it is admittedly quite doubtful whether an idea of individuality in the Occidental sense can be evidenced among most Japanese people. Not only do they seem to have a much stronger loyalty and solidarity to the group to which they belong, as is generally known, but, roughly speaking, dedication to a larger group than the individual seems still to form the main purpose of their lives.

Perhaps not unrelated to this fact, Japanese philosophers traditionally have been strongly inclined to seek the philosophical ground of human relationships or of human in-betweenness, in contrast to the strong egocentric tendency of Western philosophers. In spite of the variety of their manner of expression, however, Japanese philosophers, with only a few exceptions, did not use the term "I-Thou" relationship as a philosophical category at all. I will discuss the reasons for this salient fact later.

In this chapter, I will first take up several examples of Japanese theories seeking the philosophical ground of human relationships.

(1) THE INCOMPARABLY BRILLIANT FIGURE Tetsuro Watsuji (1889–1960), who taught at Kyoto and Tokyo Universities, wrote many excellent works addressing diverse domains of the human sciences, including the ancient and modern history of Japan, the history of major world religions, the history of Oriental and Occidental philosophy, philosophical anthropology, ethics, ethnology, comparative cultural studies, the history of the arts, and aesthetics. (His book on philosophical anthropology, *Fudo (Climate)*, has recently been translated into English and German.) He reached the highest level of study at that time in all of these areas. His methodological tool of hermeneutical phenomenology was inspired by Heidegger's *Being and Time*, which he read during his stay in Europe (1927–1928). Throughout his diverse studies, he consistently sought "the human being," a being which, he believed, cherished two sides, individual and social. Human Being is from the beginning not a closed substance or *cogito*, but a dialectical relationship between these two sides, which cannot originally remain in the immanence of the ego, but which reaches out to the transcendence of other human beings. Watsuji points out that the Japanese word "human" *(nin-gen)* etymologically means "between human and human." The human being is, therefore, a priori a relational Being or a Being in-between.

Watsuji describes the relation between hermeneutics and phenomenology as follows: Heidegger defines "phenomenon" as what manifests itself in itself. However, what Heidegger really seeks is Being by way of beings. Thus, from his standpoint, beings must be called the "phenomena" of Being. But as Heidegger himself tells us, beings are essentially different from Being itself (the ontological difference). They are not the "itself" of Being, but rather its "other."

Thus, Being could often conceal itself from its phenomena. Through this hidden state of Being, the insufficiency of Heidegger's definition of "phenomenon" becomes clear. In fact, Being manifests itself not "in itself," but "in others." What manifests itself does so only in what is other to itself. The act of letting something manifest itself in others (as others) is called "interpretation," whereas these others are called "its expression." Heidegger's original intention may be made clearer, Watsuji claims, through a hermeneutical transformation of his phenomenon-concept, while the necessity of the phenomenological reduction that guides our eyes from beings to Being must still be affirmed. Furthermore, Watsuji wants to ultimately substitute his conception of the "human being" as the intra- and intersubjective relationship *(aida-gara)* for Heidegger's "Being."[1]

(2) Wataru Hiromatsu (1933–1994), who died only recently, was a Marxist with an extremely broad range of interests. He tried to found a Marxist theory of the human being as "species-being" *(Gattungswesen)* by means of various philosophical methods, including the phenomenological one. He accepts that my body (or bodily schema) extends into the tools I use, or into another body when I feel the pain of another I (he calls the latter case the Siamese-twin structure). Such experiences are not illusions, even though some philosophers would like to think so, but rather genuine experiences that constitute our daily life. Furthermore, Hiromatsu denies both the simple substantiality of any subject (ego) and that of any object (things). For him, the "phenomenon" is not only "that which manifests itself," as Heidegger stated, but also "that which manifests something other than itself." For example, this fine wooden block manifests "the pencil." The former (the wooden block) is real and individual, but the latter (the pencil) is ideal and universal. Both together constitute the essential double (ideal-real) structure of the object, namely, this pencil. Correspondingly, the subject-ego who recognizes this object-pencil is something more than a simple ego. On the one hand, the ego confronts the object individually here and now; on the other hand, however, it is universally concerned with the ideality of the object beyond here and now, that is, as one of many congruent subjects: we. Thus, the subject-ego, too, has a double structure: I as we, or we as I. Hiromatsu calls this structure "communal subjectivity" as the *conditio sine qua non* of any role-taking and role-playing within our social life. In this way, he reexpresses Marx's well-known thesis in

Thesen über Feuerbach: "In reality, the essence of the human is the totality of the social relationship."[2]

(3) Bin Kimura (1931–) is a phenomenological psychopathologist who is strongly influenced by Nishida's philosophy. He tried to gain an insight into the unique depth of the human relationships of Japanese people. As a specialist in the treatment of schizophrenia, Kimura pays special attention to the phenomenon of self-awareness. Phenomenology means for him "to let that which shows itself be seen from itself in the way in which it shows itself from itself," exactly following Heidegger. However, what manifests itself here is not Being but the self of human Being. Through such a phenomenology, insofar as a doctor becomes self-aware of what manifests itself from his or her patient, the patient will be helped to see what manifests itself from itself, namely, this desired self of him or her.

In this way, Kimura becomes aware of the particular multiplicity of first- and second-person pronouns in the Japanese language. In contrast to the simplicity of European languages, the Japanese language uses about ten different ways of pairing these pronouns in daily usage:

First-person pronoun	Second-person pronoun
ware————————	—nanji
watakushi/watashi————	—anata/anta
boku—————————	—kimi
ore/washi——————	—omae/kisama
uchi—————————	—otaku
etc.	etc.

The use of these pairs is strictly distinguished according to the situation in which a dialogue or communication occurs. The main standard of distinction is the social pecking order between the speaker and the listener.

In Kimura's opinion, this phenomenon manifests not only the comparatively strong dependence of a Japanese self on social order and status, but also the ontological reliance, so to speak, of the Japanese self not upon himself or herself but upon something "between" himself or herself and others. He or she is very flexible and is able to adjust himself or herself to a variety of situations, because unlike the European, he or she has no rigid identity in himself or herself, and instead has a "soft" identity that is always relative to the mediate sphere in which I and others are not yet clearly distinguished. This sphere of "in-between" must not be confused with that of dialogical philosophy (e.g., of Buber), Kimura insists, because while the latter emerges only on the premise of existing individuals (I and He, She, It), the former genetically precedes each individual self and then brings them forth. The individual self must strive to establish even his or her soft identity from this mediate sphere, while he or she is developing, but, having failed to establish it, he or she is threatened by the primitive others who remain undistinguished in themselves. Kimura says, "In the case of schizophrenia, others have already permeated the basis or the home of the self."[3]

I HAVE VERY BRIEFLY DISCUSSED three representative theories of human relationships in modern Japanese philosophy, those of Watsuji, Hiromatsu, and Kimura. The feature common to these theories becomes evident when we pay attention to the mutual stance between the I (ego) and others. There is no absolute difference in the relationship between the individual moment and the social moment in Watsuji, in that between the I and the we of Hiromatsu, or in that between the I and others of Kimura's in-between, that would allow us to decisively divide these poles and contrast them.[4] Rather, these thinkers share a more or less common inclination to reduce the individual moment in some way to the social or universal, even if this should be a primitive, preconscious moment. In my opinion, this is the very reason why they almost never use the term "I-Thou" as a philosophical category, for the I-Thou relation always presupposes the microcosmic or monadic Being of both the I and the Thou. For example, Buber writes in *Das Problem des Menschen*, "[For Aristotle] a man is simply included in the world, and *does not include the world in himself* at the same time" (emphasis added).[5] The latter half of this sentence suggests the human monadic structure that Buber is thinking of. In *I and Thou*, Buber also writes, "The Thou is not a thing among things . . . but has no neighborhood, nor seam, and fills the heavenly sky."[6] These words can be seen as another expression of the monadic structure of the human. However, the coexistence of the human and others as monads in itself implies a kind of contradiction, because every monad contains the unique center of one and the same world. The contradiction between human and human as monads cannot be mediated by Hegelian dialectics, because genuine individuality can never be progressively reduced to anything particular, even if motivated by its inner and outer contradiction. The contradiction among monadic individuals necessitates a new dialectic. Perhaps the only philosopher in modern Japan who clearly recognized this fact exceptionally was Kitaro Nishida (1870–1945), the founder of the Kyoto school of philosophy.

Nishida became the greatest figure of modern Japanese philosophy through his broad influence on the philosophical thinking of Japan. Hardly any Japanese philosopher who shows any originality is out of the range of the influence of Nishida's thought. This fascination seems to arise out of his deep insight into reality, or into the ultimate unity that prevails throughout the multiplicity of world phenomena. This unity is not a mere object of cognition, but rather something that demands the whole personality of its observers. Perhaps Nishida reached this insight through his years-long practice of Zen. He expressed this unity of the universe, as well as of the human personality, first by the phrase "pure experience" *(junsui-keiken)*, and then by "seated field" *(basho)* in his later thought. This unity is described, on the one hand, as the unity of an anonymous, cosmological consciousness and true Being, and, on the other hand, as the unity of coexisting monads. In this unity every opposition and even every contradiction is reconciled, because every difference always presupposes a unity. Nishida grasped this unity as "Nothingness," because any kind of Being in the Occidental sense could not reconcile or mediate the contradiction between monad and monad.

The Hegelian contradiction between master and slave does not yet express the contradiction between monads, and the Leibnizian preestablished harmony among monads only evades the problem. I will follow Nishida's argument in accordance with his article "Watashi to Nanji"[7] ("I and You") (1932).[8] This article seems to have been inspired by his reading of Friedrich Gogarten's book *Ich glaube an den drei-einigen Gott (I Believe in the Trinity of God)* (1926), but the argument itself reflects the development of Nishida's original thought. Nishida compares *basho,* the ultimate unity, to a circle without circumference, which is to have its own numberless centers everywhere in itself, while individuals are compared to circles with infinite circumferences (monads), which identify their centers with the centers of the above-mentioned circle without circumference *(basho)*. This metaphor signifies that each individual cannot be defined as a moment of any finite world, but must rather be defined as a unique center of the infinite world, while accepting, at the same time, the coexistence with one another in Nothingness. The circle without any circumference, which alone secures the coexistence of its innumerable centers, is a metaphor for Nothingness. Yet how does this Nothingness make the encounter of two individuals as I and Thou possible? According to Nishida, Nothingness defines the individual ego not from the outside, but from the inside. I encounter the Nothingness that negates my identity deep in my depths as an absolute otherness. I accept the other through the basis of my whole Being, including my body. Otherwise expressed, I see an absolute other in myself, while still retaining my identity. Nishida calls this condition *the absolutely contradictory self-identity of myself.* However, because this occurs through the mediation of Nothingness, which is also transcendent to me, to see the other in myself means precisely to see myself in the transcendent other at the same time. However, this is completely different from projecting my empathy into the other, because there is no continuity between the I and the other. I and the other break off from each other completely, as monads without windows. Mediation by Nothingness is no analogical inference, either, because the existence of the other is given as something more than the object of inference. Rather, I possess an absolute other in my fundament and I turn from my fundament to the other in his or her totality. This is a leap mediated by Nothingness: an *im-mediate* leap. Nishida calls this seeming paradox the genuine dialectic of *basho.*

Thus I find the other before me not through any natural givenness, nor by empathy, nor by any analogical inference, but only through the Nothingness in me that negates my identity. From the temporal point of view an eternal *nunc stans* corresponds to the Nothingness, while a present temporal moment corresponds to individual motivation. Authentic determination occurs at the intersection of these two types of present.

Nishida calls the other who is found in this way "Thou," and he refers to the true love that emerges between I and Thou. Though he does not mention the I-It relation that contrasts to the I-Thou relation, Nishida's conception of I-Thou can be understood to almost coincide with that of Martin Buber. It is especially worthwhile to mention that Nishida's I and Thou are both monads, individuals in their totality (circles with infinite circumferences), and in this point they are identical with the I and Thou of Buber, who says that they can establish their mutual relationship "only with total Being." Nishida's Nothingness as mediation without mediator is parallel to Buber's "Kingdom of Betweenness," which is the anonymous field that prevails between I and Thou, but is not a mediator in the ordinary sense (because Buber denies any mediation between I and Thou). Nishida's discontinuous (absolutely negated) continuity between I and Thou corresponds to Buber's primeval distance *(Ur-distanz)* and the connection *(Beziehung)* between I and Thou. In this way, although Nishida seems not to have read Buber's works, his new dialectic of *basho* could be regarded as providing a deeper philosophical ground for Buber's idea of a dialogical principle.

Now one question still remains for us, concerning Nishida as well as Buber: What is the ultimate relation between this Nothingness as Betweenness and the Thou who appears face to face with me? Nothingness will indeed be a *conditio sine qua non*, a necessary condition for the appearing of Thou. But is it also an adequate condition?

BUBER'S WORKS WERE INTRODUCED into Japan at the end of the 1950s. The first translation of *I and Thou* appeared in 1958, and my translation of *Das Problem des Menschen* was published in 1961. I was fascinated by his dialogical thought. However, as I studied Buber, the above-mentioned question, namely, that of the ultimate relation between the Kingdom of Between and the Thou, arose and became more and more intense. Indeed, the Thou must be mediated to me by Nothingness, but then this Thou must necessarily appear or occur to me through the natural world (Buber's world of It), and particularly through the body. Now this interrelation is quite reciprocal, and at the moment of Thou's appearance for me, I myself already become another Thou that is just then appearing for another I. Or rather, the Thou also appears from inside me, penetrating my body, toward another I. Neither Buber nor Nishida sufficiently considers the reciprocity and coincidence of this appearing of the Thou on both sides. Thence arose this question: Is it not the case that the Thou on both sides is the same Thou? Is this Thou not a kind of supermonad that mediates the individual I and I? What is the relation between Nothingness as Betweenness and this Thou?

Before answering these questions directly, recall once more the problem proper to Buber's Thou mentioned in the previous chapter. It will help to understand the aporia of the dimension of Thou better. The urgent problem that is left to us is to overcome the dichotomy between the I-Thou relation and the I-It relation in Buber's thought, since, insofar as both relations are separate, it will be impossible to connect Thou and In-Betweenness in general.

Buber believes that our attitude toward the world is double according to these dual relations between I and the world. The I-Thou relation is established only with the totality of I, while the I-It relation is established merely with a part of I. Therefore, these two I's are not the same. Buber continues, "'It' is a pupa. Thou is a butterfly."[9] Thou and It succeed each other alternately. It is the melancholic destiny of the human Thou to become It (or He or She) from time to time.

Furthermore, according to Buber, the Thou is not an object among many objects; the Thou fulfills the heavenly sky with its presence. The Thou is exclusive, but everything is embraced in its light. Soon after that, Buber also says that when I see the color of one's hair, hear the tone of one's speech, and feel the goodness of one's nature, then he/she is already not my Thou.

If a human with its various attributes and my Thou are related like a pupa and a butterfly, then a human is not yet or no longer my Thou, and my Thou is not yet or no longer a human. But in our daily experience, the matter seems quite different. For example, when I encounter one of my friends, Mr. A., and, during our conversation, I feel his real presence, then he still remains my friend A. He never becomes an anonymous Thou.

Therefore, we can see that Buber's dichotomous view of the I-Thou and the I-It relation must give way to his other view: *everything lives in the light of Thou.* I will say more clearly that Thou always comes to us through the "He, She, It = World." Even Buber himself says, "The tree itself ... encounters me."[10] My friend A. becomes Thou only by the presencing of the Thou through him. Mr. A. does not disappear when he becomes my Thou; he is still there. But everything he has now appears in a new light. They have become the phenomena of Thou.

We must not misunderstand this Thou as his "I" or his alter ego.

His I is, from my point of view, nothing other than He himself. Thou appears through or by way of his self. He is surely the unifying center of phenomena: his words, his gestures, his looks, his expressions, and so forth. He as monad (as a whole) is therefore not in the same dimension as the He as those merely partial, dispersed, objectifiable phenomena. It is therefore not justifiable to absolutely deny the Being of the monadic whole (Being seen from inside by the Other) to He, She, and It, and to identify them simply with partial, objectifiable phenomena (Being seen from the outside), as Buber did. Rather, we must differentiate between at least two dimensions here: The I-He (or -She, -It) relation as an intermonadic relation between whole Beings, and the I-He (or -She, -It) relation as my relation to partial, dispersed phenomena (e.g., kinesthetic movement, color, shape, and sound). Furthermore, my Thou always appears through the former monadic dimension: He himself, She Herself, and It Itself.

Apparently, then, three dimensions should be distinguished: (1) The I-Thou relation, (2) the I-He (or -She, -It) relation as intermonadic, and (3) the I-He (or -She, -It) relation as my relation to objectifiable, dispersed phenomena. However, this is not the case.

It is very important to recognize that with the phenomenon of Thou, to be aware of Thou in him or her is at the same time to be aware of the silent call from him or her to me as his or her Thou! Both these kinds of awareness not only occur at the same time but are two aspects of one and the same thing. By the fact that, in this encounter, he or she as a monad changes into the phenomenon of Thou for me, I also change into Thou for him or her, while still keeping my identity. His or her Thou toward himself or herself occurs in me as a monad. This is the fact that Buber expresses very inadequately by the words "The primary words I-Thou can only be spoken with the totality of Being."[11]

Thus, in reality, those who meet here are not I and Thou, but my Thou and his (or her) Thou through I and he or she (as monads and phenomena). I think that the Thou who abides potentially between I and he or she must separate into two directions and meet each other again between us. Then it becomes clear that Thou is not my face-to-face partner. Rather "He" or "She" had better be called my partner. When in his or her face, look, or word Thou appears, then I, too, inwardly become a passage of Thou, and now Thou and Thou encounter each other between us. Hence, the first dimension, to which the two dimensions of I-He (She, It) — as an intermonadic relation and as a relation to dispersed phenomena — are to be added, is not I-Thou, but simply Thou, who happens only by way of these two I-He (She, It) relations.

In this way, the dichotomy in Buber's thought is decisively overcome. The most serious mistake of all kinds of dialogical philosophy, including that of Buber and Nishida, is to confuse the appeal to my Thou with my wholeness, or the discovery of Thou by the inner self-negation of the I through Nothingness with the core fact of a real, actual encounter itself. From here the simple identification of the I-Thou relation with the genuine encounter erroneously arises. However, my appealing with the word "Thou," or my discovering of the external other, is still a one-way act of mine and not yet a real, actual encounter with Thou. It is only a precondition of it, for those who are appealed to or acknowledged as I are still He or She or It (as monad or phenomena) as the possible topos of the appearance of my real Thou. And this real, occurring Thou in him or her immediately awakens another Thou in me, to encounter Thyself.

Thus the dialogical philosophy of Buber must necessarily be transformed into the *phenomenology of Thou*. Consequently, it becomes clear that Nishida's Nothingness provides the field of appearance for this deepened Thou: the intermonadic relation.

WE BEGAN BY CONSIDERING THREE Japanese philosophers who were very concerned with human relations but who did not refer to the I-Thou relation at all. Then we introduced the I-Thou relation conceived by Nishida, which is very close to Buber's idea. Nishida's idea of the inner self-negation of the monadic I, which provides this relation, can be regarded as the ontological foundation of the I-Thou relation and as the deepening of Buber's view of the simple whole Being of I in the I-Thou relation. Nishida's theory might justly be called the *Buddhistic contribution* to dialogical philosophy.

We have also raised questions about the relation between Nishda's Nothingness and the Thou. This Nothingness makes the intermonadic relation between I and the Other possible through the inner self-negation of I. However, the Other as monad found in this way is only a possible Thou in our sense, because the real, actual

encounter with Thou through him (her, it) is still virtually suspended. While Nishida mentions intermonadic actions such as expression and intuition that are very similar to artistic creation, he
never refers to the reciprocity and the coincidence of the appearing
of the same Thou on both sides. Buber also does not address this
problem. However, it has still been Nishida's remarkable achieve-
ment in the history of philosophy that he monadologically founded
the precondition of the real, actual encounter as the monad-
complex between I and a possible Thou. Needless to say, Buber's
great accomplishment was the inauguration of what now needs to
become "the phenomenology of Thou."

Chapter Fourteen

Some Phenomenological Elements of the Japanese Cultural Tradition

THE MOST DIFFICULT THING FOR US is to know ourselves, as the ancient Greeks were already aware.[1] For the Japanese, this is also true. To investigate the fundamental nature of the Japanese way of thinking in general would be a theme that is too difficult and too broad to address in the scope of this chapter. Therefore, let us rather take up quite selectively some traditional cultural aspects that clearly manifest Japanese characteristics, and then try to suggest what underlies them as their common philosophical basis. I hope that their relation to phenomenology will become clear in the course of the argument itself.

The first aspect of Japanese culture I will take up is the "haiku," the world's shortest poetic form, consisting of only seventeen syllables, which are divided into three lines of five, seven, and five syllables, respectively. The tradition of the haiku goes back more than a thousand years in Japan, but it was restored and raised to a standard of genuine art by Basho Matsuo (1644-1694), the greatest haiku master who ever lived. In Japan, the haiku is not merely a legacy of the past but is still a favorite medium for ordinary people, and many big newspapers reserve a space for their contributions every week.

It is almost impossible to translate haiku into European languages, but I must try in order to suggest what is sung there.

Basho wrote a famous haiku about a frog that reads as follows:

By an old pond—   Furuike ya
Hark! a sound of water   Kawazu tobikomu
Of jumping frog   Mizu no oto
          (1686)

To appreciate a haiku, one must distinguish between a thing and an occurrence. We live in the world of things: buildings, trees, tables, ballpoint pens, flowers, cars, clouds, smog, oxygen, bread, newspapers, cigarettes, and so forth. All of these are things. The word "thing" does not always refer to a material thing. A human being is a living thing, and I myself, according to Descartes, am a thinking thing *(res cogitans)*. In general, whatever functions as the subject of a sentence may be called a thing. When we say "The house is . . ." or "The flower is . . . ," we regard these subjects, which are expressed by words, as dense, lasting, and substantial things. The human being's way of thinking exhibits a strong tendency to substantialize every subject as a thing.

But do we ever encounter a thing itself? For example, when we recognize a flower, we see its color and shape, but we never see the flower itself. That is to say, when we encounter a flower, we encounter first its color and shape, namely the qualities that are predicated of it. Then and only then, based on these elements, can we reach the flower itself. Thus, we really only encounter not the substantial flower but rather the fact of "being red" or "blooming." We call such facts, which are not substantial things, but only predicative occurrences, "phenomena." A phenomenon is a fact and an occurrence. It is quite different from a thing. It has no inertia and no weight. It occurs only in the present moment of the encounter between *x* and me. Furthermore, these occurrences in their purest mode (antepredicative mode) are only encountered when they are freed from any substance or subject, namely, they are encountered only in "Nothingness" or in the absence of the Being of the material world as the natural ground of human beings.

According to Husserl's phenomenology, the natural world of things must be reduced through the phenomenological reduction to phenomena. These phenomena are regarded as the material *(hyle)* of the world-constituting acts of intentionality, and have their place of occurrence only in the stream of my consciousness. Husserl's grasp of the phenomenon is insufficient and too narrow, because the phenomenon in its purest mode, which is not yet even the predicate of any subject, but rather is ante-predicative, is not the occurrence of any intentional object, but that of the natural world as a whole, which conceals itself behind the Nothingness. Even in his later thought, when Husserl located phenomena in the life-world, he still insisted upon the stance of the onlooker, and hence the bracketing of the world remains so inadequate that he never reached the Nothingness that is the mask or veil of the Being of the natural world. Therefore, we can say that the haiku is the result of a more radical phenomenological reduction than any Husserl ever performed. This Nothingness is completely different from the infinite space of Newtonian physics, however, because the latter is the place where the material world is not absent, but is retained as dispersed and scattered into innumerable individual things.

In Nothingness the pure phenomenon is ante-predicative. It has no proper subject. When we are struck by the beauty of the sunset, we are indifferent as to whether it is the sky or the cloud that is red. Red is red: that is all. In this moment of encounter with the pure phenomenon, time never flows, but rather springs forth.

At the moment in which we escape from our situation of being surrounded by things, we enter the dimension of the encounter with pure phenomena and find a completely new world. In the dimension of physical things, it is things that are most substantial, while the space surrounding them is empty. By contrast, in the dimension of pure phenomena, the horizonal Nothingness has the richest content, and each phenomenon is an occurrence of it intuitively and hermeneutically. The "red" becomes an occurrence of the Nothingness that horizons it. It is no longer an attribute of the substance "flower." Here, even the flower itself has already become one of the occurrences of Nothingness.

Let us return to the frog haiku of Basho. In this poem there is no subject, as ordinarily found in a sentence: neither pond, nor frog, nor sound, nor water, is a "subject." All of them are ante-predicates of an anonymous nature that is concealed behind the Nothingness before us. They are occurrences of one and the same universe. Basho, who was standing by the pond, unexpectedly encountered the sound of water as a pure phenomenon. Simultaneously, he felt the age of the pond, the lives of small creatures in the water, the smell of moss and the embracing tranquility of the area, all integrated into the single sound of water. Moreover, even the ego of the poet himself who heard the sound was intuited in this sound. When the sound of water is regarded as something physical, it is impossible to intuit any subject of the consciousness in an object-thing. But a sound regarded as a pure phenomenon is a place where the conscious ego directly encounters the universe as a whole. Thus, it seems as if this poem itself is a silent song of veiled nature through the voice of the poet.

The famous Japanese philosopher Nishida once expressed his viewpoint in this way: "To see the shapes of the shapeless, and to hear the voices of the voiceless." The shapeless or the voiceless is the universe, which is originally infinite and eternally silent. We see and hear universal nature only through its occurrences, namely, through pure phenomena that are transient and frail, but are sometimes fixed and expressed, through good fortune, by great artists in their immortal masterpieces.

The second traditional Japanese aspect we will consider is body-surface consciousness, which constitutes the fundamental stance of various traditional Japanese athletic arts (e.g., judo or karate) and also of traditional dances.

Generally speaking, there has been a strong tendency in Japanese philosophical thought to criticize and protest against the Cartesian dualism between mind and body. For Japanese philosophers, it is difficult to think of consciousness without any bodily foundation. This criticism has its origin in our traditional stance in the practical dimension.

Here the matter concerns only daily practical experiences, but in order to clarify it and to become aware of it, it is necessary to perform a radical phenomenological reduction of the kind described above. In the Nothingness as the absence of Being of the natural world, my body reveals itself in two different aspects: as an extensional phantom, on the one hand, and as the noninterchangeable center of an individual monad on the other. Here, the term "phantom" refers not to a lack of reality but to a pure extensionality without weight, tangibility, or hardness. It is also a kind of pure phenomenon. As a body, however, it is not only an object of consciousness but also the seat of consciousness. Particularly in the practical dimension, when we are unreflectively absorbed in an action, what is the relation between consciousness and its body? It is clear that it is no longer the epistemological relation between subject and object, but Occidental philosophy, including Husserl's phenomenology, has not come up with any effective new category to explain it.

Let us begin with the reflective stance of my bodily consciousness. My reflective perspective stands some distance apart from my phantom body, which is objectified to there. However, the more my attention concentrates on the object of action, and not on my body, the narrower becomes the reflective gap between my perspective and my body, until it eventually disappears. What happens then? We believe that one's consciousness adheres to and is distributed over the entire surface of one's phantom body. Here, subject becomes object and object becomes subject, or consciousness becomes body and body becomes consciousness. Insofar as the perceiver and the perceived coincide with each other, we can call it a completely double sensation. This new complex of subject and object, or of consciousness and body, is the genuine agent of our praxis. I would like to call this consciousness, which is united completely with its body, the body-surface consciousness (or the apperceptive body). One might understand it as consciousness wearing its body. It looks at the world and its various objects only through the surface of the body. We say "The world is around me," but how do we know it with our limited narrow visible perspective? We "look" around the world even with our backs, because our backs, too, have consciousness upon their surfaces. When we sit down on a chair, it goes out of sight at the last moment, but we nevertheless continue "looking" at it with our hips and waist. Or, when we are sitting in a classroom, we usually "look" at the ceiling of the room with the tops of our head, and the rear wall of the room with our backs. Otherwise, we could not behave as freely as we do. When we are sitting in front of a piano and playing a piece of music by looking at the score, then the keys of the piano are more or less visible, not through the eyes but through the tips of our fingers. The sense or intuition of extensionality is not identical with the vision of the eyes, but rather is the foundation of the latter. Even blind people have a sense of extensionality and can play the piano, because they have body-surface consciousness too. A good shortstop in baseball can see with his body where a runner is going, even while he is looking at the ground ball in order to field it. In the Japanese traditional Noh dance, the actor wears a mask on stage, and when he looks at the moon in the sky, he is instructed to look with his belly, not his eyes.

When we look at an object, it is always present in its solidity together with its invisible sides. Husserl called the appearance of these invisible sides appresentation, namely, as an addition to the object's presentation, but he was unable to explain this phenomenon adequately. Our body-surface consciousness looks at an object in accordance and in analogy with its own solidity as an extensional body. Nishida says we must "look at a thing by becoming a thing." The whole surface of my body corresponds to the whole surface of the object, whether it is visible or not. I have never seen my back and shall never see it directly with my eyes, but nevertheless it is always visible to my body-surface consciousness. In the same way, the back of an object is invisible to my eyes, but it is still visible to my body-surface consciousness.

In the practical dimension, the phantom body is extremely flexible and changeable in scale and shape. When I drive my car, my body expands to the size of the car, and I feel the width of the car as if it were of my body, so that I can instantaneously judge whether a way is passable or not. When I use a ballpoint, my finger extends to the top of the pen in contact with the paper and feels a tangibility there, unthinkable from a purely physiological standpoint. In general, my body expands and envelops the tool it is using into itself. In this sense, it is very plausible to call both the extensional body and the tool-object by the same name, *Körper,* or physical body. Bodily action is nothing other than the dynamic and continuous change of the shape of the phantom body, which must be controlled by bodily apperception in accordance with the kinesthetic schema stored as nondated memory in the body-surface consciousness. The body-surface consciousness lives in the ever-standing present and is open to the future, that is, it is practical only in its nonreflective stance. Therefore, in traditional Japanese athletic arts the most important thing is to concentrate on the present moment, where time never flows but is absorbed or springs forth.

We have taken up two issues, haiku and body-surface consciousness, as examples of the Japanese cultural tradition, which might be called phenomenological. They concern, respectively, natural and bodily phenomena, which are revealed only by way of a certain reduction of the Being of the natural material world. This reduction is indeed closely akin to Husserlian phenomenology, insofar as it is concerned with the *epoché* of the naive belief in the Being of the world. This similarity notwithstanding, they are very different. In the case of Husserl, the Being that is bracketed is said to cease its effect with the bracketing, but in the case we are describing, the Being that is bracketed or veiled by Nothingness does not cease to have an effect. Rather, it expresses itself through natural phenomena and exercises its influence as the arbitrary, impulsive motivation of bodily action, in which case bodily apperception feels itself to be subject to an anonymous subject beyond its ego. The difference between these two reductions seems to mainly arise from the difference between the eminently theoretical stance of Husserlian phenomenology and the more practical nature of ours.

Through this comparative investigation of phenomenological reductions we are made aware that there can be various phenomenological reductions with different effects. For example, Heidegger's phenomenological ontology claims literally no reduction as its method, and is usually regarded as a phenomenology that employs no reduction, yet his definition of anxiety as the revelation of the Nothingness of the world suggests that the mood of anxiety could virtually be a kind of phenomenological reduction that transforms our naive confidence in the Being of the world.

The Japanese phenomenological tradition, which has been revealed in haiku and in body-surface consciousness, has its historical basis in Buddhism, especially in Zen Buddhism beginning in the thirteenth century. The Being of the natural material world that is to be reduced to Nothingness is originally not only outside of us, but also inside of the body, and underlying it as its ontological basis. It is the Being of the individual ego in the natural attitude. Buddhist teachings ask us to find complete otherness that does not belong to us, not only outside of us, but also in our very Being. Our phenomenological reduction is performed along these lines, and thus individual Being is necessarily shifted away, distanced, and opened up all the more to the otherness of others. Now I am removed from the natural world, which is essentially egocentric, into a new horizon called Nothingness, which is essentially intersubjective because this Nothingness always points my Being, now alienated to our Being, through its veil far in the distance. Nothingness is the veil of Being-together. How eminently this situation is symbolized by the traditional Japanese tea ceremony! In a small, clean room of a plain wooden teahouse, the host and a few guests gather and are seated on the same straw mat. There is very little decoration: only a vase with a flower on a stand or one black and white drawing on the wall. The host boils the water and serves tea with etiquette to the guests in turn with one and the same cup! The guests receive the tea and drink it in turn, also according to etiquette, and praise the valuable cup. This single cup seems to symbolize the common Being participated in by all the members, a Being that is also pointed to by the plainness (Nothingness) of the surroundings as its veil. Being must be veiled; it must remain at a distance, for a too-near approach would necessarily threaten its commonness. The ontological distance of Being is the very proof of the communion of our society.

We began with haiku and body-surface consciousness in Japanese culture, both of which are concerned with the pure phenomenon by way of a kind of phenomenological reduction. Nothingness, rather than the natural world, is the horizon where these pure phenomena occur. However, from an ontological standpoint, Nothingness is the disclosure of the Being of our communalized world, which is far distant and absent here at this moment. By living in Nothingness rather than in Being, we Japanese have had a very unique relation to phenomenalized things through the concentrated skill of body-surface consciousness. Even in the dimension of modern technology, this fundamental relation proved to be advantageous. For example, to understand the mechanism of a machine, we can and must grasp it as an analogon of our body-phantom.

Moreover, the phenomenalization of things has helped the Japanese to absorb foreign culture more easily. We use several thousand Chinese characters together with Japanese alphabets in our writing, and we use chopsticks alternately with knife and fork according to what we eat. We walk in shoes on the street and in the office, but once we return home we remove our shoes. However one might evaluate such a mixed culture, no one can deny the eminent adaptability of our people.

However, as the above discussion already suggests, a fundamental problem lies explicitly in our culture. This is the absence of a Being that is mine. Our kind of phenomenological reduction not only brings forth Nothingness but also shifts the Being of the individual ego away, negating its self-identity and opening it to the otherness of the other. This is the ontological basis of Japanese life. Notwithstanding the efforts of many modern Japanese Buddhist philosophers, including Nishida, the Being of individuality has never been adequately recovered. In other words, the Japanese people have long had an ontological basis for their society, but not one for individuality. This is the historically necessary consequence of our phenomenal naturalism. This lack of an ontological basis of individuality has already been proved by the undeniable comparative weakness in creativity and individual responsibility. It is well known that our people have shown more ability in the area of improvement than in creative invention. In addition, the ambivalent attitude of the Japanese toward responsibility for World War II cannot be separated from the weakness of the individual consciousness. How can we recover the Being of individuality while retaining the Nothingness and the ontological distance gained through our type of phenomenological reduction? This is the theme that is given to us. This is not only a theme for education, but first and foremost, for phenomenological ontology.

NOTES

CHAPTER 1

1. Edmund Husserl, *Cartesianische Meditationen*, Husserliana 1 (The Hague: Martinus Nijhoff, 1950), 121-22. *Cartesian Meditations*, trans. Dorion Cairns (The Hague: Martinus Nijhoff, 1960), 89ff. Both editions are hereafter abbreviated CM, with citations first from the German, and then from the English edition. After initial introduction by title, publisher, and date, all volumes of Husserliana will subsequently be referred to as *Hua*, followed by volume and page number.

2. CM 121/89.

3. Michael Theunissen, *Der Andere* (Berlin: de Gruyter, 1965), 58.

4. Ibid., 94ff.

5. *CM* 139/109.

6. *CM* 145-46/116.

7. The phenomenological description of the mode of the absolute Here as the monad will be given in chapters 5, 6, and 7.

8. *CM* 148/119.

9. *CM* 146/116-17.

10. This is just the open horizonality of the world.

11. Cf. Sartre, *L'être et le néant* (Paris: Gallimard, 1953), 336-40.

CHAPTER 2

1. "Es ist eine Naivität, anthropologisch weltlich bei der Subjekt-Objekt-Korrelation stehenzubleiben und die phänomenologischen Aufweisungen meiner ersten Schriften als die dieser Korrelation zu mißdeuten." *Die Krisis der europäischen Wissenschaften und die transzendentale Phänomenologie* (The Hague: Martinus Nijhoff, 1954), *Hua* 6:265.

Note: In-text translations are those of the author unless otherwise indicated.

2. "Es is dann aber klar, daß diese Beziehung [von der vollen Noesis auf das volle Noema] nicht diejenige sein kann, welche in der Rede von der Beziehung des Bewußtseins auf sein intentional Gegenständliches gemeint ist. . . . Wir werden darauf aufmerksam, daß wir mit der Rede von der Beziehung des Bewußtseins auf sein Gegenständliches verwiesen auf ein innerstes Moment des Noema. Es ist nicht der . . . Kern selbst, sondern etwas, das sozusagen den notwendigen Zentralpunkt des Kerns ausmacht." *Ideen zu einer reinen Phänomenologie und phänomenologische Philosophie, Erstes Buch* (The Hague: Martinus Nijhoff, 1950), *Hua* 3:318.

3. "Von seinen Beziehungsweisen oder Verhaltungsweisen abgesehen, ist es völlig leer an Wesenskomponenten, es hat gar keinen explikabeln

Inhalt, es ist an und für sich unbeschreiblich: reines Ich und nichts weiter" (*Hua* 3:135).

4. "Die Reflexion (ist das) sich Richten des Ich auf seine Erlebnisse und in eins damit das Vollziehen von Akten des cogito, in denen sich das Ich auf seine Erlebnisse richtet" (*Hua* 3:183).

5. *Hua* 3:212.

6. "Ich bemerke nebenbei, daß der viel kürzere Weg zur transzendentale Epoché in meinem *Ideen* . . . den großen Nachteil hat, daß er zwar wie in einem Sprunge schon zum transzendentalen ego führt, dieses aber . . . in einer scheinbaren Inhaltsleer zur Sicht bringt, in der man zunächst ratlos ist, was damit gewonnen sein soll" (Hua 6:157f). This translation was taken from Edmund Husserl, *The Crisis of European Sciences and Transcendental Phenomenology*, trans. David Carr (Evanston: Northwestern University Press, 1970), 155.

7. "Von dem reinen oder transzendentalen Ich unterscheiden wir . . . das reale seelische Subject, bzw. die Seele, das identische psychische Wesen, das verknüpft mit dem jeweiligen Menschen und Tierleib das substantiel-reale Doppelwesen Mensch oder Tier, Animal, ausmacht." *Ideen zu einer reinen Phänomenologie und phänomenologische Philosophie, Zweites Buch* (The Hague: Martinus Nijhoff, 1952), *Hua* 4:120.

8. "Wir unterscheiden also von der reinen Reflexion, der Reflexion auf das wesensmäßig zu jedem cogito gehörige reine Ich, die reflexive thematische Erfahrung auf Grund der erwachsenen Erfahrungsapperzeption, deren intentionaler Gegenstand dieses empirische Ich, das Ich der empirischen Intentionalität ist" (*Hua* 4:249).

9. "Jedes entwickelte Subjekt is nich bloß Bewußtseinsstrom mit reinem Ich, sondern es hat sich auch eine Zentrierung in der Form 'Ich' vollzogen. Das Ich ist aus eigenen Stellungsnahmen und aus eigenen Gewohnheiten und Vermögen konstutuierte apperzeptive Einheit, deren Kern das reine Ich ist" (*Hua* 4:265).

10. "Der geistige Sinn ist, die sinnlichen Erscheinungen beseelend, mit ihnen in gewisser Weise verschmolzen statt in einem verbundenen Nebeneinander nur verbunden" (*Hua* 4:238).

11. "Die Seele gehört zur Person als fundierender Untergrund" (*Hua* 4:280).

12. "Die Person ist das Sujekt, das selbstverantwortlich ist, das frei und geknechtet, unfrei ist" (*Hua* 4:257).

13. "Also reine Psychologie in sich selbst ist identisch mit Transzendentalphilosophie als Wissenschaft von der transzendentalen Subjektivität" (*Hua* 6:261).

14. *Erste Philosophie, Zweiter Teil* (The Hague: Martinus Nijhoff, 1959), *Hua* 8:82ff.

15. "Und erst in den letzten Tagen begann ich zu übersehen, inwiefern Ihre Betonung der reinen Psychologie den Boden gibt, die Fragen der transzendentalen Subjektivität und ihres Verhältnis zum rein Seelischen zu klären, bzw. allererst in voller Bestimmtheit aufzurollen." *Phänomenologische Psychologie* (The Hague: Martinus Nijhoff, 1962), *Hua* 9:600.

16. "Aus der methodischen transzendentalen Epoché entsprungen, eröffnet die transzendentale 'innere' Erfahrung das endlose transzendentale Seinsfeld. Es ist die Parallele zum endlosen psychologischen Feld. . . . Und wieder ebenso ist das transzendentale Ich . . . gefaßt in der vollen Konkretion des transzendentalen Lebens, die transzendentale Parallele zum Ich und Wir im gewöhnlichen und psychologischen Sinn, wieder konkret gefaßt als Seele mit dem zugehörigen psychologischen Bewußtseinsleben. Mein transzendentales Ich ist also evident 'verschieden' vom natürlichen Ich, aber keineswegs als ein zweites, als ein davon getrenntes im natürlichen Wortsinn, wie umgekehrt auch keineswegs ein im natürlichen Sinne damit verbundenes oder mit ihm verflochtenes. Es ist eben das Feld der transzendentalen Selbsterfahrung, die jederzeit *durch bloße Änderung der Einstellung* in psychologische Selbsterfahrung zu wandeln ist. In diesem Übergang stellt sich notwendig eine Identität des Ich her; in transzendentaler Reflexion auf ihn wird die psychologische Objektivierung als Selbstobjektivierung des transzendentales Ich sichtlich, und so findet es (transzendentales Ich) sich als wie es in jedem Moment natürlicher Einstellung sich eine Apprezeption auferlegt hat" (*Hua* 9:294). Translation by Richard E. Palmer, in *Husserl: Shorter Works*, ed. Peter McCormick and Frederick Elliston (Notre Dame, Indiana: University of Notre Dame Press, 1981), 30–31, with minor modifications.

17. "Aber können wir uns damit beruhigen, uns mit der bloßen Tatsächlichkeit begnügen, daß die Menschen Subjekte für die Welt sind und zugleich Objekte in der Welt?" (*Hua* 6:184).

18. "Ich bin es, Ich, der Ich über allem natürlichen Dasein . . . stehe und der Ichpol bin des jeweils transzendentalen Lebens" (*Hua* 6:188).

19. *Hua* 1:102ff.

20. "Das Ur-Ich, das Ego meiner Epoché, das seine Einzigkeit und persönliche Undeklinierbarkeit nie verlieren kann. Dem widerspricht nur scheinbar, daß es sich . . . für sich selbst transzendental deklinierbar macht" (*Hua* 6:188).

21. It seems clear that if the agent of phenomenological reflection (reduction) is not the transcendental ego but life itself, this reflection should necessarily return to the nonreflective mode of life.

22. See Seiji Kato, *Husserl* [in Japanese] (Tokyo: Shimizu-Shoin, 1983), 175.

23. Cf. Hiroshi Kojima, "Die doppel-einheitliche Struktur des menschlichen ego und die transzendentale Reduktion" in *Japanische Beiträge zur Phänomenologie*, ed. Yoshihiro Nitta (Freiburg/Munich: Alber, 1984), 143–65.

CHAPTER 3

1. Cf. Klaus Held, *Lebendige Gegenwart*, Phaenomenologica 23 (The Hague: Kluwer, 1966), 94ff.

2. Edmund Husserl, *Zur Phänomenologie des inneren Zeitbewußtseins*, (The Hague: Martinus Nijhoff, 1966), *Hua* 10:80ff.

3. Cf. Henri Bergson, *Essai sur les données immédiates de la conscience* (Paris: Presses universitaires de France, 1948), 167–80.

4. *Hua* 10:113.

5. Cf. John Brough, "Husserl's Phenomenology of Time Consciousness," in *Husserl's Phenomenology: A Textbook*, ed. J. N. Mohanty and William R. McKenna (Washington, D.C.: University Press of America, 1989).

6. Held, *Lebendige Gegenwart*, 28.

7. Cf. Jacques Derrida, *La voix et le phénomene* (Paris: Presses universitaires de France, 1967), 58ff.

8. Husserl, *Cartesiansiche Meditationen, Hua* 1:100–101.

9. Husserl, *Ideen zu einer reinen Phänomenologie und phänomenologischen Philosophie, Erstes Buch, Hua* 3:157.

10. Husserl, *Umsturz der kopernikanischen Lehre*, in *Philosophical Essays in Memory of Edmund Husserl*, ed. Marvin Farber (New York: Greenwood Press, 1968).

11. Cf. Maurice Merleau-Ponty, *Le visible et l'invisible* (Paris: Gallimard, 1964), 130ff.

12. Cf. Merleau-Ponty, *Le visible et l'invisible*, 201.

13. *Hua* 3:370.

14. Husserl, *Logische Untersuchungen* Volume II, Part 1 (Tübingen: Max Niemeyer Verlag, 1968), 343–508 and Volume II, Part 2 (Tübingen: Max Niemeyer Verlag, 1968), 1–218. Hereafter abbreviated as Lu II/1 and LU II/2.

15. LU II/2:219.

16. *Hua* 3:290.

17. Cf. chapter 1 of this book.

18. *LU* II/1:416.

19. *LU* II/2:87.

20. Cf. J. N. Mohanty, *Edmund Husserl's Theory of Meaning* (The Hague: Martinus Nijhoff, 1976), 143ff.

21. Cf. Donn Welton, *The Origins of Meaning* (The Hague: Martinus Nijhoff, 1983), 298ff.

CHAPTER 4

1. Cf. *Hua* 7 and 8.

2. Husserl, *Ideen zu einer reinen Phänomenologie und phänomenologischen Philosophie, Erstes Buch, Hua* 3:64–66.

3. *Hua* 3:67.

4. This latter is the tendency of the epistemological idealism that has constituted the main stream of modern European philosophy.

5. *Hua* 3:72.

6. *Hua* 3:119.

7. *Hua* 3:116.

8. *Hua* 3:115.

9. *Hua* 3:115–16.

10. *Hua* 3:135

11. *Hua* 3:135.

12. *Hua* 3:117.

13. *Hua* 3:117.

14. *Die Krisis der europäische Wissenschaften und die transzendentale Phänomenologie, Hua* 6:157-58.

15. *Hua* 6:154.

16. *Erste Philosophie II, Hua* 8:157.

17. *Hua* 8:157.

18. Ludwig Landgrebe, *Der Weg der Phänomenologie* (Gütersloh: Gütersloher Verlagshaus Gerd Mohn, 1963), 182.

19. Immanuel Kant, *Critique of Pure Reason*, 2nd ed., trans. Norman Kemp Smith (New York: St. Martin's Press, 1965), 36.

20. *Hua* 3:87.

21. *Hua* 3:92-93.

22. *Hua* 3:106.

23. *Hua* 3:316.

24. *Hua* 3:320.

25. *Hua* 3:320.

26. Cf. *Hua* 3:368-72.

27. *Hua* 3:320-21.

28. *Hua* 3:323.

29. Husserl, *Erfahrung und Urteil* (Hamburg: Felix Meiner Verlag, 1972), 23. Hereafter abbreviated as *EU*.

30. *EU* 23.

31. *EU* 24.

32. *EU* 24.

33. *EU* 25.

34. Cf. *Krisis, Hua* 6:182-85.

35. *EU* 75.

36. *EU* 75.

37. *EU* 79.

38. *EU* 88.

39. *Hua* 3:269f.

40. Kitaro Nishida, *Zen no Kenkyu [An Inquiry into the Good]* (Tokyo: Iwanami-bunko, 1950), 74.

41. Martin Heidegger, *Sein und Zeit* (Tübingen: Max Niemeyer Verlag, 1953), 34. Hereafter abbreviated as *SZ*.

42. *SZ* 42.

43. *SZ* 42.

44. Heidegger, *Vom Wesen des Grundes* in *Wegmarken*, Gesamtausgabe 9 (Frankfurt a.M.: Vittorio Klostermann, 1949), 36.

45. Heidegger, *Grundprobleme der Phänomenologie*, Gesamtausgabe 24 (Frankfurt a.M.: Vittorio Klostermann, 1975), 452.

46. Heidegger, *Vom Wesen des Grundes*, 19.

47. Heidegger, *Grundprobleme der Phänomenologie*, 40.

48. *SZ* 108.

49. *SZ* 135.

50. Heidegger, "Was ist Metaphysik?" in Wegmarken, Gesamtausgabe 9 (Frankfurt a.M.: Vittorio Klostermann, 1951), 28.

51. *SZ* 137–38.

52. *SZ* 188.

53. The pre-thetic dimension does not always have a monadic structure. We must distinguish between at least two kinds of pre-thetic world, one of which is strictly bound to the kinesthetic dimension and which has an a priori intersubjective structure as the terrain of the life world. The pre-thetic self and image in it have a direct relation to thetic extensionality. What Husserl reached by way of the reduction must have been this type of pre-thetic world. His "perceptive image," too, must belong to this world. On the other hand, some kind of image, for example, a free fantasy, has no direct and necessary relation to thetic extensionality and belongs to the monadic (solipsistic) type of pre-thetic world. The pre-thetic world, which is eminently concerned with Existence as *"solus ipse"* and its projection, is of this type. Heidegger knows only this kind of pre-thetic world. However, the same image seems capable of belonging to both of these different worlds. Cf. my article "On the Semantic Duplicity of the First Person Pronoun 'I'" in the special edition "Phenomenology in Japan" of *Continental Philosophy Review*, vol. 31, no. 3 (1998): 307–20.

54. *SZ* 83–8.

55. Sartre, *L'être et le néant*, 139. Hereafter abbreviated as *EN*.

56. Sartre, *La transcendance de l'ego* (Paris: J. Vrin, 1966), 77.

57. *EN* 57.

58. *EN* 29.

59. Cf. *EN* 145–46.

60. *EN* 19.

61. *EN* 132.

62. Sartre, *L'imaginaire* (Paris: Gallimard, 1940), 30.

63. Ibid., 30.

64. Ibid., 30.

65. Though Sartre's decisive introduction of the thetic act into the imagination surpasses Husserl's theory of neutrality modification, he still remains in the sterile dichotomy of perception and imagination on account of his total exclusion of transcendental subjectivity.

66. Cf. chapter 6 of this book.

67. Kitaro Nishida, *Zenshu*, vol. 4 (Tokyo: Iwanami, 1949), Preface 5.

CHAPTER 5

1. René Descartes, *Meditationes de prima philosophia*, Vol. 7 of *Oeuvres de Descartes*, ed. Charles Adam et Paul Tannery (Paris: Librairie Philosophique J. Vrin, 1973), 19.

2. Ibid., 22ff.

3. Ibid., 28.

4. Descartes, *Principia philosophiae,* Vol. 8-1 of *Oeuvres de Descartes,* 17.

5. Descartes, *Meditationes, Oeuvres* 7:38–39.

6. Cf. chapters 11 and 12.

7. Husserl, *Die Krisis der Europaischen Wissenschaften und die Transzendentale Phanomenologie, Hua* 6:112.

8. *Hua* 6:145.

9. Husserl, *Erste Philosophie* II, *Hua* 8:6ff.

10. *Hua* 8:23-24.

11. Husserl, Manuskript EIII5. Cited in Klaus Held, *Lebendige Gegenwart* (The Hague: Martinus Nijhoff, 1966), 132-33.

12. *CM* 134.

13. *CM* 145, 152.

14. Ulrich Claesges, *Edmund Husserls Theorie der Raumkonstitution* (The Hague: Martinus Nijhoff, 1964), 144.

15. Husserl, Manuskript C3V. Cited in Gerd Brand, *Welt, Ich, und Zeit* (The Hague: Martinus Nijhoff, 1969), 90-91.

16. Cf. chapters 1 and 7 of this book. Homogeneous space is not an aggregate of Theres, but one of Here = Theres, where indefinite impersonal perspectives radiate from everywhere in every direction.

17. Suzuki Daisetsu, *Zenshu,* vol. 5 (Tokyo: Iwanami, 1968), 393.

18. Suzuki Daisetsu, *Zenshu,* vol. 13 (Tokyo: Iwanami, 1969), 231.

19. Suzuki Daisetsu, *Zenshu,* vol. 12 (Tokyo: Iwanami, 1969), 419.

20. Suzuki Daisetsu, *Zenshu* 12:385-86.

21. Dogen I— *Shobogenzo* (Tokyo: Iwanami, 1970), 75; 85.

22. Dogen II— *Shobogenzo* (Tokyo: Iwanami, 1972), 31.

23. Suzuki Daisetsu, *Zenshu,* 12:402.

24. Dogen, *Shobogenzo* 1:258.

25. Suzuki Daisetsu, *Zenshu,* 5:431.

26. Suzuki Daisetsu, *Zenshu,* 5:429.

27. Suzuki Daisetsu, *Zenshu,* 5:429.

28. Suzuki Daisetsu, *Zenshu,* 12:364.

29. Suzuki Daisetsu, *Zenshu,* 5:172.

CHAPTER 6

1. Jean-Paul Sartre, *L'etre et le neant,* 594.

2. Husserl, *Philosophie als strenge Wissenschaft,* ed. W. Szilasi (Frankfurt a.M.: Vittorio Klostermann, 1965), 35.

3. Ibid., 36-37.

4. *CM* 124-25.

5. *CM* 131.

6. *CM* 134.

7. *CM* 102.

8. *CM* 128.

9. *CM* 145.

10. *CM* 146.

11. *CM* 157.

12. *CM* 157.

13. Cf. chapter 1 of this book.

14. *CM* 147.

15. *CM* 149.

16. *CM* 157.

17. *CM* 157-58.

18. *CM* 158.

19. *CM* 166-67.

20. *CM* 167.

21. Kant, *Kritik der Urteilskraft* (Berlin: Königlich Preußliche Akademie der Wissenschaften, 1908), 115.

22. Ibid., 115.

23. Ibid., 116.

24. Husserl, *Erfahrung und Urteil*, 88.

25. Ibid., 138.

26. Husserl, *Ideen zu einer reinen Phänomenologie und phänomenologischen Philosophie, Erstes Buch, Hua* 3:256.

27. Ibid., 265-66.

28. Ibid., 51.

29. My concept of monad resembles Sartre's *être-pour-soi*, which is also a *jemeinig*, closed whole. The biggest difference between them, however, lies in the fact that my monad has only the mode of potential Being, while Sartre's *être-pour-soi* consists of real Being and nothingness. For me this potential Being is nothing other than the Being of the image; for Sartre, however, an image is nothingness. He recognizes as Being only the real Being that he simply identified with the Being of the material world.

30. Heidegger, *Sein und Zeit*, 136.

31. Ibid., 180-81.

32. Martin Heidegger, "Was ist Metaphysik?" in *Wegmarken*, Gesamtausgabe 9 (Frankfurt a.M.: Vittorio Klostermann, 1951), 27-29.

33. Namely, it consists of three lines with five, seven, and five syllables respectively. This division gives rise to a special kind of rhythm peculiar to the haiku. See the first translated poem in the text: Na-tsu-ku-sa-ya/Tsu-wa-mo-no-do-mo-ga/Yu-me-no-a-to.

CHAPTER 7

1. Cf. Husserl, *Erste Philosophie* II, *Hua* 8:157-63.

2. Ibid., 190.

3. Cf. Husserl, *CM* 124-31.

4. *CM* 182.

5. Cf. Husserl, *Die Krisis der europäischen Wissenschaften und die transzendentale Phänomenologie, Hua* 6:185-90, 212-13. Hereafter abbreviated as *Krisis.*

6. *Krisis*, 190.

7. In *Krisis* §55 (191): "In diesem systematischen Vorgehen gewinnt man zunächst die Korrelation der Welt und der transzendentalen, in der Menschheit objektivierten Subjektivität" ("In this procedure, we first gain the correlation of the world and the transcendental subjectivitiy objectified in humanity").

Also in §71 (260): "Somit führt die radikale und vollkommene Reduktion auf das *absolut einzige ego des* sich damit zunächst absolut vereinsamenden reinen Psychologen" ("Thus the radical and perfect reduction leads us to the absolutely individual ego of the pure psychologist who makes himself absolutely solitary through it").

8. *CM* 125.

9. *CM* 167.

10. *CM* 102. Given such a definition of the monad, the following question must immediately be raised: Is the monad as ego in its full concreteness the general mode of the ego preceding the ownness *(eigenheitlich)* reduction, and does the primordial sphere emerge only after the application of this reduction to the monad? Or is this reduction the necessary condition of the constitution of the monad, such that the monad is necessarily primordial? At first the former assertion seems to be more faithful to Husserl's own conviction, and even in accordance with the order of his description. But as "I as the [monadic] ego have the surrounding-world *(Umwelt)* persistently around me" (CM §33), and I am the sole functional center as "the absolute Here" (§53), it will not be necessary to exclude the possible meaning-nexus "we" or "the surrounding world for everyone" from the monad anew. Rather, as given in §45, the distinguishing division of "the universe of experiences" into the primordial sphere and the alien sphere by the transcendental ego will be nothing other than the ownness reduction, and only through this distinction (reduction) will the ego as the psycho-physical human being appear in the former sphere by means of the incarnation of the transcendental ego into the center of the monad. Therefore, in our opinion the monad is always and a priori the primordial sphere peculiar to me.

11. *Krisis*, 190–91.

12. Cf. Husserl, *Phänomenologische Psychologie, Hua* 9:216: "in denen [Genesen] innerhalb der Monad das monadische Ich seine personale Einheit gewinnt und zum Subjekt einer Umwelt, einer ihm teils passiv vorgegebenen, teils von ihm selbst aktiv gestalteten Umwelt wird" ("in this genesis, inside of the monad, the monadic I gains its personal unity and becomes the subject of a surrounding world that is partially pregiven to it passively and partly formed actively by it").

13. Gabriel Marcel writes in his *Journal métaphysique and Être et Avoir* of the ontological fusion between the incarnated ego and the world.

14. *CM* 125.

15. *CM* 125.

16. Iso Kern, Introduction to *Zur Phänomenologie der Intersubjektivität*, vol. 3 (The Hague: Martinus Nijhoff, 1973), *Hua* 15:xviii–xx.

17. *CM* 142.

18. *CM* 157.

19. *CM* 144-45.

20. *CM* 147.

21. The spatial objectification of my body is the result of the alienation of my perceptive consciousness. I see my objectified body There, as if my consciousness seeing it were another's and not mine. This normal and routine alienation of the ego is thinkable only under the universal situation of interintentionality. (Cf. chapter 1 of this book.)

22. Mood is the monad appresented through objective space. Therefore it always contains the nuance that expresses one's accessibility to one's own concealed monad.

23. Empathy is not the act of actively throwing the Being of my monad into other bodies, as is usually thought, but rather that of appresentatively rediscovering the already passively alienated and dispersed Being of my monad in other bodies through the objectification of my bodily flesh.

24. Claesges's assertion, "Der Begriff der Lebenswelt bei Husserl . . . ist von vornherein ein *ontologisch-transzendentaler Zwitterbegriff*" ("The concept of the life-world in Husserl is from the beginning an ontologico-transcendental hybrid-concept") in *Perspektiven tranzendentalphänomenologischer Forschung* (The Hague: Martinus Nijhoff, 1972), 97, supports my conclusion.

25. I must emphasize the importance of "project" as underlying every perspectivity of life-world consciousness.

26. Cf. chapter 9 of this book.

27. As shown in chapter 1, from the standpoint of the interintentionality of the perceptive consciousness a pure inner (immanent) time-consciousness becomes a rather extraordinary abstraction, while the ordinary flow of time is already defined by spatial extension.

28. *CM* 145-46, 152.

29. *CM* 129.

30. *CM* 152.

31. *CM* 157.

CHAPTER 8

1. Cf. Aristotle, *De anima* (Oxford: Oxford University Press, 1979), 29, and Thomas Aquinas, *Summa Theologica* (Torino: Marietti, 1963), 350.

2. Cf. Descartes, *Discours de la méthode*, vol. 6 of *Oeuvres*, ed. Charles Adam and Paul Tannery (Paris: Librairie Philosophique J. Vrin, 1974), 56.

3. Descartes, *Meditationes de prima philosophia*, 18-25, 76.

4. Cf. chapter 5 of this book.

5. Without the imagination, which is the mediate stage between the thesis and the anti-thesis, there will be no "doubt," which is essentially the floating condition between them.

6. Cf. chapter 9 of this book.

7. Ludwig Feuerbach, *Grundsätze der Philosophie der Zukunft* (Frankfurt a.M.: Vittorio Klostermann, 1967), 91.

8. Ludwig Feuerbach, *Das Wesen des Christentums* (Frankfurt a.M.: Suhrkamp, 1976), 17ff.

9. Karl Marx, *Ökonomisch-philosophische Manuskripte aus dem Jahre 1844, Ergänzungsband,* vol. 1 of Marx-Engels *Werke* (Berlin: Dietz, 1968), 515. Hereafter abbreviated *OPM.*

10. Feuerbach, *Grundsätze,* 18.

11. Karl Marx, *Thesen über Feuerbach,* vol. 3 of Marx-Engels *Werke* (Berlin: Dietz, 1962), 5.

12. Feuerbach, *Grundsätze,* 110ff.

13. Feuerbach, *Grundsätze,* 105.

14. *OPM* 515.

15. *OPM* 517.

16. *OPM* 538.

17. *OPM* 539.

18. *OPM* 539.

19. *OPM* 539.

20. Marx, *Das Kapital,* vol. 22 of Marx-Engels *Werke* (Berlin: Dietz, 1968), 193.

21. Arthur Schopenhauer, *Die Welt als Wille und Vorstellung,* vol. 1 of *Schopenhauers Werke in zwei Bände,* ed. W. Brede (Munich: Hanser, 1977), 150.

22. Henri Bergson, *Matière et mémoire* (Paris: Presses Universitaires de France, 1953), 11. Hereafter abbreviated *MM.*

23. *MM* 33.

24. *MM* 35.

25. *MM* 86.

26. *MM* 87.

27. *MM* 86.

28. *MM* 82.

29. *MM* 82–83.

30. *MM* 173.

31. Max Scheler, *Vom Umsturz der Werte* (Bern and Munich: Francke Verlag, 1972), 339.

32. Max Scheler, *Der Formalismus in der Ethik und die materielle Wertethik* (Bern/Munich: Francke Verlag, 1966), 158. Hereafter abbreviated *FE.*

33. *FE* 400.

34. *FE* 410.

35. *FE* 409.

36. *FE* 417.

37. *FE* 417-18.

38. Max Scheler, Die Stellung des Menschen im Kosmos (Munich: Nymphenburger Verlagshandlung, 1949), 72.

39. Scheler, *Die Stellung des Menschen im Kosmos,* 74.

40. Cf. Scheler, "Idealismus-Realismus," in *Späte Schriften* (Bern/Munich: Francke Verlag, 1976), 126.

41. Martin Heidegger, *Sein und Zeit,* 305.

42. *SZ* 126.

43. *SZ* 192.

44. *SZ* 339.

45. *SZ* 105.

46. *SZ* 119.

47. *SZ* 117–18.

48. *SZ* 84–85.

49. *SZ* 85.

50. Jean-Paul Sartre, *L'être et le néant*, 30–34.

51. *EN* 404.

52. I later found an example of such a consciousness in Levinas's concept of *"il y a,"* but this still has nothing to do with the freedom to transcend itself.

53. *EN* 115–49.

54. *EN* 19.

55. Cf. Sartre, "Le tramway-devant-être-rejoint" in *La transcendence de l'ego*, 194.

56. Maurice Merleau-Ponty, *Phénoménologie de la perception* (Paris: Gallimard, 1945), 194. Hereafter abbreviated *PP.*

57. *PP* 395.

58. *PP* 158.

59. *PP* 115.

60. *PP* 513.

61. *PP* 109.

62. Merleau-Ponty, *Le visible et l'invisible*, ed. Claude Lefort (Paris: Gallimard, 1964), 325. English translation by Alphonso Lingis in *The Visible and the Invisible* (Evanston: Northwestern University Press, 1968), 272.

63. *Le visible et l'invisible*, 183f./139f.

CHAPTER 9

1. Cf. Keiji Yamada, *Kagaku to Gijutsu no Kindai* [The Modern Age of Science and Technology] (Tokyo: Asahi Shinbun, 1982), 274.

2. "Enframing" is the Heideggerian idea of the essence of modern technology, which designates the fundamental objectifying of nature and the world.

3. Martin Heidegger, *Die Technik und die Kehre* (Pfullingen: Günther Neske, 1962), 21–22.

4. *Die Technik und die Kehre*, 23.

5. The title is, namely, *Meditatio de prima philosophia in quibus Dei existentia et animae a corpore distinctio demonstrantur.*

6. René Descartes, *Principia philosophiae*, vol. 8-1 of *Oeuvres de Descartes*, ed. Charles Adam and Paul Tannery (Paris: Librairie Philosophique J. Vrin, 1965), 41.

7. Descartes, *Principia philosophiae*, 78.

8. Descartes, *Principia philosophiae*, 79.

9. Cf. Yoitsu Kondo, *Dekaruto no Shizenzo [Descartes's View of Nature]* (Tokyo: Iwanami, 1959).

10. *Ideen zu einer reinen Phänomenologie und phänomenologischen Philosophie, Erstes Buch, Hua* 3:62–63.

11. Cf. *Hua* 3:363–68.

12. On the other hand, I also refrain from monistic objectivism, because it is unable to found the epistemological dimension itself.

13. Here the word "phantom" does not refer to any unreal character. It signifies only an abstract reality of pure extensionality.

14. Karl Marx, *Economic and Philosophical Manuscript of 1844* (Moscow: Progress Publishers, 1967), 72.

15. The decomposition of the world into homogeneous elements is nothing other than the "annihilation of value."

CHAPTER 10

1. In my opinion, this is why phenomenology must necessarily return to ontology as the investigation of Being itself.

2. Husserl, *Ideen zu einer reinen Phänomenologie und phänomenologischen Philosophie, Erstes Buch, Hua* 3:58–59.

3. Husserl, *Erste Philosophie* II, *Hua* 8:157–63.

4. *Hua* 3:350–53.

5. *Hua* 3:118.

6. Husserl, *Erfahrung und Urteil*, 25.

7. Emmanuel Levinas, *Le temps et l'autre* (Paris: Presses Universitaires, 1983), 24–30.

8. Jean-Paul Sartre, *Critique de la raison dialectique* (Paris: Gallimard, 1960), 358–77.

9. Max Scheler, *Die Stellung des Menschen im Kosmos*, 54.

10. Maine de Biran, *Nouveaux essais d'anthropologie, in Oeuvres Complètes*, vol. 14 (Geneva and Paris: Slatkine, 1982), 168.

11. Gabriel Marcel, *Être et Avoir* (Paris: F. Aubier, 1935), 239–40.

12. Sartre, *L'Être et le néant*, 495–500.

13. Leibniz, *Monadologie* (Hamburg: Reclam, 1954), 30.

14. Cf. chapter 3 of this book.

15. Husserl, *Erfahrung und Urteil*, 311.

16. Husserl, *Krisis, Hua* 6:176–77.

CHAPTER 11

1. In Martin Buber, *Werke*, vol.1 (Munich and Heidelberg: Kösel Verlag, 1962), 75–170. Hereafter abbreviated as *BuW*.

2. *BuW* 1:79.

3. *BuW* 1:79.

4. *BuW* 1:80.

5. *BuW* 1:89.

6. *BuW* 1:158.

7. *BuW* 1:101.

8. *BuW* 1:120.

9. *BuW* 1:120.

10. *BuW* 1:120.

11. *BuW* 1:121.

12. *BuW* 1:122.

13. *BuW* 1:83.

14. *BuW* 1:83.

15. *BuW* 1:145.

16. *BuW* 1:153-54.

17. Schopenhauer, *Die Welt als Wille und Vorstellung*, 1:149.

18. Albert Schweitzer, *Das Christentum und die Weltreligionen* (Munich: Biederstein Verlag, 1950), 51.

19. Ibid.

20. Schweitzer, *Aus meinem Leben und Denken* (Hamburg: R. Meiner, 1955), 133.

21. Schweitzer, *Kultur und Ethik* (Munich: Biederstein Verlag, 1948), 242-43.

22. Henri Bergson, *Essai sur les données immédiates de la conscience* (Paris: Presses universitaires de France, 1948), 102-3.

23. *Essai sur les données immédiates de la conscience*, 173-74.

24. Cf. chapter 6 of this book.

25. This sight of the Other from inside of me is completely different from the sight of the Other from outside of Me. The former is a deeper negation of my identity than mere objectification by the latter.

26. *BuW* 1:120

27. *BuW* 1:104.

28. *BuW* 1:83.

CHAPTER 12

1. See Bloch and Gordon, eds., *Martin Buber—Bilanz seines Denkens* (Freiburg: Herder, 1983), articles by W. Kaufmann, 22-39, J. Bloch, 62-81, R. Horwitz, 141-56, and B. Casper, 159-175.

2. *BuW* 1:79.

3. *BuW* 1:89.

4. *BuW* 1:89.

5. *BuW* 1:83.

6. *BuW* 1:83.

7. *BuW* 1:83.

8. *BuW* 1:83.

9. Martin Buber, *Werke*, vol.3 (Munich/Heidelberg: Kösel, 1963), 799.

10. Jochanan Bloch, *Die Aporie des Du: Probleme der Dialogik Martin Bubers* (Heidelberg: Lambert Schneider, 1977), 78.

11. *BuW* 1:82.

12. *BuW* 1:84.

13. Nishida Kitaro, *Zenshu,* vol. 6 (Tokyo: Iwanami, 1948), 341ff. Cf. chapter 13 of this book.

14. *BuW*1:154.

15. *BuW*1:103.

16. *BuW*1:87.

17. *BuW*1:81; 83–84.

18. Cf. *Martin Buber—Bilanz seines Denkens,* 160ff.

19. Emmanuel Levinas, *Totalité et infini* (The Hague: Martinus Nijhoff, 1984), 50.

20. Levinas, *En découvrant l'existance avec Husserl et Heidegger* (Paris: Libraire Philosophique J. Vrin, 1967), 194.

21. Buber, *Briefwechsel aus sieben Jahrzehnten,* vol. 3 (Heidelberg: Schneider, 1975), 582.

22. Ibid.

23. Levinas, "Martin Buber und Erkenntnistheorie," in *Martin Buber,* ed. Paul Schilpp and Maurice Friedman (Stuttgart: Kohlhammer, 1963), 131.

24. Cf. Buber, *Briefwechsel,* 3:528–84.

25. Cf. chapter 13 of this book.

26. Cf. chapter 9 of this book.

27. Cf. chapter 10 of this book.

28. Cf. chapters 3 and 4 of this book.

29. *BuW*1:134–35.

CHAPTER 13

1. Tetsuro Watsuji, *Ningen no Gaku toshiteno Rinrigaku [Ethics as the Science of Human Being]* (Tokyo: Iwanami, 1934).

2. Wataru Hiromatsu, *Sekai no Kyodo-shukanteki Sonzai-kozo [The Communal-Subjective Structure of the World]* (Tokyo: Keiso-shobo, 1972).

3. Bin Kimura, *Hito to Hito no Aida [Between Human and Human]* (Tokyo: Kobundo, 1972).

4. Consider the soft identity claimed by Kimura.

5. *BuW*1:318.

6. *BuW*1:83.

7. It seems somewhat strange that Nishida used Japanese words for I and Thou (*watashi to nanji*) that are not exactly congruent with each other. See the table on p. 240.

8. Nishida Kitaro, *Zenshu,* 6:341–427.

9. *BuW*1:89.

10. *BuW*1:82.

11. *BuW*1:79.

CHAPTER 14

1. This chapter is a slightly revised version of a speech given by the author at Colombia National University, Santa Fe de Bogota, on September 22, 1994.

INDEX

apperceptive unity: and pseudodualism, 147-48; pure I, 12-13; as schematic body against dualism, 150-52

appresentation: coupling, 110-11; other's perspective, 5-6, 8, 77-79, 88; time, 77

Basho Matsuo, 99-102, 217-19

Being: anonymous *il y a*, 162; body, 79, 177; cogito, 40; consciousness, 176-79; continuity in monad, 94; Descartes, 69-73; detotalized, 35; as field, 16; Heidegger, 46, 53-54, 160, 206; individual and religiousness, 81; from inside or from outside, 78, 177-78, 181-87; insufficient in Husserl, 158-59; Japanese philosophy (Watsuji), 206-7; mood and potential, 117-18; noema, 35; nothing, 46, 57, 223-24; as object of reduction, 32; power (force), 158-60, 165-69; pre-thetic, 45, 140-41, 160; real and potential, 94-97; reason in Husserl, 159; Sartre, 22, 57-58, 140; species-being, 127-29, 207; teleology, 161; thetic, 58; Thou and whole Being, 174, 183-84, 192; whole, 96; will, 178; of world, 158-60

Bergson, Henri, 25, 27, 179-80, 130-33

between: nothingness, 212; personal as mediator, 72, 185-88; Thou as mediator, 72, 185-88, 193-95, 198, 213-15

Biran, Maine de, 163

Bloch, Jochanan, 191

body: Aristotelian-Thomistic, 125; Being, 79, 177; Bergson, 130-32; Buber's lack of, 201; central Here, 7, 23, 90-91, 97, 113; conflict of forces, 163; Descartes, 125-26; doubt, 126; Heidegger, 55, 138-39; human Existence in Merleau-Ponty, 141-42; intersubjectivity, 33, 88, 116, 120; Japanese philosophy, 220-24; *Leib-Körper*, 116-20; life-world, 117-18;

look of other, 112-14; mediating community, 97; monad, 74-75, 87, 106-7; potential Being, 94; praxis, 220-22; Sartre, 59, 61, 140; Scheler, 133-37; schema, 28-30, 33-34, 150-51; Schopenhauer, 130; in scientific view, 57, 127; standing present, 23, 27-28, 33; technology, 154-57; time, 119; union of pure and psychological ego, 13. *See also* somatic ego

Brough, John, 25.

Buber, Martin, 72, 173-76, 184-98, 201, 209-15

Cartesianism in Husserl, 38-48

Chao-Chou (or Johshu), 82-83

Claesges, Ulrich, 75

consciousness: Being, 176-79; Husserl and Leibniz, 115-16; objectifying and non-objectifying, 33-34; of others, 4-5; reflective and non-reflective, 22-23; transcendental as intersubjective, 114-15. *See also* intentionality

constitution: of back, 5-6; of sense, 29-31, 35. *See also* transcendental ego; language

continuum: immanence in Zen, 81-82, 223; life, 25-29, 68, 80-84; monad, 94

coupling: appresentation, 110-11; Being from inside and outside, 182; *Leib-Körper*, 116-20; of monads, 97, 188

Dasein: Heidegger, 54-57; monad, 85

Derrida, Jacques, 28

Descartes, René, 38-40, 44-45, 68-73, 146-47

Dogen, 82-83

dualism: body/mind (pseudodualism), 146-53; body against dualism, 150-52; body in technology, 154-57; in Descartes, 68, 146-47; genuine dualism, 156-57; Husserl and pseudo-dualism, 148-49; I-Thou and I-It,